Seeking the Compassionate Life

Recent Titles in
Psychology, Religion, and Spirituality
J. Harold Ellens, Series Editor

Married to an Opposite: Making Personality Differences Work for You
Ron Shackelford

Sin against the Innocents: Sexual Abuse by Priests and the Role of the
Catholic Church
Thomas G. Plante, editor

SEEKING THE COMPASSIONATE LIFE

The Moral Crisis for Psychotherapy and Society

Carl Goldberg with Virginia Crespo

Psychology, Religion, and Spirituality
J. Harold Ellens, Series Editor

Westport, Connecticut
London

Library of Congress Cataloging-in-Publication Data

Goldberg, Carl.
   Seeking the compassionate life : the moral crisis for psychotherapy and society / Carl
Goldberg with Virginia Crespo.
       p. cm.— (Psychology, religion, and spirituality, ISSN 1546–8070)
   Includes bibliographical references.
   ISBN 0–275–98196–7
   1. Psychotherapy. 2. Psychoanalysis. 3. Compassion. I. Crespo, Virginia. II. Title.
   III. Series.
RC480.5.G5863 2004
616.89′14—dc22   2004005803

Library of Congress Catalog Card Number: 2004005803
ISBN: 0–275–98196–7
ISSN: 1546–8070

First published in 2004

Praeger Publishers, 88 Post Road West, Westport, CT 06881
An imprint of Greenwood Publishing Group, Inc.
www.praeger.com

Printed in the United States of America

The paper used in this book complies with the
Permanent Paper Standard issued by the National
Infirmations Standards Organization (Z39.48-1984).

10   9   8   7   6   5   4   3   2   1

Haskell Felsenstein and Anna Meyer Crespo
Our predecessors who exemplified the virtues we strive
to convey in this book:
Curiosity, courage, compassion, and emotional wisdom.

CONTENTS

SERIES FOREWORD

The interface between psychology, religion, and spirituality has been of great interest to scholars for a century. In the last three decades a broad general interest has developed in books which make practical sense out of the sophisticated research on these three subjects.

This series intends to define the terms and explore the interface of psychology and religion or spirituality at an operational level of daily human experience. Each volume identifies, analyzes, describes, and evaluates a range of issues, of both popular and professional interest, that deal with the psychological factors at play in the way spirituality functions within humans, in the ways that spirituality may be shaped and expressed, or the ways religion takes shape and is expressed.

These books are written for the general reader, local library, and undergraduate university student. They are also of significant interest to the informed professional, particularly in corollary fields. These volumes have great value for clinical settings and treatment models.

This series editor has spent his professional lifetime focused upon research into the interface of psychology, religion and spirituality. These matters are of the highest urgency in human affairs today when religious motivation seems to be playing an increasing role, constructively and destructively, in the arena from personal and social ethics to national politics and world affairs.

It is just as urgent that we discover and understand better what the psychological forces are which empower people of genuine spirituality to give themselves to all the creative and constructive enterprises which, throughout the centuries, have made of human life the humane, ordered, prosperous, and aesthetic experience it can be at its best. Surely the forces for good in both psychology and spirituality far exceed the powers and proclivities toward the evil that we see so prominently in our world today.

This series of Praeger volumes is dedicated to the greater understanding of *Psychology, Religion and Spirituality,* and thus to the profound understanding and empowerment of those psycho-spiritual drivers which can help us transcend the malignancy of our pilgrimage and enormously enhance the majesty of the human spirit, indeed, the potential for magnificence in human life.

J. Harold Ellens, Ph.D.
Series Editor

ADVISORY BOARD

PREFACE

The path to the compassionate life is the focal concern of this book. I investigate here how each of us can best recognize, respond to, and sustain the personal, interpersonal, and social requirements of the compassionate life. The stories and vignettes presented here—of people from all walks of life, through the centuries and among all the cultures of the world—reveal the crucial importance of the presence of *seven factors* for achieving the compassionate life. They are *constructive shame, curiosity, self-reflection, moral courage, personal agency,* and *social* and *moral responsibility.* These stories and vignettes provide evidence for the central thesis of this book: People cannot live a satisfying life in the midst of others' suffering and despair. Consequently, *living compassionately is a functional requirement of a satisfying existence.*

For the most part, psychotherapists and psychoanalysts have failed to recognize the importance of compassion in the struggle to be human. Consequently, the precise ways that psychotherapists must heed more efficaciously the need for compassion and decency in how people conduct their existence, in order to inspire their clients toward the life lived fully and well, is the second concern here. I explore these interactions in a series of case studies.

In the late 1970s, when I practiced psychotherapy in Washington, DC, I was a member of a peer supervision group—consisting of six psychiatrists and me. We met biweekly over savory lunches in Georgetown restaurants. Every few months one or another of a cadre of four of these psychiatrists would announce in a hushed voice that he and the other three would be absent for the next meeting. Neither I nor the other two psychiatrists needed to ask why. We knew that this group, as members of a special psychiatric team that consulted for the Central Intelligence Agency, would be abroad—usually in the Middle East—profiling the personalities of important foreign national leaders. I shuddered when informed of their intended absence. None of these psychiatrists, who were psychoanalytically oriented, was expert in political science, sociology, history, comparative religion, or philosophy—subjects required to competently evaluate the Middle Eastern leaders. At least, in part, because of their lack of qualification as political advisors, I believe ill-advised decisions were made by our State Department. In other words, I attribute our failed political policy that resulted in the Iran hostage situation to the misconceived advice of this psychiatric team.

It is not surprising that these psychiatrists were professionally poorly prepared to efficaciously handle their unfamiliar task. At that time few clinicians were asked to step out of their consulting rooms and participate as active agents in societal crises. Today, especially, after September 11, the situation has changed considerably. Psychology and psychotherapy are undergoing a severe change—if not a crisis—in regard to their aims, values, and methods of inquiry. The good news is that psychotherapists in increasing numbers are being called to act as psychological advisors in helping societal agents sort out and deal with pressing social issues. So, for example, psychotherapists are now participating in conflict resolution—ranging from negotiations between Arabs and Israelis to Estonians and Russians. And in therapists' consulting rooms today they more clearly recognize the need to acknowledge their own, as well as their clients', moral and spiritual values and to use them clinically, at least in part, as a guide to a meaningful life.

The bad news is that, like the group of psychiatrists discussed above, probably few psychotherapists today are comfortable dealing with the moral, spiritual, and political concerns of their clients. If for no other reason, this is because psychology and psychotherapy have in the past eschewed moral and spiritual concerns as beyond the pale of scientific investigation, and as such, an improper purview of the psychotherapist.

As a psychologist, I investigate here the ways that my colleagues can more efficaciously address the moral, spiritual, and societal values and concerns of their clients. However, as a social theorist, I wrote this book also for all those who are concerned with the moral crises in contemporary society and seek personal and social solutions to constructively deal with these issues. As such, the reader need not be a professional behavioral scientist in order to identify readily with the issues under discussion here. In this regard, the term *Seeking the Compassionate Life* in the title of the book represents the ongoing struggle within most of us to find a beacon to guide our way to living decently and virtuously amidst the phalanx of hatred, fear, and doubt that pervade our daily world. Compassion is a personal trait that people—across all social, political, and philosophical persuasions—seem to wish to embody, including everyone, for example, from the compassionate conservatives to the radically liberal.

If ever there were a need to find constructive ways of dissuading the forces of hatred and misunderstanding from their destructive pathways that may lead to a series of calamities capable of consuming the entire planet, it is in our day. In almost every region of our world, in fact, we are witness to the fierce mortal storm between destructive forces, each of which claims to have legitimate and righteous moral authority.

Indeed, whereas many of the moral struggles of our age are global, far more are personal battles. Self-honesty impels us to recognize that within virtually every human breast hatred and arrogance battle compassion and decency as the driving force of our personal identity. As such, each of us is challenged to find for ourselves the mainsprings of our humanity—that which is noble, courageous, and loving in the human spirit—so that decency and compassion may serve as our personal agency. And for the psychotherapist reader, I explore here how these virtues may find their way into the lives of those who are treated in their consulting rooms, as well as for those with whom they consult in the world at large.

PSYCHOTHERAPY'S MORAL AGENDA

Psychotherapy's original mission, although rarely openly discussed as such, had a moral impetus—to transform society from a hostile, fearful place to a world in which goodwill and reason would prevail. In recent years psychotherapy has come upon hard times. Caught in the snare of political, bureaucratic, and economic issues on the one side, accused of clinical inefficacy, social irrelevancy, and a lack of moral responsibility on the other, psychotherapy has lost the sweep and profundity of Freud and other leading psychological theorists' vision of psychotherapy's mission. In short, the public no longer regards intensive psychotherapy as the panacea it was held to be for decades. Consequently, the opportunities for maintaining a large practice of intensive psychotherapy have been considerably decreased for most practitioners. Today psychodynamic psychotherapy stands far behind short-term therapy and psychopharmacology as the treatment of choice for psychological problems.

Psychotherapy's tarnished reputation is unfortunate in light of our contemporary international and American societal issues. Psychotherapeutic understanding has the capacity to provide profound insights to enable us to comprehend and competently deal with these difficult social problems. For example, as psychotherapy is potentially the most knowledgeable discipline for seeking out the motivations that encourage us to cooperate with and join in communion in others' well-being, psychotherapists are well appointed as trusted advisors in the establishment of a well-functioning society. It is in regard to the capacity of psychotherapists to recognize the underlying factors that foster societal salubrity that I here speak out about the roles and functions psychotherapists can and must assume to address the social and moral challenges of the new millennium. I don't want the light to fail: I wish to see realized the vital ideas and intentions that psychotherapy early in its history held up as a guide to a more constructive society.

Perhaps the subject of importance most neglected by modern psychological investigation is that of *morality*. Given this, I am concerned in this book with how to efficaciously investigate the crucial question: How best does a person live a compassionate and decent life?

Long ago the eminent Harvard University psychologist Gordon Allport (1950) identified two basic approaches to the investigation of psychological issues. The investigator, he indicated, may choose to study in general terms a select number of variables among a large group of research subjects, or he may focus instead on a few individual people and explore in depth their interests, concerns, and motivations as case studies. In this book I have chosen the case study approach and seek to explore the significant existential issues on the path to the compassionate life.

STUDY OF VIRTUE

Admittedly, a probing moral inquiry of our personal and societal crises is a complex and elusive endeavor. Why a person acts honorably (or heinously) is one of the most puzzling issues in the study of human behavior. Throughout history numerous explanations have been offered, but no consensus of opinion has prevailed. Our lack of understanding of how virtue actually develops has prevented far too many of us from living as we believe we should and no less importantly has impeded a knowledgeable encouragement of the necessary considerations in the development of virtue in our children.

Societal events within the United States in recent years illustrate the great difficulty of finding a guide for our quest of the virtuous life. Statements by both public officials and average citizens about these events suggest that they believe the solutions to our serious societal problems—and by implication, the reparation of our moral failings—require that these villains be severely punished by long-term imprisonment. Furthermore, as preventive strategies, those calling out for social reform reveal that we Americans as a nation believe that by strengthening the observational and punishing components of the superego of the American psyche we can successfully overthrow our moral failings. Nevertheless, as I discuss in chapter 4, tightening the demands of the American superego will not accomplish our moral aims.

Here I take a new direction in unraveling the mystery of virtuous behavior. In this regard, I examine one of the most puzzling findings in the history of moral inquiry. This mystery concerns the Nazis. Most people have described the Nazis' brutality and inhumanity toward those they regarded as outsiders and enemies as that of immoral, demented brutes. However, psychiatric interviews and sophisticated psychological testing of leading Nazi officials reveal that such a facile depiction of the Nazis does not hold up to psychological investigation. When leading psychological experts were asked to interview and test the Nuremberg trial Nazi defendants, the results were not what most people would have expected. None of the Nazis was shown to be a hostile, impulse-driven sadist.

The contrasting picture between what our commonsense notions about the Nazis and other such destructive people are, and the results of the psychological assessment of them, needs to be sensibly explained—as it is crucial to our understanding of the moral failings in society then and to this day. The reason for this seemingly astounding contradiction, as I show in the chapters to follow, is that most of us—even the most eminent philosophers—have not recognized that there are different systems of morality at work within each of us.

The central thesis of this book is that there are strong competing systems of morality within every society with which most of us continually struggle to reconcile. Only when we recognize this fact and begin to understand the appeal of each of the different moralities can we begin a constructive quest for a virtuous existence.

The two major systems of morality I am concerned with here are *righteousness* as a refluent morality (the unreflective enactment of the values and mores of one's society) and *conscience* as a reflective consciousness (in which one suspends the certainty of righteous behavior and seeks a more noble and humane vision of proper behavior than one has been taught). Thus, for example, the good Nazi was loyal, obedient, even willing to sacrifice his life to carry out the prescriptive norms of his society. He didn't lack a strong superego (a sense of righteousness); rather, it was a deficiency in the development of empathy, compassion, and concern for other people who were not like him (in those ways his uncurious and limited insights about humanity impressed upon him) that impelled him toward heinous deeds.

In the chapters to follow I show that morality based upon reflective consciousness (conscience) consists of seven major factors that differentiate it from refluent (righteous) morality. From historical cases, from case studies of people I have encountered in my work as a psychologist/ psychoanalyst, and from vignettes of my personal life, as well as the intuitions of the master literary psychologists—such as Leo Tolstoy, Mark Twain, and J-J. Rousseau—I show how these crucial factors come together to foster virtuous behavior. These insights and hunches are not simply impressionistic notions; I show that they are demonstrable from empirical evidence as gleaned from a purview of the existent psychological research on the development of altruism, empathy, and learned concern for others in children and adults.

ACKNOWLEDGMENTS

I would like to acknowledge the thoughtfulness and useful suggestions provided by friends and colleagues in the preparation of this book: Howard Book, M.D., Merri Goldberg, M.S.W., John Graham, M.D., Carole Turoff, Esq., and Heward Wilkinson, M.S.

Chapter 1

CONSTRUCTIVE SHAME: AN ENCOUNTER WITH AN UNFORTUNATE CHILD

Shame opens a pathway to ourselves.
—Max Scheler (1874–1928, German philosopher)

Why a person acts honorably is one of the most puzzling issues in the study of morality. Throughout history numerous explanations have been offered, but no consensus of opinion has prevailed. Some believe a person acts properly because that person has been instilled early in life with good values. Others claim that direct life experiences are more crucial than childhood teachings; still more point to the presence of exemplary role models as exceeding that which has been taught or personally experienced. And, finally, there are those who maintain that learned factors are of minimal importance in fostering human virtue. After all, they indicate, we expect virtuous behavior from humans, but not animals. Even the most intelligent and best-trained animals don't act protectively toward humans from a sense of righteousness, no matter what they are taught, but from a bond of affection and loyalty with those with whom they are familiar. Consequently, it is reasonable to assume, these philosophers claim, that a moral sentiment is a unique, inherent quality of the human mind. In this regard, the eminent eighteenth-century German philosopher Immanuel Kant (1956) postulated that it was the human capacity to reason rather than to respond emotionally that fosters virtue. By this he meant that social and emotional experiences are unnecessary—and often interfere—given the mind's inherent capacity to recognize the superiority of virtue over immorality.

Obviously the explanation we endorse in regard to virtue's mainspring has significant implications for psychology and education: If the capacity for moral behavior is an inherent quality of the human mind, a course of rational training would be the most appropriate way to free malefactors' minds of misconceived assumptions about human existence that have impelled their wrongful and destructive behavior. If, on the other hand, virtue is a psychological induction from direct experience and/or the emulation of exemplary role models, then we must shape those experiences and models that best impress our children with the appropriate moral messages.

The vignette that follows concerns the question of why we act virtuously. It suggests that constructive shame may play a crucial role as a guardian of virtuous behavior because of its role in the development of empathy and identification with others.

The story takes place in a distant land. The specific location should not divert our attention from the recognition that the crucial elements of the situation are similar to those with which many of us are routinely confronted.

He was a slight lad of nine or ten. His tan, rough hemp shirt was tattered and his trousers, a couple of sizes too large, held by a length of cord. He may have been wearing shoes, although the impression I have of him was that he was barefoot. What I remember best was his immutable, sad demeanor and that he tightly clutched in his left hand a picture postcard and a small box of plastic-covered matches. The tenacity with which he held these meager items suggested that they were all he materially possessed.

The photo on the postcard was that of the city plaza of Cuzco, Peru—once the sacred city of the Incas—now a teeming South American metropolis, high in the Andes mountain range, visited by tourists for its historical sites and awe-inspiring churches filled with priceless religious relics.

The picture postcard was carefully wrapped in a piece of clear plastic. The matches were the type manufactured throughout Latin America, purchased in shops for the equivalent of a North American nickel.

The child had approached our table as a female friend and I were dining late one summer evening in a popular Cuzco restaurant. Three musicians, young men of Cachapayan Indian descent from the Andes, were playing haunting ancient tunes on a small stage in the front of the restaurant. We were captivated by the music, new to us, as it was a number of years before musicians from the Andes would become a ubiquitous feature of North American metropolitan life.

Throughout the evening we had watched small children, in groups of twos and threes, slip into the restaurant and approach the patrons' tables, heavily laden with delicious Peruvian dishes. They were acrimoniously scooted away by the patrons and then ousted from the establishment by stocky waiters wearing white smocks around their dark suits and no-nonsense grimaces.

A few of these poorly dressed children, first casting furtive glances, returned. Carefully making their way to where the patron families sat, they looked up with their sad child faces at the customers consuming their food with apparent gusto and abandon.

The boy who approached our table stood silently for a long moment. His large brown eyes seemed filled with tears. Or were they mine that countenanced despair? By what quirk of fate was I well educated and able to travel frequently to South America, while at the same time this small child stood before me impoverished and uneducated? I had no doubt that by his socioeconomic circumstances he was destined to a life of hardship—perhaps not a very long life at that. Were he to live long enough to have children of his own in this land of disadvantage and violent political strife, his unhappy legacy to his offspring would be to have no real hope for better things in life, perhaps not even the necessities. The pack of cigarettes my friend smoked each day undoubtedly was more costly than the price of food his family, if indeed he had one, could afford him that day.

We spoke to him in Spanish. He told us that his name was Pedro, but it was difficult to ascertain where he lived in the city. Pedro was quite inarticulate in his own native tongue, but conversation was not his immediate interest.

Remaining mute, he thrust his left hand toward me, revealing his postcard and matchbox. I asked whether he was selling the items. He slowly nodded. Not speaking, he hadn't stated a price. I assumed that he wanted me to exact the proper value of his items. But I was reluctant to do so, for if he sold the two spare items he held, what besides his shabby clothes would he possess?

Not surprisingly, he looked malnourished. The food on our plates was simple fare but plentiful and savory. I realized it would be more reasonable to feed the child than to purchase his only salable holdings.

I invited Pedro to sit at our table. He fretfully looked around at the occupants of the other tables, then vigorously shook his head. In retracing the sweep of Pedro's glance, two things were evident: First, my friend and I were the only foreigners present, and second, if Pedro sat at our table it would be a breach of local customs. The other waifs were standing by the customers' tables, rapidly consuming with their bare hands leftovers from the patrons' dinner plates. Not one child had been invited to sit down at a table.

A look at my companion confirmed my sense that we were too uncomfortable with Pedro standing by our table, eating the scraps from our plates, to respect local mores. I cringed, embarrassed to associate myself with the rich stranger in a white suit, played by the actor John Huston in the 1940s film *The Treasure of the Sierra Madre,* who disdainfully flipped silver coins to the beggars in a shabby Mexican seaport; nor did I wish to act like a feudal lord casting unwanted food from my table to starving peasants. I wanted to respond to Pedro in a humane way. But I didn't know how to proceed.

After a few awkward moments pondering upon my discomfort, my course of action was clear: The climate between Pedro and my companion and myself would not be benevolent unless we were all seated. So I more emphatically repeated my invitation to Pedro to sit down at our table, pulling out a chair for him next to me. With measured movements he complied. We ordered food from a waiter, who disapprovingly kept his eyes on Pedro as he served him a glass of milk and a plate of food. Pedro consumed the food with rapid thrusts of his right hand; he held fast his two possessions, as if someone might steal them if he were to loosen his grip on them for even an instant.

When he had finished eating he looked up at us and then stared ahead with the same unhappy expression as when he had first appeared at our table. I sensed that this inarticulate child was feeling embarrassed sitting with us, not knowing how to thank us or what he should say or do in taking leave of us.

In recognizing Pedro's distress, I again became aware of my own uneasiness. Although the restaurant was quite cool, my face felt flushed, my hands and neck wet with perspiration. I also was close to tears. The symptoms I was exhibiting, my years of clinical experience suggested, were those of *shame.* But why, I puzzled, was I ashamed? I had not done something wrong. Indeed, I was trying to act decently as best I could.

Then I remembered the words of G.W.F. Hegel. One of the best definitions to help us understand the decisive factors involved in shame was offered by that famous nineteenth-century German philosopher (1892). He tells us that shame is an anger against what *ought not to be.*

Applied to everyday life, Hegel's definition seems exceedingly accurate. We all know of the notorious father who viciously slapped his daughter who had tearfully returned home having fallen from a tree she was climbing, badly abrading her knees. His angry words and actions imply that she was being punished for having done something wrong. Viewed from the outside, the father as educator was attempting to discipline his daughter to take proper care of herself. The father's anger and the daughter's guilt manifestly seem to be the major emotional players in this allegorical scenario.

However, quite a different psychology ensues when viewing the drama from the psyche of the father. He is the caretaker of his child; he cares deeply about her. Not surprisingly, he becomes frightened and upset from seeing how vulnerable his child is to injury. Moreover, he not only fears for her, he is ashamed that he has failed as her protector. His fleeting awareness of his inability to shelter his child sufficiently stirs his anger against what ought not to be. In short, the father feels self-recrimination that he is not an adequate father at such times, when he is forced to recognize that he can do little to protect his beloved child from being vulnerable to life's hurts.

To divest himself from his sense of painful impotence, which he neither understands nor knows how to deal with, the father strikes out at his daughter. By blaming her for his uncomfortable feelings (of helplessness), he unwittingly has transposed his child from a victim of injury to a perpetrator of a wrongful act: behaving as an irresponsible child (no wonder that the waiters in the restaurant treated the children so badly!). Moreover, by becoming angry at his child, the father insulates himself from his daughter's hurt.

Unfortunately, in the transformation of feeling helpless to blaming the person who arouses one's sense of inadequacy, a destructive interpersonal pattern is established. Emotionally separating himself from a child who has awakened his sense of vulnerability makes it difficult for the father to be empathetically in touch with his daughter's needs, or anyone else's, for that matter.

The allegorical story of the angry father had important implications for me. It was not until my encounter with Pedro that I became sufficiently aware of how strongly demonstrations of unfairness and injustice affected me. I was angry at the conditions that militated against children like Pedro having the same opportunity as those born more socioeconomically fortunate to survive, to live fully and well.

To ease my shamefulness in having affluence in the face of the dire impoverishment that this child represented, I needed some way to bridge the vast cultural gap between the child and myself. In other words, I felt pressed to find a way of indicating to this inarticulate, intellectually limited, and seemingly despondent lad that our brief encounter together was mutually beneficial. Do I mean satisfying? Hardly! Indeed, I was only too aware that the time with Pedro was exceedingly difficult for me!

I had started on this trip to South America as a reward for a successful year of psychoanalytic practice during which I had completed a number of projects that I regarded as ensuring my recognition as a highly regarded psychoanalytic writer and practitioner, including a well-received book. However, the experience of shame I felt with Pedro interrupted the placid and unprobed self-satisfaction I was feeling the moment prior to meeting him.

What had disturbed my unexamined satisfaction with myself was a sense of *sadness*. Baruch Spinoza (1949), the excommunicated and exiled Jewish philosopher of the seventeenth century, noted in his *Ethics* that there is sadness that accompanies the uneasy self-consciousness of shame. In his view, shame as sadness expresses the tension between what *is* in one's current existential condition and the *ought* of one's sense of who one is or should be. In other words, we are valuing beings. Our sense of shame, if we allow it, can play a constructive role in recognizing the responsibilities of virtue by reflecting upon the discrepancy between the person we seek to be and who we experience ourselves being at that moment.

I realized that I was still struggling with the need to justify who I was—in this instance someone who cared about the suffering of others, undoubtedly the emotional component that directed me to a career as a psychologist and psychoanalyst.

My experience with Pedro revealed something of my own inner being in such a way that I was in closer touch with my deeper sensibilities and convictions than I had been prior to our encounter. I came to recognize at that moment that my caring about the separation between myself and some other who was deprived was not an indication of some pallid sentimentality but the affirmation of my sense of agency—my striving to be the person I wished to be. It is our sense of agency that leads us to virtue—those attitudes that enable us to be more enlightened, compassionate, and responsible to both self and other.

And, fortunately, I was not helpless against what ought not to be. No, not as long as I recognized my shame as my willingness to care! Consequently, I needed to inform Pedro that he wasn't given food because of our pity for him, but that all three of us had gained something from our shared moment. But how, I wondered, could I convey this idea to him in a way he would understand?

My eye again caught the scene of Pedro clutching his postcard and matchbox and my friend's pack of cigarettes on the table before her. She routinely lit up a cigarette after a satisfying meal.

The solution suddenly struck me. I asked Pedro whether he would allow me to examine his matchbox. He readily handed it over. The cardboard container had a pretty design on it, but the matches had only ignition value. I said to Pedro in carefully chosen Spanish idiom that my friend, as he could see, smoked cigarettes, but she had forgotten her matches back at her hotel. I suggested that we exchange the food we had bought him for his matchbox. He instantly nodded in agreement. It also appeared as if his facial expression had changed following my offer. For a brief moment it seemed as if he was faintly smiling. But I am not certain. In an instant after our negotiation, still gripping his postcard, Pedro had bolted up out of his chair and was through the door of the restaurant into the chilly Peruvian night.

The agreement of a swap of goods had freed Pedro, my companion, and myself from an embarrassing moment. But more importantly for me, it provided a means for responding to my sense of agency. We all have choices about good and bad every day of our lives. How we approach and choose to deal with these daily issues will shape the more difficult moral choices we face later on. If we respond in ways that are indifferent, callous, or contemptuous, we begin to lose the ability to be virtuous as well. And though we continue to have an opportunity to behave well, to do so becomes more strange—unlike the person we are now experiencing our self to be. In short, our characters are forged by the choices we make. We change as we choose.

Shame may serve admirably as a mark of our humanity (Schneider, 1977). In fact, the experience of shame is like a mirror that reflects back to us parts of ourselves that are typically hidden. Shame experiences are vivid and painful because they foster an accentuated and disturbing sense of self-consciousness. These are moments in which we become aware, as I experienced in struggling to examine my feeling of concern for Pedro, of aspects of ourselves—our ambitions, longings, and sentiments—that are both valuable to our sense of who we are and, at the same time, prone to misunderstanding and derision by other people. In the Pedro story I am referring to the disapproving waiters in the restaurant and even the other customers who didn't seem overly concerned about the welfare of the children begging at their tables. At the time, I imagined that they regarded me with scorn for what they viewed as my overly sentimental behavior toward Pedro. What they probably didn't realize (even if they cared) was that my reflection on the incident in the restaurant enabled me to recognize that I did not know myself and other people sufficiently to live fully, well, and with pride. I had *hidden from myself* my most basic values: social justice and compassion. Accordingly, the French existential philosopher Jean-Paul Sartre (1966, p. 73) in *Being and Nothingness* admits: "I am ashamed of what I am. Shame therefore realizes an intimate relation of myself to myself. Through shame I have discovered an aspect of my being."

The desire for wisdom, like other virtues, has its roots in a sense of shame. It begins with the realization that one does *not* know something that is of importance to living well, and that which is not known is knowable and *should* be known. Shame is positive if it enables us to choose and act. In short, shame becomes constructive upon a reflection on my ignorance and my resolve to learn that which until now I have failed to recognize as important to how I intend to live my life. The major benefit of my shame in the incident discussed here is that it began my conscious awareness that two areas of existence should be of paramount importance to me: friendship and community (that is to say, the community of humanity)—all the rest is vanity.

CONCLUSION

A thorough examination of the etiology and clinical implications of shame is a neglected area of psychological investigation. *The Psychological Abstracts,* the yearly compendium of books on psychological subjects and articles contained in psychological and psychiatric journals, does not have a separate subject category for it, placing this elusive affect under the category of guilt. In short, shame and its variants are the most seriously neglected and misunderstood emotions in contemporary society.

Psychoanalysts traditionally have attributed the most complex and difficult cases (which they would now evaluate as impinged with shame and despair) to the agent of guilt rather than the steward of shame. Due to an overabundance of clinical studies of guilt, the emotional workings of shame have only recently received some of the careful psychological attention they deserve.

LOOK AHEAD

In the next chapter I show by means of social philosopher Martin Buber's notion of an authentic dialogue how I was able to bridge the fault that lay between a seriously disturbed woman and me.

Chapter 2

HEALING SUFFERING AND DESPAIR THROUGH COMMUNION: THE REMARKABLE PSYCHIATRIC CASE CONFERENCE

When in doubt, be human.
—Karl Menninger (contemporary American psychiatrist)

Because of the difficulty I had early in my career as a psychotherapy educator in finding psychotherapy training methods that adequately explored and dealt with the existential roots of psychotherapeutic practice, I decided to design and conduct experiential workshops for mental health practitioners that focused on these concerns. For the past 30 years I have conducted these workshops at professional conferences and in psychotherapy training workshops throughout the world. In these workshops I utilize existential situations and experiential exercises to focus on such issues as separation, loss, aloneness, temporality, limitation, and finitude. Here I confine my discussion to the most important of the experiential exercises I have used in these workshops, the lifeboat situation, and the experiential process that usually is fostered during this exercise—a process that I contend lies at the core of the healing process but that is virtually ignored in the psychoanalytic and psychotherapeutic literature.

THE LIFEBOAT SITUATION

To accentuate a phenomenological sense of time, I ask the participants of an existential workshop to remove their watches and other objective standards of movement and time (e.g., message beepers). I darken the room and relate the instructions for the exercise in a slow cadence. The participants are assigned randomly to small groups of no more than six or seven people. Whenever possible, these groups are sent to separate rooms or locations within a large room where they will be the least distracted by the other groups.

Before the participants move into their groups, I tell them:

> In keeping with the notion that only the immediate moment is presently available to us, I would like each of you as best you can to consider as immediate and real the following situation: You and the people in your group are in a lifeboat in the Atlantic Ocean, far off from the shore and without any real prospect for rescue. To make things worse—you find that your boat is taking on water. There is too much weight in the boat. For the purposes of this exercise, someone has to be dropped overboard, cast away, and lost. This is because of the fact that without casting off one of the people in your boat, your small craft will submerge and everyone will be lost. Again, for the purposes of the exercise, there is no way to avoid this problem; so please don't spend your time planning clever ways to avert this dilemma. You have 30 minutes to deal with this immediate situation.

I move from group to group trying to discourage any intellectual or even practical solutions that would deny the "reality" of the lifeboat situation. Nevertheless, invariably, the participants first view the situation with amusement and intellectual excitement. Accordingly, they usually spend the first moments in the situation planning ways to avoid having to consciously struggle with what their lives mean to them, and whether or not they wish to fight for or even justify their existence in the presence of other people who are also wrestling with the meaning of their existence. However, once other occupants of the lifeboat or I discourage intellectual solutions, the feeling tone in these groups takes on an emotional gravity, similar in my experience to what happens in long-term psychotherapy.

Near the end of the 30 minutes the participants initially are given for their task, I say to the members of each of the groups, separately: "Apparently a serious error has been made! Your boat is taking in water at too rapid a rate. It appears that only *one* person can be saved. You have 15 minutes to handle this situation." This twist of the exercise is designed to discourage the participants from facile solutions, such as one of the participants volunteering or being chosen by the group to "commit suicide" by jumping off—so that the other participants wouldn't need to investigate their existential concerns in depth.

At the end of the 15 minutes, I move the participants out of their small groups and have them join the other participants in a large group. There I encourage a discussion in terms of the following questions:

Were any of you actually able to get yourself into the situation and experience it as immediate and real?

What was the situation like for you?

What did you learn about yourself?

What values and meanings in your life did you get in touch with during this experience?

Do you have any sense how this experience may alter the way you will practice psychotherapy after you leave the workshop? If so, how?

The ways that each participant responds to the lifeboat situation and even the behavior of the participants as a group varies considerably, of course. In the first workshop in which I used the lifeboat situation, the following occurred: Considerable shouting and arguing came from one of the groups. One of the participants was angrily complaining to the other occupants in his boat about the behavior of another participant seated across from him: "Goddamn it!" he said to the accused, "Why are you always putting yourself down? If you want to sacrifice yourself and make it easier for the rest of us, big deal! But in every [professional] meeting I see you, you're doing the same thing—making yourself out to be worthless. Don't you have any ego at all? Don't you have any self-esteem?"

During the general discussion that followed, the blamed participant—who, because he had chosen himself in the early moments of the exercise to jump overboard, had been accused of no self-esteem—explained, in his distinctive German accent, and with considerable animated surprise, that until he found himself in the lifeboat he had completely suppressed the memory that a favorite uncle of his, just prior to the United States' entrance into World War II, had given up his place in a lifeboat to a woman in the water, after his ocean liner had been torpedoed on its crossing from Europe. Without realizing it, he was colluding with a family role.

A few weeks later in a workshop I conducted for the department of psychiatry of a medical school, a highly respected psychiatrist and educator told the others in his group of the rapid loss of his vision. His colleagues assembled around him in his boat spoke of their admiration for him, while at the same time avoiding any discussion of his value to them in dealing with the lifeboat situation. He responded by speaking poignantly to them of his sense of increased distance and separation from people who said that they respected him but treated him as handicapped. His complaint led the others in the boat to speak about the loss of eyesight as a metaphor for the slow but steady progression of finitude for each of them.

Most frequently, at least in the earlier moments of the lifeboat situation, especially when all the occupants of a lifeboat are men, there is considerable competition in regard to who is best qualified to survive for the duration in an open lifeboat in a perilous sea. So, for example, often men who have had naval experience or are skippers of their own sailing boats forcefully indicate they are the best suited to survive alone or to even to save the other occupants' lives by their nautical skills. In other instances, senior occupants or those with serious illnesses may volunteer or be volunteered by the others in the boat to be cast off because of their already diminished future. On the other hand, those who are mothers of small children are usually told by the others in the lifeboat situation that they are the most legitimately qualified among the occupants to be saved because their children need them.

Perhaps the most remarkable lifeboat situation solution occurred when I conducted a workshop on existential psychotherapy for a group of highly seasoned psychotherapists in the southeast of the United States. Given the intense competitiveness, the ambivalence about the value of one's own life and those of other occupants in the lifeboat situation that characterized at least the opening minutes of most of the situations in which I had conducted the exercise, I was taken by surprise to observe the participants in one of the lifeboats from the very beginning of the exercise speaking softly, gently, and, in what appeared to be from my vantage place, an intimate conversation with one another. The calm atmosphere in this group persisted throughout the 45-minute exercise.

I took particular interest in this lifeboat because the senior member of the boat had been a mentor to me—a kind and caring friend who was supportive to me in regard to my early professional writing and, although he lived in a city distant from mine, had often gone out of his way to attend lectures and presentations I had given.

Later, when all of the participants of the workshop reassembled in a large group, one of the occupants of my friend's lifeboat, with tears filling his eyes, told us that each of the occupants of his lifeboat were former students and/or former analytic clients of my friend. As colleagues, they were all acquainted with one another. But what none of them knew was that my friend had recently been diagnosed as suffering from a very serious cancer condition. My friend had told occupants of his boat of his illness and his concern that he had only a limited future. Without much discussion they had come to an agreement in the boat that because life was short and precious, they would spend their time together without struggling about who shall survive and who shall not. All they had for certain was the present moment together, and they would spend this opportunity getting to know one another—and, perhaps, themselves—in ways they had not heretofore. Perhaps that meant the whole boat of occupants would sink, but that would happen later; now each wished to celebrate their all being together and experience their friendship in a way that they had never done before.

What these occupants of the lifeboat participated in I refer to as communion. *Communion* is a moment shared with another person(s) in which each recognizes that all that is important at this moment is the authentic caring of friendship and their shared humanity and common fate as human beings; all the rest at the moment is vanity and vacuous.

COMMUNION AS DIALOGUE

Communion is an I–Thou relationship. In short, we come to know ourselves through the other. Communion is that bond with the other that renders our differentiation from the other both possible and bearable. This is to say, we become a sentient being through participation with another sentient being. Without this authentic dialogue one's suffering is intolerable, an adverse condition the social philosopher Martin Buber calls the I–It sphere (Buber, 1970). It is a world of restricted boundaries, limitations, and finitude. The events of this world are distant, manipulated, objectified. As such, communion is the suspension of inquiry, doubt, or need for certainty. It is the acceptance and recognition of the unique being of the other, which gives a reciprocal validation to the personal worth of one's own being. As such, communion is experienced phenomenologically as the converse of the unbearable obliqueness of unshared being, that is to say, the aloneness and loneliness of ordinary existence. The felt sense by those involved in communion is that "this moment go on forever!"

COMMUNION AND THE PRESENT MOMENT

Communion is the aim toward which every healing and spiritual endeavor intends—usually without its agents' conscious recognition. So, for example, many seek a spiritual communion with a deity to the extent that they lack human communion.

Communion informs us in an unmistakable way that neither our past nor our future shall have dominion over us if we recognize the preciousness of the present moment. In other words, most of us have spent our lives antic-ipating the future, reliving the past. But the present moment has advantage over the past and future—as shown in the experience in my friend's lifeboat—it is our own to do with as we will, provided that we adhere to its requirements and opportunities.

British analyst W.R. Bion (1967), in his terse depiction of the analytic sit-uation, brilliantly brings to light the importance of suspending memory and desire so that both client and analyst may be more fully in the present moment. I regard Bion's paper as a masterful statement of the spiritual com-munion possible in psychotherapeutic and psychoanalytic endeavor in which both client and analyst uphold the requirements of a real relationship rather than regard it as merely a transferential arrangement (Greenson, 1981).

Communion in psychoanalysis and psychotherapy as a spiritual endeavor is unlike religious communion; it is not a process toward something else—such as a union with God or a pathway to salvation. In psychoanalysis and psychotherapy communion also differs from other notable psychological experiences for the client—such as a flash of insight about repressed mate-rial, an emotional recognition of a transferential relationship, or an alter-ation in perception about behavioral options—in that communion is not necessarily a process to another therapeutic moment, but a moment that is sufficient in and of itself. In other words, communion is an appreciation of the other's unique and personal efforts to make sense and to give meaning to our shared present moment. As such, it is a bonding of two beings with-out the submergence of either. As in my friend's lifeboat, it is usually a quiet moment. The agents in the therapeutic encounter may have been struggling contentiously to achieve some rapprochement in their being together, but at this moment they have reached an accentuated recognition that the presence of another caring person is instrumental in assuaging the unbearably oppressive moments of being. In contrast, loneliness is the lack of communion, not only the absence of validation by another, but the feared sense of unawareness of one's being by the other.

Communion may be a moment without explicit language or even overt expression. There will be opportunities later to psychologically investigate the intricacies of this shared experience. But for the present, the shared moment is sensed as complete in and of itself; it is the fulfillment of one's shared humanity with another being.

What does the psychotherapist need to do to render the moment of com-munion possible? A person's energetic presence in a dialogue comes from a harmonious balance of natural rhythm—passivity and activity, thought and emotion, intense involvement and objective observation, and so forth. In other words, one's full presence in a dialogue comes from the articulation of denied and underrepresented aspects of one's personal identity. Creative growth, as the ancient Greeks well understood, requires the reconciliation of oppositional forces within oneself. Advancement in psychological maturity is thwarted by one's failure to harmoniously amalgamate psychologically antagonistic trends in oneself. In other words, too much emphasis given to one side or the other of one's natural dichotomies fosters personal imbalance and tension, creating conflict between those in intimate relating. Consequently, each agent in communion can enable the other to be more fully present by enabling the other to experience those aspects of himself that are underrepresented in their dialogue.

American psychoanalyst Harold Searles (1975) has shown in elaborate detail how the client is or should be an equitable contributor to therapeutic communion by enabling the therapist to recognize and utilize aspects of the therapist's self that he or she has suppressed or has underdeveloped.

The work of British psychologist Peter Fonagy is of importance here, as well. In a series of studies Fonagy (Target & Fonagy, 1996) has shown that the development of the capacity to understand another's mental state in turn fosters the ability to acquire one's own mental agency. In the psychotherapeutic situation it requires the practitioner to comment explicitly on his own processes so that the client is shown a model for articulating his or her own inner experience. Consequently, communion requires a practitioner who not only listens but speaks tellingly as well. In listening to the client's struggles with suffering, despair, loneliness, unrequited love, or whatever the issue is, the practitioner speaks of his own struggles—past and present—and does so with the wisdom and compassion derived from his own experience. The practitioner's ethos may be along the lines that "I endeavor that my efforts will be worthy of my struggle to cherish the being of the other, by enabling me to disclose myself as unconfined and undisguised as I expect of the other in disclosing herself to me." Direct personal statements, discussed in the next chapter, are required in this endeavor.

Are psychoanalysis and psychotherapy unsuccessful without the event of communion? It depends upon the goals of that treatment. If they are simply to alleviate some disturbing symptoms, as practiced in short-term psychotherapy or psychopharmacology, communion may not be a necessary consideration. But genuine healing, similar to genuine intimacy, requires communion.

MOTHER–CHILD BONDING OPTIONS

Communion is at its core the essence of intimacy. As such, for a clue to its earliest development or a lack thereof, I suggest we review the options of the mother–child bonding.

The self, as conceptualized by the early twentieth-century American sociologist Charles H. Cooley and American philosopher George H. Meade, is a "looking-glass self," created from the reflected appraisals of other people, particularly those of early caretakers. In other words, the infant forms an early sense of self from the responses of significant others. Each serves as a psychological mirror, and in these mirrors the infant invents himself.

The earliest and most basic aim of social behavior is the striving for intimate relations with a caring other. The capacity for intimacy usually develops in the infant by means of the mother's mirroring functions. In other words, the mother's responses to her infant serve to represent how other people, in subsequent years, will behave toward the child.

Evidence from developmental studies clearly indicates that the child learns to recognize him- or herself in the eyes and facial expressions of the mother. From the earliest months of the infant's life, the compelling attraction of the probe of the mother's face may take on such riveting captivation for the child as to constitute a powerful need state for the child's existence (Stern, 1985), characterized by "the desire to be known by and to know another, to be understood by and to understand another" (Shane and Shane, 1989).

Infant research (Stern, 1985) also indicates that a very crucial arena for the child's feeling discounted (shamed) comes from finding an incongruity between his own experiences of excitement and joy and what is expressed on his mother's face. The discordance between his experiences and those of his caretaker have been found to effect a disruption in the child's trust of his own judgments as well as an incapacity to recognize his own personal worth (Goldberg, 1991). In short, the infant *needs* to be looked at, smiled at, and approved of by an active, loving, and supportive caretaker. Without this emotional nurturance the infant experiences the world as persecutory and regards aspects of his personal identity as unacceptable. Consequently, individuals who are subjected to an unresponsive or distorted mirroring relationship with a significant other will be handicapped to a greater or lesser degree by their limited capacity to experience their inner being freely, creatively, and courageously.

We can sense the scope of these ideas by recognizing the different ways a mother and her child bond. Prototypically, the mother offers her child *one* of three very distinct and important options in relatedness. In their early relationship, the child may be given unrestricted *permission* by the mother to look into her depths *through* her eyes and by means of her facial expressions. By so doing, she metaphorically gives her child access into the mystery of her psyche. The child's witnessing of the mother's relationship with her own depths allows the child to have a relationship with the mystery of another person and, in turn, to find beauty and contentment within himself.

In sharp contrast with the first option, the child may be provided the restricted opportunity of solely looking *at* the mother's eyes and facial expressions and, as a consequence, be allowed to perceive only his reflection as the mother's limited view of the child. By withholding her mystery from her child, the mother simultaneously discourages the child from trusting his own psyche as a place to foster an enriched inner being. These inner psychic urges to which the child will have access will be experienced as painful and troublesome.

In the third option, the mother allows her child into her depths. But, in the process, she overwhelms him with her anxieties and fears. She treats her child as if he were her own imaginary parent, there to assuage her loneliness and desperation. Because she doesn't recognize her child as separate from herself, or perhaps even as real, she doesn't allow the child the freedom to have his own mystery.

I am proposing that open intimacy between the mother and her child in their early bonding requires the mother's ability to be intimate with her own depths. She must be able to struggle with, or at least not to deny aspects of, her totality as a person. Significant in their relationship, therefore, is the child's witnessing the mother's fortitude in bearing pain and suffering in her caring functions. This perspective has important bearings on the individual's capacity for intimacy.

German American psychoanalyst Hans Kohut (1977) has shown us that children who are denied the open, inner being of their mother for identifying their own psychic experience—because the mother possesses an agenda in which her child is not given sufficient consideration—will be in continual search for external mirrors: other people and objective reflections, such as glass mirrors and photographs, in order to find who they are. Of primary importance, they seek experiences that will reflect acceptable parts of themselves, thereby validating and justifying their existence. It has been my clinical experience, as one might expect, that those who have been nurtured in the first mother–child bonding described above find communion a considerably more easily obtainable experience in everyday life and as a psychotherapy client than those who are products of the other two bonding options. Unfortunately, communion is not a process many clinical settings support.

PSYCHOANALYTIC CLINICAL CONFERENCES

More than 35 years ago in my clinical internship at a renowned medical center, I attended clinical conferences on patients who were hospitalized in the psychiatric and forensic units. The conferences, conducted by eminent psychoanalytic practitioner discussants, were well attended by all the psychiatric disciplines and their trainees. Sitting in, as well, were other prominent analysts who were consultants to the psychiatric department.

The discussant at the case conference had overall charge of the case. His assessment of the patient presented was used as a guide for the patient's care in the hospital. He conveyed his assessment by his didactic remarks about the psychodynamics in the patient's condition and/or from a demonstration of these issues by his skillful interview of the patient. The particular circumstances of the case determined which approach the discussant used. If the psychiatric resident who interviewed the patient early in the conference was adept and/or if the patient was relatively cooperative, the discussant would ask only a few questions—sometimes perhaps only one—broaching information still unclear.

Few members of the audience remained in the room for the entire conference if not directly involved in the patient's care—unless there was a heated controversy among the prominent professionals in attendance about how to understand the case. Consequently, if the patient was highly resistant to being queried in front of an audience or if the case was boring, the discussant usually took an active role in the patient interview.

Frequently, most of the conference was taken up with theoretical disagreements about the childhood factors that caused the patient's present morbid behavior. Little was said about the patient's immediate and future prospects.

With all these eminent analysts present observing the patient, I found it morally and professionally disgraceful that not one was willing to tell us (better yet, show us)—the trainees responsible for these patients—how to help the patients. When I or some other trainee inquired, "But what should I do to treat this patient?" the discussant would usually shrug his shoulders and say, "Just do your best! These sort of patients are virtually untreatable, but they make excellent teaching cases." It was as if these analysts regarded the patients presented at the conference as fictional characters in a novel or film to be studied rather than as real, suffering people who deserved to be helped.

My disdain for analytic attitudes toward human suffering during my internship and later in my psychoanalytic training led me to the writings of

Martin Buber, Albert Camus, and other existential and humanistic philosophers. The centrality of Buber's I–Thou dialogue made eminent sense in
regard to how I wanted to treat other people—both in my analytic practice
and in my personal life.

I discuss here two events to explore what is personally required of a
healer if he or she is to engage in an I–Thou dialogue with an emotionally
disturbed other.

The first event took place during my appointment to the teaching faculty
of a medical school. Several senior psychiatric residents asked me to be the
faculty discussant at a clinical case conference. I was flattered by the request
and determined to behave more wisely and compassionately than the discussants I witnessed in the clinical conferences during my own training.

The conference was held in a room filled with psychiatric residents,
medical students, psychiatric staff, and some members of the teaching faculty. The chief resident of the psychiatric inpatient unit presented the
patient's history.

Use and Misuse of Communion

The patient, whom I shall call Mrs. Franz, was a very intelligent, middle-
aged, upper-middle-class mother of two daughters. Well educated in con-
vent schools in Europe, she was the co-owner of a highly regarded art
gallery in the city. Her partner was Dr. Danton, a family friend and an influential faculty member of this medical school. He sat in the back of the room
during the conference. Her husband, described as a very attractive and
urbane man, was a highly regarded history professor at a local university.

Rather rigid and punitive parents, who used humiliation and ridicule to
discipline her and her siblings, brought up Mrs. Franz. An overriding motif
of her upbringing was that she should associate exclusively with people of
high moral and intellectual character. She was taught that people who have
not developed sufficient intellectual and aesthetic sensibilities are prone to
be derisive about what they cannot appreciate or understand. She conducted herself and her gallery accordingly, unwilling, for example, to sell
or even show her paintings to anyone she regarded as uncultured.

Mrs. Franz had been hospitalized 10 days before the conference. She
had become increasingly secretive and hostile. Flatly refusing to communicate what was troubling her, neither her family nor Dr. Danton had been
able to reach her.

When the reading of her psychiatric history was completed, Mrs. Franz
was led into the conference room by a medical student and given a chair at

the far end of the conference table around which the principals in her treatment were seated. Her drab attire startled me. We had been told that she was a very stylish dresser who wore expensive diamond earrings and rings. She now was dressed in a dark gray hospital dress with no jewelry. In the midst of the assembled mental health professionals, peering inquisitively at her, she looked quite pale, lost, and alone.

Dr. Levy, a mild-mannered and loquacious resident, then took over the interview of Mrs. Franz. But, although he had spoken to her several times before, she remained unresponsive to his questions about her guarded behavior. Throughout his attempts at interviewing her, I heard hushed whispers of annoyance and disapproval around me. Recalcitrant patients do not make stimulating conferences!

Dr. Levy was flushed with exasperation. After a few indecisive moments of wondering what to do, he turned to me and asked whether I would take over the interview.

During Dr. Levy's attempts at interviewing, I had closely studied Mrs. Franz. Her appearance was remarkably similar to the qualities of her guarded self. She was quite thin. I surmised that her slender build had resulted neither from a lack of appetite nor from salubrious considerations of dieting; it was tied into some moral requirements of her upbringing in the home of highly critical parents. In short, her appearance seemed to convey a conviction that it was too painful and unseemly to allow anyone to see too much of her.

Because I sensed that she was proud of her ability to stay thin, asking her first about her diet seemed to me to be a less-threatening line of questioning than to inquire about other aspects of her life. Nevertheless, she said nothing to my questions. I was at the time not overly concerned. I then asked her about how she found the conditions in the hospital. Few patients, even in a well-run hospital like the one in which she was hospitalized, enjoy their stays on a psychiatric ward. I had previously found this sort of question effective in getting angry and withholding patients to speak freely.

To my dismay, Mrs. Franz refused to respond to my questions about the conditions in the hospital. For that matter, although I felt my questions and my manner were clinically sensitive and caring, she would not converse on any subject I broached. Her contemptuous expressions and gestures made it clear that she neither wanted to be in the hospital nor wanted to be questioned in a clinical conference. Indeed, the few words she did utter conveyed her conviction that she didn't belong in the psychiatric ward, but if she needed help, I would not be the person to do so.

I was becoming increasingly self-conscious about how poorly I was doing in trying to reach her. Needless to say, my idealized imago of myself as a competent clinician was quickly dissipating under the critical scrutiny of my colleagues. Because I regarded my difficulties as not caused by any lack in my clinical skills but by Mrs. Franz's intractable psychopathology, I viewed what was happening to me as grossly unfair to my teaching career at the medical school.

The embarrassment of my position caused me stage fright. For a few long moments I was uncertain about what I should say to Mrs. Franz or the audience. Amidst my indecision I found a direction, aided by a strange inner resource: The anxiety of how poorly I was doing as a clinician loosened in my mind an association of memories of past humiliating moments in my life. These events flashed through my consciousness in a rapid kaleidoscope of emotions until my attention focused on a particular event. I realized only afterward that the atmosphere of the conference room—my colleagues' disdain for a difficult patient—had directed the recollection. So, too, was my hope that despite Mrs. Franz's distancing defenses, she desired to be understood.

I describe this event with mixed emotions: an amalgamation of pride at my clever dispatch of a disturbing social situation and, at the same time, chagrin at my deceit.

Some time before, I consulted at a hospital in the upper reaches of the Bronx. The trip to the hospital was long and unpleasant. I rode an old, dirty, crowded subway train from Manhattan to the hospital. The only distraction from the disagreeable travel experience was reading the *New York Times*.

Early one morning as I began reading the newspaper, I observed a heavy, middle-aged African American woman entering the subway car in which I rode. She was garbed in black, wore a strange sort of bird's nest hat to one side of her head, and held a black-covered Bible. A queasy feeling was set off in my gut by the sight of her. I had worked with many such chronically disturbed people in my career. Now I wished simply to read my newspaper. My day as a consultant would be long and demanding; in the afternoon I would be taking the same long trip back to my office in Manhattan to work with analysands until late in the evening.

There were a few empty seats in the subway car. The woman in black did not seat herself. She slowly strolled back and forth the length of the car, with a slightly rocking cadence to her stride, calling out in a loud flat voice, "God speaks to me. God speaks to me."

People in the train, mostly African Americans and Hispanics on their way to work or school, turned their faces away. I, too, attempted to avoid her and concentrate on my newspaper. It was to no avail. I could not ignore her loud, monotonous voice. After 10 or 15 minutes of her further religious recital, I was willing to do anything, short of getting off the train in some unknown (to me) part of the Bronx and, by so doing, miss my work at the hospital. The cars were locked, so I could not readily change cars.

I called the woman over to where I sat and asked her, "Did you say that God speaks to you?" She replied in a loud voice, although she was standing close to me, "God speaks to me."

"Well," I responded, "God speaks to me, too. And if you believe in God you will listen to what He said to me. He told me to tell you that you 'should get off at the next station stop.' "

She looked straight at me. Her appearance seemed altered—her eyes no longer held the fixed, glassy gaze she had when she paced the car. And when the train stopped at the next station, she promptly left the train. Perhaps her exit was a coincidence between my statement and her destination. But I assumed at that moment that her delusional system induced her to believe me.

After she left the train, the other passengers stared over at me as if I were even more demented than the Bible lady. Nevertheless, I felt a sense of considerable relief. I assumed that I would have some tranquillity for the remainder of the trip. I was mistaken. I didn't feel at peace; a disquieting feeling arose in me. I had denied a hapless person my humanity. By using my technical knowledge about psychopathology to insulate myself from my annoyance, I had shown cleverness, not wisdom. Wisdom requires compassion, decency, and common sense.

If I had acted more compassionately on the train, I might have realized that the Bible lady, like many ostensibly sane people, endures her daily struggles, frustrations, and disappointments in the silent hope that her suffering will someday entitle her to a caring closeness with another person. I now believe that the woman's heeding my contrived command came not from a religious delusion but from her desperate wish to believe that my stating that God speaks to me, too, was my statement of communion with her. I surmise that she fervently needed to believe that I understood her, and, as a consequence, cared about her. She was willing to get off at the wrong stop, to what considerable inconvenience I'll never know, as the price for communion with my caring.

In turning my attention back to Mrs. Franz at the conference, I realized at that moment I had the opportunity to utilize my untoward experience on the train to reach another human being in a compassionate way. However,

I could no longer present myself as a professionally aloof being, but as a fellow sojourner. Buber (1970) is quoted as saying, "The origins of all conflicts between me and my fellowmen is that I do not say what I mean, and I don't mean what I say" (p. 26).

Accordingly, I needed to reveal my feelings candidly about my difficult impasse with Mrs. Franz. Yet, to openly disclose my feelings to her, I would at the same time be revealing my personal vulnerabilities to the scrutinizing eyes of my colleagues assembled around me, who were, I feared, critically judging my every word and action. I felt at the moment considerably more comfortable divulging uneasy aspects of myself to Mrs. Franz than to my colleagues. It was best, then, that I turn my thoughts and concerns away from the audience and act as if Mrs. Franz and I were alone in my consulting room.

My initial discomfort with Mrs. Franz had come from my need to act as if I were in control of the clinical situation, and in so doing, deny what was obvious to everyone present: Mrs. Franz was directing the interview, not me. I further recognized that my need to conceal my feelings of professional ineptitude had augmented my dysfunctional anxiety. I decided, whether or not I succeeded in doing a better job of interviewing her, it made no sense for me to remain anxious—certainly not if I could do something about it!

I indicated to Mrs. Franz that I had been asked to interview her because supposedly I had some expertise in cases like hers. I added that I had no idea from where this absurd notion had come. I smiled and pointed to the audience, while saying to her that she must be aware, as were the others in the room, how poorly I was doing.

For a moment Mrs. Franz appeared not to know what to make of my statement. Then, for the first time in the interview, a slow smile crept across her face. Her smile evolved awhile into a quiet laugh. The softening of her face conveyed a warm and approachable person. I told her in earnest that I appreciated her tolerating my ineptitude. Her smile broadened, and her body appeared for the first time to be at ease.

In the process of liberating myself in order to express myself more freely, I became aware that I had been more concerned during the interview with my persona to the professionals present at the conference than in how difficult and shameful this exposure of herself must be for her in front of so many strangers. If I felt uneasy revealing my vulnerabilities to colleagues, some of whom I already knew, her embarrassment must have been even more manifold.

Curiously, as I spoke increasingly of my shameful feelings, she became more responsive to me. She told me, "Dr. Goldberg, I am now willing to talk with you."

But before she spoke of her feelings and the disturbing events that had caused her to become recalcitrant, Mrs. Franz told me the following, as if she were commenting upon a painting hanging in her gallery:

> I should tell you that you are not doing such a poor job interviewing me as you have presented yourself to me and the doctors here. My lack of cooperation, if you want to call it that, is simply because I don't want to be the only person in this room who is going to admit to having feelings. To speak of my troublesome feelings in a room of professionals, who are acting inaccessibly, makes me feel ashamed of my problems and terribly alone.

After a moment's hesitation and with a deep sigh or two, she spoke of what drove her into seclusion. Her words were an admixture of venom and sadness:

> I know that my husband is having an affair with a younger woman. I assume he no longer finds me attractive and interesting. Just as the doctors in this hospital, he expresses his concern about me as if his caring is some damn formal obligation rather than from some personal warmth and interest. He has been rottenly cold and indifferent to me. I have this dreadful feeling as if my personality is crumbling away, without a sense of something to replace it. I feel gripped by the feeling that I am unwelcome to everyone. I feel doomed to a limited life. I guess it is because my husband has been the only person I have ever completely trusted. His betrayal of me has devastated me. There is no one else who cares for me or understands me. I feel isolated and don't know how to reach out to anyone.

I asked Mrs. Franz how she was feeling at that moment. My changing the way I was interacting with her had made a decisive impression on her, she said. By expressing my shameful feelings openly, she was able to express her own vulnerable concerns. Indeed, I had tacitly conveyed to her, by expressing my emotions freely, that it was both safe and proper to express dissatisfactions with oneself at a clinical conference.

Only a few minutes after I started speaking of my anxiety, she and I were involved in the kind of intimate dialogue that a therapist may not achieve until after several months of therapy. Unfortunately, the clinical conference had drawn to a close; our conversation had to be stopped. I never saw or heard from her again. Nevertheless, my time with Mrs. Franz left an indelible impression on how I practiced my profession.

CONCLUSION

Intensive psychological endeavors now stand far behind short-term psychotherapy and psychopharmacology as the treatment of choice in the amelioration of suffering and despair. But these now more-favored approaches cannot achieve what I have referred to as the essential core of the healing endeavor—communion. Communion can take place only where there is sufficient time and interest in the shared humanity and common fate of those who seek to fully share the immediate moment together.

It is noteworthy to point out that nowhere in my purview of the psychoanalytic and psychotherapeutic literature has this elusive but crucial process of communion been explicitly discussed.

An objection by clinicians to the view of therapeutic communion I am describing is that what appears to be communion may be instead, or more importantly, a mutual collusion by client and therapist to avoid some important conflictual issue and its powerful affects. This is an appropriate concern that is no less relevant to all seemingly positive events in psychoanalysis and psychotherapy. However, alert to its possibility, *after* the communion event, the therapist can pursue this possibility. Because as pursuant to the self-validating experience of communion, and with the support of a therapist she or he is now more likely to trust than in the past, the client who has experienced communion with her therapist is far more available for the difficult work of therapeutic exploration than in her past psychotherapeutic work. In other words, communion, like any other clinical material, may be an analytic guide to repressed and well-guarded issues that has been beyond the pale heretofore.

The ideas of British psychoanalysts W. H. Winnicott (1958) and W. R. Bion (1962) are relevant here. In Winnicott's terms the psychotherapeutic situation has the structure of a "holding environment," or what Bion calls a "container." Within this sanctuary both client and therapist are enabled and permitted to explore the entirety of their immediate being in a process of play. In therapeutic play the unrestricted expression of the fantasies of each participant invites a response from the other. In other words, all aspects of the participant's being are given permission to be revealed. But, of course, this encounter would remain only emotive and, perhaps, at best cathartic, without the imposition of *comment*. Comment on the process transforms the intimate moment, which I have previously described, "as if time stopped," to a context that has the attributes of time and space. This is to say, explicit comment on the immediate being together of client and therapist reveals the meaning of the experience to the ongoing lives of its constituents. So, for example, each of those in my friend's group discussed in the large group the personal meaning that the experience of communion had for them.

We live in a world inundated with man's inhumanity to man. So let us stop, pause, and celebrate for a change those moments, those too-few precious moments, that give humanity and nobility to human existence! Is there any human achievement more worthy of psychoanalytic and psychotherapeutic endeavor than the fostering of communion?

Analytic and psychotherapeutic training and experience, it is hoped, will help practitioners guide their torch to a greater awareness and appreciation of why and how presence and communion can be fostered in their consulting rooms, and even more importantly, in the world beyond.

LOOK AHEAD

What makes communion possible, I show in the next three chapters, is a reflective consciousness fostered by constructive shame. These three chapters provide the conceptual and theoretical ideas that have guided my investigation during my psychological career toward an understanding of the compassionate life.

Chapter 3

MORAL INQUIRY:
THE INVESTIGATION OF HUMAN
SUFFERING AND PERSONAL
AGENCY

Suffering is the surest means of making us truthful to ourselves.
—J. C. Sismondi (1773–1842, Swiss historian)

A system of morality is a statement of how a person ought to behave. Morality, as such, is derived from a conception of the necessary responsibilities members of an ideal society must establish and maintain in concert with one another in order to lessen human suffering.

In this chapter I discuss the ideal conditions that would allow the sufferer to constructively define himself in relation to others and in doing so to maintain personal agency.

Nothing accompanies human striving so constantly as suffering—humankind's most puzzling and persistent concern. As such, one would expect that behavioral scientists have been concerned with human adversity as part and parcel of their daily professional endeavors. Therefore, we might also assume that behavioral scientists expend considerable effort in explanations of why we suffer. But in fact few contemporary behavioral scientists have attempted probing examinations of the problem of suffering. They have done little more than treating the symptoms of suffering. Eschewing its etiology as a moral issue—beyond the legitimate bounds of scientific investigation—behavioral scientists have left it to philosophers and theologians to account for the presence of suffering.

Philosophers, however, have been no more diligent in this regard than have behavioral scientists. The presence of suffering of others can easily be avoided. Unlike related subjects that require an audience, such as evil, suffering is usually borne silently and alone. Accordingly, for example, the German seminal philosopher of science, George Simmel, claims that suffering is not what philosophy is about—as if there is something tainted or unseemly about a thoughtful concern with untoward experience (Natanson, 1981).

An investigation of those who suffer yields readily to the observation that many sufferers undergo and remain in a disabled and anguished state in regard to their suffering, while others find personal meaning in their plight that allows them to transcend their anguish. My contention here is that the capacity to find meaning in one's suffering is not a singular endeavor—entirely the product of a personal assessment of one's state of being. As importantly, the meaning attributed to suffering is a socioemotional process that involves the sufferer's willingness to define himself to himself and others in ways that respect his personal agency.

To investigate my thesis, I explore two concerns: One, what is our responsibility in regard to another's suffering? Two, what is the sufferer's responsibility to self and others in regard to his suffering? The experiential material I use to explore our responsibilities to a sufferer are the thoughts and feelings of the protagonist of Russian novelist Leo Tolstoy's masterful novella *The Death of Ivan Ilyich*. The data I build upon in suggesting the responsibilities of the sufferer to self and others is the dialogue between Job and God found in the Book of Job in the Jewish Bible.

HUMAN SUFFERING IN MODERNITY

In the past people generally regarded suffering as an immutable component of human existence; we no longer do. Contemporary attitudes toward human suffering, according to Harvard University theologian Arthur McGill (1982), reveal the pernicious

> conviction that suffering is somehow utterly incompatible with being genuinely human. It is widely believed that no human growth and no human development are possible in suffering.... Not only is it assumed that affliction enervates our humanity, it is also assumed that those who suffer have nothing of value to offer us.... [T]o many suffering has become the most dreaded and most overwhelming form of evil. While earlier ages were preoccupied with the moral evil that issues from the misdirection of human freedom, our times look upon moral evil as secondary to the evil of suffering.... Since suffering effectively destroys our humanity, those who exercise their humanity to help the sufferers can only do so from a vantage point

apart from suffering. In the prevailing view, then, there are two domains, as it were. There is the domain of successful humanity, characterized by people who are healthy, confident, outgoing, and capable of serving others.... On the other hand, there is the domain of suffering.... We can see a vivid example of this dualism [with helpers who behave] in such a way that traces of their fragility and suffering are carefully hidden.... There is an incredible pretense involved in this stance, but it is believed to be essential, so that [helpers of those who suffer] hardly ever present themselves as sharing the same misery as [those they assist]. (pp. 159–163)

Attitudes that stigmatize and objectify those who suffer, obviously, violate the codes of morality found in every culture that entreat us to regard the other as we, ourselves, would wish to be regarded. To gain a constructive context in order to recognize our responsibilities to the sufferer we need to closely examine the avoidance and objectifying responses in ourselves that tend to isolate the sufferer from positive human validation. There is no more excruciating articulation of this tendency than that which is found in the writings of the great novelist Leo Tolstoy. In his novella *The Death of Ivan Ilyich,* Tolstoy writes of the tragedy of living and dying without being understood and personally cared for by those closest to oneself.

Synopsis of *The Death of Ivan Ilyich*

St. Petersburg, Russia, professor of literature Lydia Ginzburg (1991) tells us that the demise of Ivan Ilyich "is merely the death of a human being. Ivan Il'ich has no individual personality; he possesses only those qualities that are typical of the middle-level reformed bureaucrat, and they are enough for the horror of his meaningless middle-level bureaucratic life to shine through in the portrayal of his death" (p. 247). People like Ilyich dwell in the ever present, their unreflecting lives taken over by trivial concerns and meaningless activity, devoid of a sense of passing time (Blythe, 1981).

Tolstoy (1987), with the use of deceptively simple language, portrays Ivan Ilyich as a man without any central purpose, whose major aim in life is to increasingly liberate himself from life's countless disturbances. He behaves in such a way that his daily trivial activities appear "innocuous and respectable. He managed to do this by spending less and less time with his family and when obliged to be at home, tried to safeguard his position through the presence of outsiders" (p. 59).

On the whole, his endeavor was successful: His life progressed in the way he desired—proper and pleasant. However, as an unreflective man, he was jolted, while progressively deteriorating in health, to find his entire family denying his medical condition—because to confirm the seriousness of his condition would keep them from engaging in the ways that they ordinarily enjoyed their lives. Tolstoy tells us that "Ivan Ilyich suffered most of all from the lie, the lie which, for some reason, everyone accepted: that he was not dying but simply ill, and if he stayed calm and underwent treatment he could expect good results.... [H]e was tortured by this lie, tortured by the fact that they refused to acknowledge what he and everyone else knew, that they wanted to lie about his horrible condition and to force him to be party to that lie" (1987, pp. 102–103).

Ilyich was also tormented that his wife and children were annoyed at him for being downcast. His confession of suffering met only with censure. Tolstoy, aware of the solitude that develops from not being accepted after confessing to others, tells us that Ilyich had to go on living like this, on the brink of doom, all by himself, without a single person (except his peasant servant Gerasim) to understand or pity him.

SUFFERING AS AN INTERPERSONAL PROCESS

Psychologists have told us that suffering, unlike happiness, is a state of anomie—"crying out for meaning" (Baumeister, 1991). In fact, this contention is phenomenologically invalid. Suffering merges the victim with others; rarely does suffering occur in a singular way outside an interpersonal context. In other words, other people participate in one's suffering as those who inflict, observe, and comment on one's painful state. This can be seen in recognizing how pain is transformed into suffering.

Medical studies indicate that universally pain is almost always described as "it"—an objective stimulus that causes varying degrees of stress (Bakan, 1968). Accordingly, in observing individual responses to pain we readily see that which is intolerable to one person may be manageable to another. This is because humans experience pain, but pain does not become suffering until it is translated into a category of meaning conveyed to us by the assumptions and expectations of others. Consequently, because suffering is a learned process transmitted to us interpersonally, we may not recognize that we are suffering without trying to see ourselves as others do. Upon taking on the perspective of the other, suffering is infused with meaning—meaning, however, that is often contradictory to how we have been led to believe that our life should unfold. In other words, our state of being is intolerable if it contradicts the conditions we have been told are required for decent human existence. Thus, Ivan Ilyich was puzzled during his illness that his friends and family treated him as a nuisance or indifferently. Such behavior was inconsistent with how he had construed his relationship with others. After all, Ilyich kept telling himself, he was a righteous person as seen by others: He had never abused his power as a magistrate, exercising it leniently and impersonally. We can see in Ilyich's confusion that suffering, rather than being devoid of meaning, is replete with a tormenting sense of injustice.

RESPONSIVENESS TO THE OTHER'S SUFFERING

The central notion in my understanding of suffering is derived from the ideas of the Danish philosopher Søren Kierkegaard, who informs us in *Sickness Unto Death* (1974) that the goal that each of us most ardently seeks is *to become who we are.* As such, "the most common despair is to be in despair of not choosing or willing, to be oneself; but that the deepest form of despair is to choose 'to be another than himself.' On the other hand, 'to will to be that self which one truly is, is indeed the opposite of despair,' and this choice is the deepest responsibility of man" (Rogers, 1961, p. 110).

In keeping with Kierkegaard's ethos, in our responsiveness to the sufferer, we must never define the other as we wont, but instead enable him to define himself to us as he intends. To do so, we must avoid regarding the sufferer primarily in a status role—as sick or well. Status relations deprive the other of his right to contract as he intends. In other words, we need to recognize and emotionally touch the other in the way the other experiences as accurately mirroring his desires for caring and understanding. Second, authentic caring is essential to a constructive responsiveness to the other's suffering. Authentic caring is a demonstration of respect for the other's complexity and mystery. It is the willingness to be there for the other rather than simply do for the other; it is exemplified in a capacity to listen responsibly to the other rather than render value judgments and act as problem solver for the other. When the other is in acute distress, our caring response is to be concerned that the other's struggles to deal with the assumptions she is making about her suffering will be sufficiently worthy to enable her to be as she intends rather than how we or anyone else want her to be.

For our relatedness to be genuine, of course, we require an authentic dialogue with the sufferer.

DIALOGUE AND HUMAN SUFFERING

According to Martin Buber, because our personalities are twofold rather than solitary, dialogue is essential to our nature. "Man exists anthropologically not in isolation, but in the completeness of the relation between man and man; what humanity is can be properly grasped only in vital reciprocity" (Buber, 1999, p. 85). In other words, human wholeness requires an authentic dialogue with another person(s) who also seeks wholeness. In this engagement the other "says something to *me,* addresses something to me, speaks something to me that enters my own life"—which requires me to participate in his being as a whole person (Buber, 1965, p. 9). As a whole person, one must enter into the primary relations that Buber calls I–Thou. Here the totality of what constitutes a human being is revealed. In Buber's words, "I require a Thou to become; becoming I, I say Thou." By evoking Thou the composite of my being is revealed: I am no longer restricted to a predictable, ordered existence, for the I–Thou has no bounds (Buber, 1970, p. 62).

There was no one in Ilyich's world (except in a limited way his servant Gerasim) with whom he was able to have a genuine dialogue. Without dialogue one's suffering is intolerable. This adverse condition is what Buber calls the I–It sphere. It is a world of restricted boundaries, limitations, and finitude. The events of this world are distant, manipulated, and objectified.

We have now examined how we may best respond to the sufferer, but not how he may best respond to his own suffering. The story of Ivan Ilyich is of little help in this regard. We need to look elsewhere.

The Book of Job

The best-known theological response to the problem of suffering is contained in the Book of Job in the Jewish Bible. The story is an extensive debate in which a series of conflicting positions about why we suffer are provided. It is included in the Jewish Bible, according to American Rabbi Neil Gilman, because all theocracies are ultimate explanations of suffering. It was as if the ancient Jewish sages reasoned: "We really don't have any conclusive answer for why human beings are doomed to suffer. So here's another approach" (Gilman, 1990, p. 211). However, the account offered in the Book of Job is intellectually demanding: No single explanation is expounded and defended as preferable; this requires "of its readers a mental flexibility and even a willingness, in the end, to be left with no unequivocal message" (Clines, 1993, p. 368).

The Book of Job is said to have its origins in a myth told by a Semite people who lived in the land of Canaan and were defeated by the invading Israelites between 600 and 300 B.C.E. In the version told in the Jewish Bible, Job is presented as upright and correct in God's eyes: Job feared the

Lord, kept His commandments, and was happy in the midst of his family and goods (Dhorme, 1984). God boasted of this man's perfection to Satan, His chief prosecutor in ferreting out impiety toward Him by His chosen flock, the Israelites. Satan counter-poses God's version of Job. He indicates the possibility that Job's virtue is directly proportional to Yahweh's (God's) generosity. Thus, if Yahweh were to deprive Job of his earthly joys and plentiful goods, Job would turn against God. Yahweh does not accept Satan's assessment of Job. So He permits Satan to test Job by causing great pain to this righteous man and his family. Job's flocks of sheep and goats are slaughtered, his cropland razed, his body afflicted with agonizing disease and disfigurement. Worst of all, his 10 children are slain by fierce winds.

The story of Job still has considerable relevance for a cogent understanding of human suffering. Job's world, replete with devastating losses, was ripe with existential possibility for psychological and spiritual growth—opportunities that were far more problematic for Ilyich. Here I discuss Job's response to his plight and compare it to that of Ivan Ilyich in seeking an answer to why some people undergo and remain in a disabled state in regard to their suffering, while others find personal meaning in their situation that enables them to transcend their anguish.

Job's Existential Plight

The Bible provides no direct help for us in recognizing the psychological factors in Job's background that enabled him to avert a psychotic decompensation. However, we are given ample description of his existential response to his adverse plight. It is my contention that it is Job's proactive stance in regard to how his suffering is being defined and explained by others that enables him to avert anguished suffering. To understand this, we must be clear about what it is that specifically causes Job to suffer. Obviously, it is not the losses and deprivation themselves visited upon him. In the first two books of the story Job seems to accept his plight with equanimity. He says that he doesn't understand the reasons for what is happening to him but will not condemn or turn away from God. But soon Job's attitude changes: He hurls angry invectives against Yahweh for the injustices done to him. What causes this abrupt change in how Job responds to his experiences?

Job's transformation seems directly related to the rhetorical questions that his friends heap upon him that imply that his plight is God's punishment for some sin or wickedness committed by Job. After all, his friends indicate, God is not whimsical but just. Job vehemently protests. He repudiates what has become the dominant biblical explanation for adverse experience: deserved retribution. Job indicates that whereas he can accept the deprivation and losses visited upon him, he will not accept inaccurate and unfair descriptions of him as immoral. It is the *mislabeling* of his behavior and intentions that causes Job to suffer, not the painful experiences themselves. The author of the Book of Job seems to agree; he has God lash out at Job's friends for their outrageous statements to him.

Job's Moral Agency

Job's existential plight is that he feels it necessary to rebel against other peoples' lack of recognition of him as a legitimate moral agent free to negotiate for himself as to how he is regarded and treated by others. Unlike Ilyich, Job actively seeks moral agency.

An individual's sense of freedom of choice of behavior is based on the recognition that he seems to be able in at least some aspects of his life to have some control over his behavior. This capacity is called *personal agency*. A belief in our freedom of will is a *functional* position; it serves to maximize our ability to choose. This is to say, the freedom of choice I experience is made possible by the fact that exercising my belief in psychological freedom enables me to act rather than remain passive. In short, if an individual believes he has some freedom over his behavior, he generally acts in ways to maximize his capacity to choose. If, in contrast, he believes that he has little or no choice, he generally behaves in ways to minimize his decisional activity. "To act is to determine; and the Agent is the determiner" (Macmurray, 1957, p. 134).

By moral agent, then, I mean a person who assumes responsibility for her own actions and inactions. So when she finds herself in adverse situations, she investigates the factors within herself that might have influenced the untoward occurrence. This is quite different from seeking blame and accepting guilt. By using her self-inquiry as a guide, she attempts to redress and correct any attitudes on her part that are incongruous with what she regards as her intended behavior. As importantly, moral agency is interpersonally directed. A moral agent realizes that his statements and actions define him. On the other hand, he is undefined to the extent that he remains passive and undisclosed. The more self-defined a person is, the less other people need to interpret his needs and intentions. Consequently, to the extent that a person addresses descriptions of himself that are inarticulate, constricting, or inauthentic definitions of what he intends, he is able to define himself in a constructive way. *Authentic personal statements* are essential to this endeavor. They are communications in which the agent conveys his perceptions and judgments in a direct and undisguised way. By so doing, authentic personal statements enable the agent to convey the composite of his regard for self and other. Personal statements are authentic insofar as they are products of the agent's struggle to self-examine and not to deny aspects of what he has learned about himself. Obviously, people who don't know themselves very well, having avoided thorough self-inquiry, are handicapped in their capacity for authentic personal statements.

A moral agent is a person, therefore, who with authentic self-awareness insists that others behave responsibly and decently with him, as he with them. Ilyich and Job are clearly distinguishable in regard to their differing capacity for moral agency.

Job enacts his moral agency not only with his friends, but also with Yahweh Himself. God has refused to provide any substantial reason for Job's fate. He seems to be saying to Job: "Who are you to think that you can tell the difference between good and evil?" Job, in response, says in effect: "You have rendered me capable of humanity, but too often you don't exercise your own. I am incapable, of course, of forcing you to do so, but as a legitimate moral agent, I will insist that you extend your compassion and humanity to me." In other words, Job acknowledges God's sovereignty over him as an omnipotent being, but not as a moral agent. Job seems to intuitively recognize that Yahweh often forgets to use His omniscience in dealing with the Jewish people. So Job insists that God negotiate with him in terms of what today we call a *social contract:* an agreement of limitation on each other's wont to wound (physically, socially, psychologically). Specifically, Job agrees to continue his piety to Yahweh and accept his fate, if in return God tempers His rage with His compassion. In asking Yahweh to use His omniscience to protect Job from God's omnipotence, Job seems to be tutoring God toward a greater sense of humanity by showing Him how to self-reflect. Initially God doesn't accept this contract. Job insists. Finally, Yahweh relents and agrees to Job's proposal.

My interpretation of Job as a moral agent has some similarities with the Swiss psychoanalyst C. G. Jung's (1971) intriguing and controversial view of God as a highly paradoxical figure in the Jewish Bible. Jung contends that Yahweh has been portrayed contradictorily throughout the earliest biblical scriptures. A deity immodest in His passions, Yahweh often suffered for His fiery temper. He frequently admits to being eaten up with instinctual rage and jealousy that have no understandable origin—an awareness that disturbs Him. He recognizes that owning to His lack of self-examination, He occasionally presents His chosen people, the Israelites, with insoluble conflicts (Jung, 1971).

In Jung's view, God could have permitted such cruel satanic mischief only because He forgot to use His omniscience. In the story of Job, for example, Yahweh did not recognize how much He actually favored His dark son, Satan, over the welfare of humanity.

However, Jung also points out that Yahweh, so often seen as raging and seeking vengeance in the Jewish Bible, is no less frequently portrayed as demonstrating loving-kindness and charity toward His chosen people. Jung contends that this paradoxical presentation of the deity manifests a psychological condition conceivable only when one does not consciously reflect upon one's actions and intentions or when one lacks a highly developed capacity for self-reflection. Jung, then, argues that Job has a better-developed consciousness and mature sense of morality than does God. Job uses these assets to cleverly encourage God to separate His loving presence from His terrible, irrational rage and to become an advocate for Job in protecting him from Yahweh's own madness (Jung, 1971).

Job's Moral Courage

Job shows considerable courage in his insistence on a social contract with Yahweh. In recognizing Ilyich's paralyzing trepidation as compared to Job in their existential plights, we can observe the crucial role that a moral imperative plays in fostering personal agency. In observing Job's courage in his struggle with Yahweh, we see that courage is not a character trait, an essentialist attribute that one person possesses and another doesn't, without which forthright behavior cannot occur.

The belief that courage is a trait or attribute that some people have, while others don't, prevents people who don't regard themselves as courageous from carrying out acts that they are capable of performing. Courage, in other words, is not a mysterious quality, bestowed at birth or metaphorically a result of being struck by lightening and as a result being forged as a brave person. In fact, courage is an empty and illusory concept except as a term to describe a series of specific behaviors and activities that all of us are capable of performing. Courage is in fact allowing our actions to be statements of our identity and purpose in life.

I agree with the American humanistic psychologist Rollo May that the act of courage has a *moral* aim. May (1978) claims that each act of courage raises the moral conscience and social consciousness of the society in which it is exhibited. Courage is necessary because the human condition is by its very nature risky and uncertain. Without courage we are apt to avert the deeper concerns of human existence. Consequently, the act of courage proclaims that the denial of certain values and ways of being are intolerable. Life without them, like an unexamined existence, is not worth living.

In the act of courage a person proclaims by means of his act(s) an implicit trust that by his audacious conduct he has created a bond with humanity to raise humanity's consciousness, to accentuate its awareness, and to challenge its unexamined assumptions about human behavior. In committing himself to a courageous act a person also makes the assertion that these acts do make a difference in the world. Accordingly, the author of the Book of Job seems to be telling us that Job by his act of courage is stating his willingness to stand up and be recognized as a responsible moral agent. And, as importantly, Job's implicit trust is that humanity will be confronted and shaken by his act and, as a result, will be more accountable.

MADNESS AND SUFFERING

It is the participation in a dialogue with God—in which Job is a legitimate moral agent—that enables Job to escape madness. In other words, whereas Job clearly is suffering, his suffering is not that of a psychologically disabled person such as Ilyich.

The great literary moral philosophers—Sophocles, Shakespeare, Goethe, Dostoevsky—intuitively understood that madness is not an illness—at least not in the medical sense of an organic system affliction. I am referring to the madness that is reactive to psychological conditions and am sidestepping here the question of the role that genetic and constitutional factors play in functional psychosis. Madness is an agonizing impairment of the ability to feel good about oneself and confident in one's relationship to others. It is a moral affliction in the sense that madness issues from a severely pained trepidation: the sufferer's inability or unwillingness to define himself as a legitimate moral agent. In other words, madness is a passive acceptance of the shame and humiliation the sufferer has endured at the hands of his caretakers. Instead of protesting and constructively defining himself to those who don't seem to understand him, Ilyich excommunicates himself from human company. Ashamed of his incapacity to deal effectively with others, Ilyich uses his excommunication as a way of hiding from the world—to keep others away from his vulnerable personal identity. Like the Irish poet Dylan Thomas's dying father, he is unwilling to "rage, rage against the dying of the light."

A number of influential writers in the past few decades have attributed a sense of existential clarity and creative energy to the mad. British existential psychiatrist Ronald Laing (1967), for example, presents madness as a mitigation of the constraints of the false self and the self-deceptions of our everyday world. There is some validity to this perspective. The absence of self-deception of the mad, American sociologist Ernest Becker (1973) shows us, is caused by their failure to "confidently deny man's real situation on this planet" (p. 63). But rather than possessing the creative power to overcome their alienation, as Laing suggests, from what he refers to as the appalling state of normality, Becker indicates that it is the misfortune of the mad that they are "burdened with extra anxieties, extra guilt, extra helplessness, an even more unpredictable and unsupportive environment" than the rest of us (Becker, 1973, p. 63). Like Ivan Ilyich, the suffering and terror of those who are mad emanate from their inability or unwillingness to constructively define their personal agency to themselves and to significant others.

CONCLUSION

Job is one of the earliest existential figures in the Jewish Bible. He finds existential satisfaction as a moral agent in responding to his own suffering. Ilyich, in contrast, remains psychologically disturbed because he does not. As such, he is prevented from finding meaningfulness in his plight in that it takes a responsive other with whom to dialogue, to touch the deeper sources of one's existence, and, in doing so, to experience one's human wholeness.

In coming to terms with our human wholeness, we are compelled to recognize that we are essentially frail, limited, vulnerable beings. The realization of our finitude may be assuaged somewhat by the busy work of our daily endeavors, together with our dishonesties about the precariousness of our situation in the world. There are moments, however, Tolstoy informs us, such as serious illness in ourselves, or those we care about, that baldly compel us to confront the impermanence of our existence. Such moments evoke more than just anxiety; they often unleash sheer terror. This terror foretells the decimation of any viable meaning for our existence.

To constructively confront this terror, Tolstoy shows us, we first need to realize that human purpose is only meaningful to an existent being—that is to say, someone who is finite and someday will cease to be. Ivan Ilyich found some meaning for his existence in the last hour of his life, by courageously struggling for the first time with what previously was his impeded love for others.

The function of suffering and despair, Tolstoy seems to be telling us, is to confront us with the reality of our tenuous existence on this planet. Without this tragic sense, we might mistakenly assume that by simply being human, we are fully taken care of by Providence. Under this illusion, we might assume that we need neither to improve ourselves nor to reform the conditions of society. Personal agency enables us to recognize and responsibly address the social and personal requirements of enlightened selfhood.

LOOK AHEAD

The role that curiosity and its impeded states play in the development of morality is shown in the next chapter to be central to how and why each of us struggles with conflicting systems of morality.

Chapter 4

THE MORTAL STORM: THE STRUGGLE BETWEEN RIGHTEOUSNESS AND COMPASSION

(N)ature hath implanted in our breasts a love of others, a sense of duty to them, a moral instinct, in short, which prompts us irresistibly to feel and to succor their distresses.
—Thomas Jefferson (1743–1826, American president)

As a social theorist as well as a psychologist, I am concerned with what each of us as a member of a troubled society can gain from a thorough study of very destructive people about the underlying causes of our complex social problems and the practical, tangible ways enlightened psychological inquiry will enable us to successfully address these issues. My contention is that we can learn a great deal about the development of virtue by an investigation of people who seem to be psychologically healthy except that they lack an important moral sense. This attribute is reflective consciousness, a crucial factor in the development of constructive moral behavior.

Three widespread social outrages during recent years have severely shaken our trust in the moral fiber of American society: Catholic priests abusing children, sexual predators abducting and murdering young girls, and officers of large corporations illegally manipulating their accounting practices in order to collect millions of dollars for themselves, while at the same time depriving their rank-and-file employees of their pensions and life savings.

Declarations by our public officials, together with citizen outcry, suggest that the solutions to these problems—and by implication, the reparation of our society's moral failings—require that these villains be severely punished by long-term imprisonment. Furthermore, as preventive strategies, those calling for reforms also demand the early detection of wrongful behavior by means of sophisticated psychological screening of candidates for the priesthood, better police tracking of sexual deviants, and strict federal laws in regard to acceptable accounting practices by corporate officers.

A psychological purview of the reforms called for above suggests that we Americans, as a nation, believe that by strengthening the observational and punishing components of the superego of the American psyche we can successfully overthrow our moral failings. My clinical experience strongly suggests that strengthening the demands of the superego of the American psyche will not accomplish our aims. To illustrate my contention, I offer the following clinical occurrence: A not unusual event in prison is the brutal beating or even killing by other inmates (including those who have been diagnosed as psychopaths) of molesters and murderers of young children, the elderly, and the severely disabled. How does one reasonably explain these reactions as self-interested behavior on the part of psychopath inmates? Indeed, this clinical example indicates that there exists even in prison populations a strong sense that certain social behaviors are unacceptable and deserve severe retribution for the offenders. In short, it would appear that a strong code of morality—emphasizing proper behavior—is alive and well even in prison. In this book I define the obedience to the values and mores of one's society as *righteous* behavior.

However, whereas righteous behavior has shaped every society since the beginning of the world, at the same time, few societies have been peaceful either in regard to their neighbors or within their own internal boundaries. Fear, hatred, and cruelty have pervaded the corridors of most societies. Not surprisingly, then, those psychopathic inmates referred to above when freed from prison usually continue to victimize and hurt other people. Obviously, there is a crucial lack in their moral development, but it is not—as I contend as my major thesis—a sense of righteous behavior.

I provide here a psychohistorical perspective in order to investigate why people who have a sense of righteous behavior are, nevertheless, willing, and often quite eager, to victimize the weak, the vulnerable, and the unprotected. I confine my purview in this chapter to Nazi Germany.

The sheer brutality and inhumanity of the Nazis' behavior toward those designated as outsiders during the Holocaust have been commonly described as the behavior of immoral, demented brutes. I seek to show here that such a facile depiction of the Nazis does not hold up to psychological scrutiny. However, by examining a spurious notion in our understanding of moral behavior, I suggest here a new direction for understanding virulent hatred/brutality and the development of virtue.

THE MENTAL STATUS OF THE NAZIS

Adolph Eichmann ranks near the top of the list of the most destructive people who have ever lived. Half a dozen Israeli psychiatrists examined Eichmann before his trial in Jerusalem, but not one was able to discern any serious abnormality in his intellectual functioning or any other indications of a mental illness. Indeed, one of the psychiatrists, emotionally agitated from having to be in close quarters with this architect of genocide for several hours, commented that Eichmann was normal, "(m)ore normal, at any rate, than I am after having examined him" (Arendt, 1963, p. 25). Another psychiatrist indicated that "his whole psychological outlook, his attitude toward his wife and children, mother and father, brothers, sisters and friends, was not only normal but most desirable" (Arendt, 1963, p. 26). As German American philosopher Arendt (1963) indicates about Eichmann, "his was obviously also no case of insane hatred of Jews, of fanatical anti-Semitism or indoctrination of any kind. He 'personally' never had anything whatever against Jews; on the contrary, he had plenty of 'private reasons' for not being a Jew hater" (p. 26).

British political scientist B. Clarke (1980) wrote that what concerned him most about Eichmann was not his madness but his sanity. Eichmann's tragedy, Clarke claims, was "that he did not inherently lack the faculties of understanding, reason and will but merely gave up the active and personal use of these faculties—that he deferred in all important aspects to the faculties of others [e.g., Hitler and Himmler]" (p. 428).

Clarke is suggesting that something important was missing in Eichmann's behavior toward his victims—a personality attribute that a purview of his life history (Arendt, 1963) seems to indicate was absent throughout his life.

I start my inquiry of the missing ingredient in Eichmann's personality, as well as other Nazis, with a question about Eichmann: What do we make of a person, of at least bright, normal intelligence, who harbors no personal animosity toward a group of people, who never seems to have made any statement that he had accepted the Nazi propaganda that this group is evil, vile, or inferior, and yet acts with no moral hesitance in initiating or condoning the mass extermination of these people?

Normally, behavioral scientists account for the heinous behavior committed by people such as Eichmann as those of a person who is either psychotic or suffering from a severe personality or character disorder. Psychosis is characterized by one or more of three major psychological disturbances: one, a severe *depressive* state, in which the sufferer's happiness and well-being is constricted to the extent that the person is incapacitated from effectively participating in everyday activities—accompanied by a belief, unsupported by reason, that the sufferer is guilty of unforgivable wicked thoughts and/or deeds; two, *paranoid* ideas—a systematic and pronounced belief that another person(s) is conspiring to harm the sufferer because of his unique capacities or eminent position in the world; and three, by a *deficiency in the ability to reason,* seriously interfering with the sufferer's ability to test reality and to relate to people in such a way as to fulfill appropriate needs and intentions.

However, the psychiatrists who examined Eichmann found no evidence that he was suffering from an agitated depression, paranoid ideas, or a thinking disorder (Arendt, 1963). People who are not psychotic and who act as malevolently as Eichmann did usually are diagnosed as psychopaths. But again, the psychiatrists who interviewed him and the minister who had an ongoing relationship with Eichmann found that his psychological outlook on life was not only appropriate but "most desirable" (Arendt, 1963, p. 26). The mystery of what is missing in the Nazi personality widens upon an inquiry of other leading Nazi officials.

Sixteen other leading Nazi officials, as war criminals, were examined by two American Army officers, psychiatrist Douglas Kelley and fluent German-speaking clinical psychologist Gustave Gilbert, soon after the Second World War—as part of the preparation for the Nuremberg trials. To determine whether the personality organization and psychological functioning of these men had incurred some form of psychopathology that could explain their behavior, they were administered the Wechsler-Bellevue Adult Intelligence Test, the Rorschach, and the Thematic Apperception Personality Test and were interviewed on numerous occasions by Kelley and Gilbert. The Nazi war criminals evaluated were:

Hans Frank—Minister of Justice and the German commander who had put down the Warsaw ghetto uprising

Hans Fritzsche—Chief deputy to Joseph Goebbels

Walter Funk—Minister of Economics

Herman Goering—Second in command to Adolph Hitler and Luftwaffe Chief

Rudolf Hess—Hitler's secretary

Ernest Kaltenbrunner—Chief of the concentration camps

Wilhelm Keitel—Chief of Staff for the Armed Forces

Constantin von Neurath—Protector of Bohemia and Moravia

Franz von Papen—Vice Chancellor under Hitler

Joachim von Ribbentrop—Foreign Minister of State

Alfred Rosenberg—Editor of the major Nazi newspaper and the leading anti-Semite propagandist in Germany

Fritz Sauckel—Plenipotentiary General of the Utilization of Labor ("slave labor")

Hjalmar Schact—Minister of Economics of the State

Baldur von Schirach—Youth Leader for the Third Reich

Artur Seyss-Inquart—Governor to occupied Poland, Austria, and the Netherlands

Albert Speer—Hitler's chief architect

Ten leading psychology projective-test experts were asked to perform a blind evaluation of the Nuremberg prisoners' protocols—that is to say, they were given the responses to the Rorschach of the prisoners without prior knowledge of whose clinical data they were examining. The results were surprising. The Rorschach protocols were interpreted as indicating that whereas the Nuremberg prisoners had a wide range of differences in their personality adjustment—from the exceptionally well-integrated personalities of Schact and von Schirach to the severely disturbed Hess and Von Ribbentrop—nevertheless, none showed any marked superego impairment. Certainly, none was shown to be a hostile, impulse-driven sadist.

On the basis of these findings, the Rorschach interpreters reported that they concluded not only that such personalities are not unique or insane, but that they could be duplicated in any country of the world today (Harrower, 1976). In keeping with this interpretation of the clinical data, American psychologist Barry Ritzler (1978) points out that "[t]he Nazi themselves, almost to a man, clung to the defense that they simply were normal victims of circumstances—loyal, well-intentioned and obedient to the perverted wills of their superiors (whoever that conveniently happened to be)" (p. 252).

In a summary chapter evaluating the multitude of clinical papers and books written about the psychological assessment of the Nuremberg prisoners, American psychologists Gerald Brofsky and Don Brand (1980) add to Rorschach expert and New York University Professor Molly Harrower's (1976) findings, "[a]t the present time we as psychologists have been unable to satisfactorily 'explain' the motivations and personality organization that prompted the NCWS [the Nazi war criminals] to such grotesque and inhuman acts" (p. 399).

Common sense surely finds a remarkable discrepancy between the psychologists' interpretation of the clinical data and the barbarism of the acts instigated or condoned by the Nazi leaders. Only two explanations seem possible. We can choose to believe, as many apparently still do, that the reports of the kinds and the numbers of atrocities during the Holocaust were greatly exaggerated—that is, the defendants at Nuremberg were not guilty of the sheer magnitude of heinous crimes attributed to them. Or we can doubt the adequacy of the interpretations of the psychological findings of these malevolent criminals.

Since the reality of the Holocaust cannot be denied by rational beings, we are left with the second conclusion: The tests and interviews failed to detect psychopathology because the theoretical assumptions upon which the psychologists interpreted the test data were inadequate for helping the psychologists recognize crucial signs of moral defect in the responses of the Nuremberg prisoners.

THE PSYCHOANALYTIC NOTION OF MORAL DEFICIT

At the time that the Nuremberg prisoners' clinical data were interpreted, Freudian psychoanalytic theory guided almost all in-depth psychodynamic assessment of personality. There simply were no other substantial theoretical competitors.

Psychoanalytic theory regards the prohibitions and commands of the superego as the primary basis of an individual's personal morality. In other words, the superego is formed from a person's identification with societal values through the incorporation of that person's parental moral authority. Consequently, immoral behavior is regarded in psychoanalytic theory as being caused by a limited or poorly functioning superego.

FREUD'S CONFUSION OF SUPEREGO AND CONSCIENCE

Viewing moral conduct as an autonomous act of healthy striving comes from the belief that its expression is a manifestation of affection for others rather than compelled from the fear of punishment for wrongful behavior.

Sigmund Freud (1905), however, mistrusting love as a binding force in mature relationships, rejected affection as a healthy mainspring of human behavior. Instead, he viewed it as a seductive, repetitive magical wish inflicting everyone. In short, he believed that intimate attachments were the rediscovery of the lost object—in which the experiences of affection and love repeat infantile patterns. Predicated upon the mother–child bonding, disappointments in adult attempts at intimacy result in inevitable narcissistic hurt and depression. As such, love sentiments were for Freud an unreliable guide for moral conduct.

Freud also did not trust altruistic behavior. In his writings (Freud, 1930, and his letters to Albert Einstein) he reduced all human strivings to conflictual drives, and by so doing, he eschewed altruism and other virtuous behavior as fundamental human attributes. He claimed, instead, that these apparent virtues are actually psychological defenses compelled by feelings of guilt and/or grandiose fantasies to mask feelings of impotence.

Someone who believes that neither affection nor altruism is genuine is left with only fear and the threat of punishment as moral guardians. Freud (1923), therefore, held that the superego—predicated on fear and threat— is the agent of morality. However, as Harvard University psychiatrist Robert Coles (1981) indicates,

> the moral texture of a life is, one suspects, not going to be fully explained by an analysis of how the ego negotiates with the id and the superego. Nor is the ego or the superego, important as they be to an understanding of moral development, quite all we need to know in the face of certain dilemmas. [As] Erik H. Erikson has shown us in his studies of Luther and Gandhi, and as any number of clinicians come to realize in the course of their everyday professional lives, neither among the great nor among ordinary people do defense mechanisms quite account for the entirety of psychological life.

A balanced purview of psychoanalytic writing on moral development should indicate, in agreement with Coles, that some psychoanalytic writers have suggested that the moral development of the child cannot properly be reduced to the inculcation of parental values from the threat and fear of punishment. These theorists (Brunswick, 1940; Greenacre, 1954; Grinker, 1957; Macalpine, 1950; McDevitt, 1979; Schafer, 1960; Spitz, 1958) have discussed the affectionate qualities of the mother–child bonding and have suggested that through a loving identification with the mother the child acquires a potential for generosity and concern for others. The import of this insight, however, is unsystematically scattered through the psychoanalytic literature. I contend, therefore, that throughout its history and until this day, psychoanalytic theory in general has regarded virtuous behavior as a defensive strategy to avert the threat of introjected parental punishment. Nevertheless, whether or not one agrees with my overall assessment, it is clear that the view I have presented of psychoanalytic notions about moral development prevailed at the time when the Nuremberg prisoners' clinical data was interpreted.

DIFFERENTIATING CONSCIENCE FROM SUPEREGO

An important lead in understanding why righteous people are willing to treat others without regard to their humanity comes from the work of American sociologist Eli Sagan—who persuasively argues that for the superego to be moral it needs the services of the *conscience*. He (Sagan, 1988) points out that "(t)he relative health or pathology of the superego is [actually] dependent on how much or how little of conscience is operative in its functioning" (p. 14) because the *superego always collaborates with its own corruption.* In contrast to superego, the conscience is fostered in love, derived from the child's strong early bonds with loving caretakers.

It should not surprise us, then, that Freud's misconception of superego and conscience makes it rather difficult to make any psychological sense of heinous acts by individuals with strong superegos. As Sagan (1988) indicates, "the mechanisms of the superego make it possible to use almost any virtue in the most horrible of human projects...the Nazis used all the trappings of the superego to promote genocide" (p. 13). In other words, the good Nazi was loyal, obedient, even willing to sacrifice his life to carry out the prescriptive norms of his society. Because his superego was not deficient, but actually too severe and punitive, he perceived life only in bold black or white dimensions.

Nevertheless, in the reality of adhering to any moral code, there arises uncertainty as whether to be more righteous or more compassionate in a particular situation. We can detect this dilemma in a speech given by Heinrich Himmler, the odious overseer of the German concentration camps, to his SS officers: "I want to talk to you quite frankly on a very grave matter.... I mean...the extermination of the Jewish race...most of you must know what it means when 100 corpses are lying side by side, or 500, or 1,000. To have stuck it out and at the same time—apart from exceptions caused by human weakness—to have remained decent fellows, that is what has made us hard. This is a page of glory in our history which has never been written and is never to be written" (Manwell & Fraenkel, 1965, p. 132).

It is prudent to consider the exploration of moral conduct rendered by the influential University of Chicago philosopher John Dewey in regard to how a person ought to respond to the dictates of the code of morality of his society. Dewey (1980) indicates that "[a] moral principle...is not a command to act in a given way; it is a tool for analyzing a special situation, the right or wrong determined by the situation in its entirety, not by the rule as such" (p. 141). In other words, causing suffering to others—because it is in keeping with a society's righteous morality—in an unreflective way isn't moral; it is merely heartless and inhuman.

It is important to recognize that Dewey's statement reveals that a morality based upon either righteousness or conscience is not categorically right or wrong in itself. Each has a place in a constructive moral behavior. This can be illustrated by the following hypothetical example: Dr. A. is a criminologist. He believes that society would be a better place if each of us upheld with courage and fortitude the highest standards of personal responsibility to the values and mores of our society (righteousness). Reverend B. is a clergyman. He contends that the social problems that plague us would be best addressed if we exhibited liberal amounts of tolerance and compassion for other people's mistakes and limitations (conscience). To properly understand the moral validity of righteousness and compassion we must investigate how each is used in actual situations.

In this regard, I contend that what the good Nazi lacked, then, was not recognition of moral options, but rather empathy, compassion, and concern for people who were not like him (in whatever ways his limited insight about the humanity of other people impressed upon him).

A person with desirable attitudes toward life can become as evil as Eichmann showed himself to be if he lacks a propensity for curiosity. In other words, Eichmann—who was in the audience during Himmler's speech— never appears to have questioned the heinous role he was asked to assume in the genocide of the Jewish people.

Curiosity, an intrinsic personality propensity with which all but an unfortunate few enter the world, furnishes us with the raw material for fostering a sense of who we are. I define curiosity as the capacity for inquisitiveness and the accompanying feeling of wonderment about those matters one does not yet understand. As such, curiosity involves the capacity to suspend judgments and to explore with passionate interest the conditions of one's private and social worlds. Over time curiosity maintains itself by a willingness to ask questions and to periodically subject to doubt everything one cherishes and holds firm.

In trying to explain the apparent contradiction between the Nazis' reported normality and their involvement in genocide, we need to recognize that the expression of righteousness alone does not result in virtuous behavior. A strong propensity for curiosity about oneself in relation to other people also is required.

Is there any evidence that verifies my notions about the differentiation of superego and conscience in the clinical data of the Nuremberg prisoners? Apparently, there is. Psychologist Barry Ritzler (1978) reports that the Nuremberg prisoners, based on the University of Chicago psychologist Samuel Beck's (Beck, Beck, Levitt, & Molish, 1961) system of analyzing the content of Rorschach responses, "were distinguished [from the other populations of whose Rorschach responses they were compared: schizophrenics, depressed patients, and state troopers] only by a significantly low percentage of human responses. In the absence of any other indication of severe psychopathology, the low human percent stands out as a suggestion of an inability to empathize with other human beings. It also suggests the Nazis may have had an incomplete sense of their own identities as human beings" (p. 349).

LITERARY ACCOUNTS OF CONSCIENCE

In the real world, the usual moral struggle is not choosing between purely good and purely evil options—it involves *competing* and *conflicting* moralities. Indeed, in extreme situations, acting in a courageous and compassionate way may, and often does, involve violating duty to family and the ostensible values of one's society.

Consider the situation of the rescuers of the Jews and other persecuted people trying to flee the Nazis. To those they saved, they were expressing the highest moral virtues. But stop and consider what the families and neighbors of these courageous people might have felt. Some may have approved, and indeed, a number of entire families were involved in aiding the oppressed. But still more families and their neighbors—especially those whose lives were threatened, if not forfeited, by the rescuer's actions—undoubtedly believed that the rescuer was violating his or her duty to protect them from harm for the sake of the welfare (in most cases) of strangers.

As is so often the case, it is the literary master psychologists, rather than professional psychologists, who have provided the most brilliant insights into our moral dilemmas.

In several passages of Mark Twain's *Huckleberry Finn,* Huck struggles with a dilemma as to whether he should turn in the runaway slave Jim—with whom he has formed a strong affectionate bond—to the authorities. Not to do so would violate the moral lessons his pre–Civil War Southern society had taught him about proper and responsible behavior. But Huck doesn't want to return his friend, who escaped to rescue his children. He feels guilty and fears punishment—the consequences of violating the demands of his sense of righteousness for considering a course of action that neglects his societal duty—especially since Jim has talked about murdering the white people who have taken away his children.

Yet, Huck realizes that if he turned in Jim, he would feel worse than if he did what he intuitively senses as proper—helping Jim to escape. Huck is uncertain about the basis of his feelings; they seem unrelated to anything he has ever been explicitly taught. As Yale University sociologist Helen Lynd (1958) points out, "Huckleberry Finn had no doubt that he was doing wrong, but, because of some wider feeling of human decency that he could not name, he could not bring himself to do what his society called right" (p. 36).

In the end, Huck follows his intuition about the right thing to do. His conscience—based on his love for Jim—enables him to regard Jim as a struggling fellow human like himself rather than as a piece of property to be returned to his owner (as his sense of duty demands), overriding his fear of punishment.

Mark Twain's insight about altruistic behavior is in firm accord with studies of actual courageous altruists, such as those who rescued the Jews during the Holocaust. These people commonly perceived themselves as strongly linked to others through a shared humanity (Fogelman, 1994; Monroe, Barton, & Klingemann, 1990; Tec, 1986).

The eighteenth-century French writer J-J. Rousseau's *Emile* is the second superb classic work of literature that can help us understand the development of human conscience. Rousseau's treatise on moral philosophy is predicated on the recognition that the human infant is born naturally good. Error and vice, he claims, imposed from the outside from the demands for private property and material wealth, subtly subvert our inherent goodness (Jimack, 2000).

The novel *Emile* consists of Rousseau's philosophy of how a tutor can successfully inspire from infancy—by didactic and dramatic lessons in living—a virtuous adult. Below I have abstracted several of the most important of Rousseau's principles in the moral education of his pupil Emile (Rousseau, 2000):

Remember you must be a man yourself before you try to train a man; you yourself must set the pattern he shall copy. [Your] authority will never suffice unless it rests upon respect for your goodness. (p. 69)

Rather than hasten to demand deeds of charity from my pupil I prefer to perform such deeds in his presence. (p. 80)

The only moral lesson which is suited for a child—the most important lesson for every time of life—is this: "never hurt anybody." (p. 81)

Men are taught by fables; children require naked truth. (p. 91)

The degrees of conscience are not judgments but feelings. Although all of our ideas come from without, the feelings by which they are weighed are within us, and it is by these feelings alone that we perceive fitness or unfitness of things in relation to ourselves, which leads us to seek or shun these things. (p. 303)

The child's first sentiment is self-love, his second, which is derived from it, is love of those around him; for in his present state of weakness he is only aware of people through the help and attention received from them. So a child is naturally disposed to kindly feelings because he sees that everyone about him is inclined to help him and from this experience he gets the habit of kindly feelings toward his species; but with the expansion of his relations, his needs, his dependence, active or passive, the consciousness of his relations to others is awakened, and leads to the sense of duties and preferences. (p. 209)

So pity is born, the first relative sentiment which touches the human heart according to the order of nature. To become sensitive and pitiful the child must know that he has fellow-creatures who suffer as he suffered, who feel the pains he has felt, and others which he can form some idea of, being capable of feeling them himself. (p. 220)

First Maxim—It is not in human nature to put ourselves in the place of those who are happier than ourselves, but only in the place of those who can claim our pity. (p. 221)

Second Maxim—We never pity another's woes unless we know that we may suffer in a like manner ourselves. (p. 222)

Third Maxim—The pity we feel for others is proportionate, not to the amount of the evil, but to the feelings we attribute to the sufferer. (p. 223)

Empirical studies of how altruism develops in the young child, as I show below, tend to confirm Rousseau's program for the development of moral behavior. Of course, critics of Rousseau's notions of moral development contend that Rousseau sidestepped the Socrates–Freud question of moral choice: whether the person who has insight into the good can still choose evil. But, as I have already shown, this issue rarely is encountered in the real world as a struggle between purely good and evil choices.

AN OVERVIEW OF ALTRUISM AS A DEVELOPMENTAL PROCESS

We know that humans intuitively feel a natural sympathy toward others. Evidence of sympathetic responsiveness has been repeatedly shown in empirical research. For example, newborn infants cry more when other infants in the same room cry than when they hear noise of a similar volume or from computer-simulated cries (Sagi & Hoffman, 1976; Simner, 1971).

Apparently, however, a genetically determined proclivity for a concern for others is insufficient alone for the development of altruism. In other words, if sympathetic responsiveness is an innate human proclivity, but if by adulthood some people demonstrate a significantly greater capacity than do others for altruistic behavior, we may reasonably conclude that nurturing and learning experiences during childhood have a crucial influence on the expression of sympathetic responsiveness toward others. In short, while we don't yet know the magnitude of importance of each of the moral lessons of childhood, it is necessary to recognize the factors required so that the child develops his or her capacity for helping behavior as opposed to more egoistic tendencies.

In their review of the literature on the child's concern for others, child researchers Yarrow, Scott, & Waxler (1973) conclude that "it appears that nurturance is more likely to have positive influence on learning when (a) it is a meaningful, warm relationship that has built up over time, (b) when it has included some withholding of nurturance, (c) when it not only precedes the adult's modeling but is continuous throughout the entire modeling sequence, and (d) when children have responded to real victims."

To elaborate on these findings, a plethora of studies has indicated that the observation of others who behave in a helpful manner elicits helpful responses from a child.

1. However, for helpful behavior to become a regular part of the child's repertoire the socializing agent must do more than espouse altruistic values; he must act in accordance with these values (Bryan, 1972).

2. Warm affection for the child by an adult—by intensifying the child's desire for approval—becomes a dependable basis for impulse control and "other-oriented discipline by inducing positive internal forces, possibly capitalizing on the child's capacity for empathy and thus leading to a more active consideration for others" (Hoffman, 1963).

3. The relationship between the mother's empathic care-giving behavior and the child's emotional responsiveness in altruistic acts reflects the emergent development of the child's empathic sensitivity (Zahn-Waxler, Radke-Yarrow, & King, 1979).

4. An assignment of responsibility that he be helpful to others enhances a child's overall concern for others, particularly if it occurs in the child's first-grade experience (Staub, 1970).

5. The most important socializing technique in acquiring concern for others is either that of role playing or the provision of cognitive perspectives separate and different from the child's previous worldview. Such diverse perspectives lead to a decreasing amount of egocentricity and an increasing, wider, and more integrated understanding of other people's needs (Rushton, 1976).

6. Expressions of generosity in the child generally increase with age. Moreover, those children within an age group who have the highest levels of moral judgment ability and role-taking capacity tend to be more generous than those children who have lower levels of moral judgment and role-taking ability (Rushton, 1976).

7. Children are capable of learning norms that dictate their assistance to others in distress (Bryan & Walbek, 1970).

8. Allegiance to a norm of helping others increases with age, at least until 9 or 10 years (Midlarsky & Bryan, 1967).

9. Altruism doesn't necessitate self-abnegation. When the child is feeling positive toward himself, self-gratification and altruism coexist. Consequently, the greater the proclivity of a child to be generous to himself, the greater is his tendency to provide for others (Rosenhan, Underwood, & Moore, 1974).

10. The rendering of one good deed increases the likelihood that a person will do another (Harris, 1972).

11. In being confronted with a decision to help, a person who has been attentive to the plight of another may, quite literally, think first about the needs and concerns of others. In contrast, those who focus primarily on

themselves think first of their own concerns (Thompson, Cowan, & Rosenhan, 1980).

12. "After joy or sadness (and quite possibly other affects) are experienced, and one is presented with an opportunity to help, tacit social comparison processes are triggered in which a person quickly examines whether his or her emotion is relatively greater or less than that of the needful other. The outcome of that examination determines the subsequent cognitions that arise. If one perceives that another's sadness is much greater than one's own, one's subsequent thoughts are more likely to be directed to the plight of the other and to the fact that the other requires help. If, however, one perceives that one's own sadness outweighs another's, then cognition that is likely to arise is '*I* need comfort and help.' Under such circumstances, altruism declines" (Rosenhan, Salovey, & Hargis, 1981).

Other psychological studies (Clary & Miller, 1986; Grinker, 1964; Hoffman, 1975; Wright, 1942; Zahn-Waxler, Radke-Yarrow, & King, 1979) indicate that for helping behavior to become integral to the child's character at least one of the child's parents (or some other highly significant caretaker) must during the child's socialization represent three attributes: a model of altruistic values; a consistent and fair agent of discipline; and a person who conveys warm affection. These findings, consistent with Rousseau's notions as to the requirements of moral training in the development of conscience in the child, also, closely correspond to the childhood factors in the lives of German anti-Nazis.

GERMAN ANTI-NAZIS

David M. Levy (1946, 1948), a child psychiatrist and psychoanalyst, in his capacity as a American military medical officer at the end of the Second World War, carried out an extensive investigation of Nazis and anti-Nazis for the purpose of determining those life history and personality factors that decisively differentiated these two types of Germans. He limited his study to males who had a choice in whether or not to affiliate with the Nazis. He included in his study both those he categorized as passive anti-Nazis and those who were active anti-Nazis. Levy defined passive anti-Nazis as "those who opposed the regime by resistance in the form of refusal to join the Nazi party and general noncompliant behavior" and active anti-Nazis as "those who opposed by organized or individual aggressive acts, ranging from public utterances and the spreading of leaflets to sabotage" (Levy, 1948). His rationale for the inclusion of both is based on his contention that the "so-called passive anti-Nazis in their non-compliance may, in special instances, show more courage and suffer severer penalties than those active anti-Nazis, whose activities were limited to sporadic outbursts of criticism in public places" (Levy, 1948).

Levy's differentiation of German Nazis and German anti-Nazis consisted of six factors: paternal, maternal, position in the family, religious crossover, political or religious anti-Nazi influences, and the influence of reading and foreign travel. His investigative hypothesis is that German anti-Nazis significantly differed from German Nazis in a predominance of these background factors. In brief, his generalization about the typical German family during the developmental years of his subjects' lives is as follows:

The typical German father is dominant in the family and uses corporal punishment in the discipline of his children. The child, in awe of the father, does not talk freely with him. The German mother typically is undemonstrative in her caring for her child after his preoedipal years. She devotes her affection to her youngest child. On the other hand, a favorite or an only child has a special position in the family. Not only is he given more attention from the mother than are children in larger families, he also is more likely to be protected by her from the father's corporal punishment. The usual German is a member of either the Evangelic or Roman Catholic church. He marries a woman of his own nationality and religious faith. In the typical family anti-Nazi sentiments are openly expressed. However, the number of families in which active opposition to the Nazis was fostered is small. Except for vacations, travel is typically confined to the homeland. Few foreign or radical books and publications are read. (Levy, 1948).

Levy's 21 case studies confirm that the life histories and personalities of his German anti-Nazi subjects significantly differed from that of the typical German: "(A)s a group the anti-Nazi Germans, in comparison with typical Germans, have escaped the conventional and rigid family structure. They have been brought up with more affection and less constraint. Their world is a broader one, less limited in terms of religion, social, and intellectual boundaries. They have a more critical attitude. They are freer from conventional thinking. [B]ecause of the absence of a disciplinary father maternal affection was more freely manifested; hence the corresponding results of more warmth and kindness. A more expansive growth occurred" (Levy, 1948).

Consistent with the findings of German anti-Nazis' life histories and personalities were those of French Catholics who saved Jews during the

Nazi occupation, even though a number of these rescuers were, in fact, members of pro-fascist, anti-Semitic organizations. Interviewers found that these rescuers came from family backgrounds of openness, compassion, and empathy (Schulweis, 1990). These virtuous people commonly perceived themselves as strongly linked to others through a shared humanity. Although they were keenly aware of the perils to themselves and their families, their first consideration seemed to be the needs of others in danger. Said one such rescuer, "You wanted to be able to look yourself in the eye the following morning" (Schneider, 2000).

What is the *more expansive growth* to which Levy alludes? I believe that it is the key to an understanding of the development of conscience. I examine this issue here from the perspective of the crucial importance of the development of a reflective capacity in moral judgment.

RIGHTEOUSNESS AS A REFLUENT MORALITY

We are captive of the verbal concepts our language provides us to shape the parameters in which we define and come to know ourselves and others. It is articulate language, after all, that enables us to be *sentient;* that is to say, capable of understanding ourselves and others and creating a caring relationship with them. In contrast, lacking the words and linguistic concepts to articulately address their sense of injustice, authoritarian-oriented individuals from childhood on feel incompetent and self-contemptuous. Unable to competently articulate their hurt feelings, they express secondary rage. As a consequence, their language is usually heavily infused with aggressive, need-oriented words and concepts. Whenever they try to express tender or caring feelings, they generally find at their disposal only crude and shallow linguistic concepts. In other words, those who are brought up in a language in which power relations and aggressive expression is the pathway to others come to know themselves as bearers of aggression, which is expressed as the only comfortable way to deal with other people. They attempt to rid themselves of their self-hatred by displacing their sense of badness onto specific vulnerable people or groups of people with social, religious, and political values different from their own.

In studying the lives of German Nazis, it appears to me that as children, they were made to feel ashamed by authoritarian parents of their "unacceptable" feelings—such as disagreement and anger at parents and other authority figures. Because they were discouraged from these and, indeed, any deeply felt emotions, they had difficulty empathizing with the pain and suffering of others. Unable to express a caring identification with others, in situations in which they subliminally sensed a similar painful vulnerability with another, they struck out viciously to silence their resurrected hurt. In other words, they tried to eliminate their unwitting mistrust of their own inner resources by adherence to a rigid obedience to the undigested (introjected) enactment of the values and mores that authoritarian figures impressed upon them since childhood. Their code of morality required minimal reflective deliberation in its application.

It is only a morality of conscience that requires reflection and a willingness to struggle with societally imbued values.

CONSCIENCE AS REFLECTIVE CONSCIOUSNESS

Crucial to the development of conscience, Rousseau seems to suggest, is the agent's self-reflectivity in regard to the interiority of the other, enabling the agent to respond to the other as if to oneself. In this regard, the word *conscience* is closely linked in many languages with the concept of consciousness—both imply the capacity to *know with*. Accordingly, the German American social philosopher Erwin Straus (1966) describes man as "the questioning being": he, who at the same moment that he exists, can question himself and the way he lives his own existence. Indeed, the essence of conscience is the capacity to look beyond the limitations of the moral values one has introjected from one's society and to envision a more compassionate and noble way of being with other people. Eichmann, with his impeded curiosity, apparently was incapable of reflective consciousness. The "banality of evil" that Hannah Arendt ascribes to him is predicated on her observation that

> Except for an extraordinary diligence in looking out for his personal advancement, he had no motives at all.... He *merely*, to put it colloquially, *never realized what he was doing*.... It was a lack of imagination. [But he] was not stupid. It was sheer thoughtlessness—something by no means identical with stupidity—that predisposed him to become one of the greatest criminals of that period. (p. 287)

In other words, a person's overriding need in the development of a constructive moral perspective is to find within himself positive qualities about himself and his life and to use this recognition to establish his own identity in a self-enhanced way. One cannot authentically love another without genuinely caring for oneself. Thus, the most difficult task, indeed, the turning point in the establishment of a morality of conscience, is to gain a trust in one's own goodness and to use this sense to find the good in the interiority of the other.

Conscience, as such, involves a courageous reflection about oneself and others. It requires us to know our limitations, to accept ourselves as less than perfect, to live to the best of our abilities, and to come caringly together with others to heal the wounds of loneliness, shame, and self-hatred. This is the stuff of which love, compassion, and virtue are made. And this is the stuff from which we must build a more caring and just world.

CONCLUSION

Encouraging moral responsibility rests upon the knowledge of virtue. Consequently, to perform a constructive role for the society it serves, a theory of morality needs to competently explain how virtuous behavior develops. Unfortunately, "(t)here has rarely been an active, systematic search for goodness" (Schulweis, 1990). Nevertheless, psychotherapists need to devote a considerable portion of their work to helping their clients gain access to their personal goodness—by enabling them to recognize and then overthrow the fears, anxieties, and shames that have impeded the realization of their goodness. In short, psychotherapists need to devote far more attention to admirable and constructive mainstreams of human development, such as conscience as an empathic and compassionate guide to moral issues. As Peter Marin (1981) points out, "the future task of therapy becomes clear: to see life once again in a context that includes the reality of a moral experience and assigns a moral significance to human action."

LOOK AHEAD

Psychology and psychotherapy today are in a serious crisis. The problem of self-examination is integral to this issue. Criticism of the ways in which psychology and psychotherapy have dealt with self-inquiry are explored in the next chapter.

Chapter 5

A CRITICAL EXAMINATION OF THE PROBLEMS OF SELF-EXAMINATION

The most difficult thing in life is to know yourself.
—Thales (640–546 B.C.E., Greek philosopher)

To a large extent, today's psychotherapeutic crisis centers on the problem of self-understanding. Critics of psychoanalysis and psychodynamic psychotherapy challenge clinicians with an important question: Do clinicians have any meaningful basis (empirical or any other kind of evidence) to support the notion that a quest of our inner life—whether alone or with a professional guide—is the best means available to us for living fully and well?

We in the Western intellectual tradition have a long history of the exultation of self-reflection; the most famous of these is Socrates' claim that "only the examined life is worth living." For the past century psychoanalysts and psychotherapists have adopted Socrates' admonition as the cornerstone of their theory and practice. They have built upon Socrates' claim the recognition that one of the most significant of human characteristics is that we are more decisively shaped by what we don't know about ourselves than what we are aware of and understand. Our ignorance of ourselves is due to the fact that while there is an innate human propensity—separating us from other creatures—to establish a causal relation in the events of our experiences, that is to say, to discover why things happen as they do, all too often our ability and willingness to be curious about ourselves is seriously impeded by self-deceptions.

SELF-DECEPTION

Self-deception is conventionally viewed as a way people use to try to protect themselves from threatening revelations about themselves by ignoring information they possess that contradicts their preferred view of themselves. The crucial importance of self-deception in how people live their lives has impressed observers at least since the oratory of the Greek moral idealist Demosthenes in the third century B.C.E. But it was Sigmund Freud who first developed a comprehensive theory to account for self-deception. Among Freud's most important clinical discoveries is the realization that the underlying cause of our psychological disturbances and interpersonal conflicts is our fear of self-knowledge: information that when consciously recognized induces us to feel ashamed, incompetent, and unworthy—leading to self-hatred. And because Freud found that an awareness of the defenses against self-hatred is crucial to our psychological well-being, the basic goal of psychoanalysis, although never stated as such, is to identify and trace the motives that induce us to mislead ourselves.

However, while the problem of self-deception is obvious, there is no evidence that self-inquiry as it is now practiced is an effective shield against self-deception. Consequently, is the claim for the paramount importance of self-examination valid or just a romantic myth? Critics of psychoanalysis and psychotherapy question whether psychoanalysts and psychotherapists have actual evidence to support this claim other than highly selective societal myths and biased anecdotal reports from their clinical practices. If this evidence is lacking, then, the critics insist, the notion that only the examined life is worth living is an unproved assumption.

Accordingly, it seems reasonable to assume that the usefulness and limitations of self-examination can be best answered by those who have knowledgeably practiced it faithfully for the longest period of time. Who are better authorities on this subject than highly seasoned psychoanalysts? It may be instructive to examine the beliefs of some eminent psychoanalytic practitioners who don't hold self-reflection in the same sacrosanct status as others do.

A decade ago (Goldberg, 1992) I conducted a research investigation of highly seasoned psychoanalysts and psychotherapists. The subjects of the study had a median average of more than 30 years of clinical experience. One of the analysts I interviewed, to whom I shall refer as Dr. R, was one of the six analysts in the study with more than 50 years of clinical practice. He is the author of numerous books on the cultural context of psychoanalysis and is the training director of one of the largest and most prestigious analytic institutes in the United States. Among the questions I had asked the subjects of my study was: "As a result of their continual examination of how other people live their lives, do psychoanalysts and psychotherapists learn anything of practical value in living their own lives more maturely and wisely?"

In regard to my query about an acquired maturity from clinical practice, Dr. R responded with a placid facial expression, but his articulate hands conveyed a sense of exasperated disbelief at what he apparently regarded as my misguided inquiry. He turned sideways, as if in deliberation—uncertain whether he should let me in on an important secret. Finally, he turned back to me and said, with what I regarded as no small amount of stridence, that

> At our institute we recognize that candidates who believe that there is a path to wisdom by being analyzed haven't received a good training analysis.... While analysis helps you understand psychological issues, it doesn't necessarily indicate what do with this understanding. I know some people at seventy-five who have never been in analysis but are quite effective, cheerful, and happy. Are they any worse off for being less self-aware than the analyzed person who is depressed from what he has discovered about life from examining it closely? All you have to do is to look at that collection of analysts who are social misfits, child molesters, and what not. And the rest of them don't have any better marriages than do ordinary people either, nor are they any better parents. Whether they are better prepared to handle aging and death than anyone else, I'm not certain. But I don't know of a single person who is an analyst who isn't afraid of dying.

Another eminent analyst and writer who appears to share Dr. R's perspective on the examined life is San Francisco psychoanalyst Allen Wheelis. His autobiographic novel *The Seeker* (1960) is the story of a popular and brilliant analyst who finds himself in a painful existential malaise that he contends is not the product of unresolved childhood trauma or other displaced intrapsychic conflicts. His despondency, Wheelis shows, issues from the pathos of a sensitive and thoughtful person who recognizes the contradictions, paradoxes, and absurdities of the human condition. Wheelis uses his novel to address a basic question about self-examination within the context of psychoanalysis: Is psychoanalysis essentially a medical treatment to repair the rents caused by psychopathology, or is it also a guide for successfully dealing with the existential dilemmas of human existence? His answer seems to be that, at best, it is the former.

The protagonist's anguish in Wheelis's novel is presented as a legitimate response to his recognition of the fraudulence of the pursuit of the examined life in analytic practice. The protagonist confesses in his self-reflections and in his analysis with a colleague that he has not harvested the savory fruits of a well-lived existence that his original faith in psychoanalysis promised—because the examined life may actually work in reverse. This is to say, continuous self-examination often results in a despairing dissatisfaction with oneself rather than in the acquisition of self-enlightenment. All of Wheelis's subsequent novels, as well as many of his professional papers, come to the same pessimistic conclusion.

A third eminent analyst who shares Dr. R and Wheelis's doubts about the examined life is the San Francisco Jungian analyst James Hillman. He is quite sanguine in his opinion that psychoanalysis and psychotherapy have for the past century been operating with spurious assumptions about the examined life. He points out that we have now had a century of psychoanalysis and psychotherapy. Our culture is saturated with their theories. Vast numbers of people have been recipients of their treatment services. And yet, in the postmodern world we are less optimistic about our future than were people prior to the psychoanalytic/ psychotherapy era (Hillman & Ventura, 1993). Hillman explains that psychoanalysis is

> only working on the 'inside' soul (p. 3).... This is not to deny that you do need to go inside—but we have to see what we're doing when we do that. By going inside we're maintaining the Cartesian view that the world out there is dead matter and the world inside is living...working with yourself, could be part of the disease, not part of the cure. I think therapy has made a philosophical mistake, which is that cognition precedes conation—that knowing precedes doing or action. I don't think that's the case. I think that reflection has always been after the event. (p. 12)

All three of these analysts speak articulately in regard to serious problems with the importance given to self-examination in clinical practice; however, Dr. R's perspective that people become depressed from what they discover about the dark side of the undiscovered self upon too close a self-examination, I believe, lies at the heart of the problem of self-deception. I refer to this perspective about self-discovery as "the dark side of curiosity."

The difficulties my clients encounter in their self-examination suggest to me that psychoanalysis imposes a perplexing existential dilemma. Human suffering arises from our mortal status and our vulnerability to pain. But pain may be assuaged or managed, our sense of finitude less easily. Most of our daily roles and activities are designed to deny and buffer us from our dreaded aloneness—the casting shadow of our eventual non-being. Accordingly, throughout our lives we seek a fund of knowledge and a place in the world that magically will forestall, if not defeat, death. In this regard, the eminent nineteenth-century German philosopher Friedrich Nietzsche explains the efforts of those who seek superiority through wisdom as the wish to be aligned with God. As an *übermensch*, there is the magical hope that one can defeat death and the shame that accompanies its recognition. Leo Tolstoy's novella *The Death of Ivan Ilyich,* discussed in chapter 3, powerfully dramatizes death as the ultimate shame because it provides undeniable evidence of our powerlessness and ultimate demise as human beings. Shame, as an ontological emotion, issues from the profound despair of recognizing that we have limited future moments as existential beings. It is the reality of death, German philosopher Martin Heidegger contends, that creates our sense of time. In short, our temporal limitations revealed in self-discovery force us to face our fearful eventual fate.

In other words, the recurring theme of human existence is our striving for personal identity, significance, and unification of our personality. We are impeded in this endeavor by the recognition that we are essentially frail, limited, vulnerable, and finite beings. This realization evokes more than just anxiety for most of us; it unleashes sheer *terror.* The dread of which I speak is concerned not only with our mortal being; it also includes questions about our achievements, our reputation, even a remembrance of us by others. In short, *the terror bared by our human vulnerability* has to do with *the fear of erasure of all that we have striven for and created: the meaning of our lives.* This underbelly of terror that we all experience, at least in some subliminal way, lies at the core of human suffering and is revealed baldly in a thorough self-exploration of our psyche.

On the other hand, in terms of Sigmund Freud's notion of the Unconscious, ironically, *to know is to be limited.* The unconscious, as Freud (1915) emphasizes, is *timeless.* Because of the sense of no limitation of time in the unconscious, there is no negation of possibility (no death) in those regions of the psyche that are still unexplored. In Freud's words, "Our unconscious, then, does not believe in its own death; it behaves as if it were immortal. What we call our 'unconscious'—the deepest strata of our minds, made up of instinctual impulses—knows nothing that is negative; in it contradictions coincide." (p. 296)

The existential perspective on human suffering, to repeat, suggests that the exploration of the underlying motives of our behavior poses a difficult dilemma for each of us. Brandeis University professor Abraham Maslow (1963) refers to this dilemma as "(t)he need to know, the fear of knowing" (p. 111). In order words, not to pursue self-examination may leave us a victim of our untoward instinctual urges; on the other hand, to vigorously self-reflect may result in inexorable despair in regard to the seemingly insoluble limitations and finitudes of human existence.

I believe that the reason for the dilemma of self-examination as I have been discussing it is rooted in the ontological assumptions underlying Western thought—a perspective that regards the human being as an encapsulated consciousness, set separately and competitively apart from other beings in the cosmos. This ontological orientation is not only the root cause of the fraudulent self-reflection in psychoanalysis that Wheelis decries, but also the crucible that spurns the pervasive societal ills ignored by psychoanalytic theory and practice that concerns Hillman.

WESTERN AND EASTERN PSYCHOLOGIES

Western psychology, in an attempt to establish itself as a legitimate scientific inquiry, operates from the premise that mastery over human existence emanates from interpreting the principles of nature. By predicting the lawful actions of objects and people, we can control and manipulate nature. But this is possible, scientific psychology cautions us, only if the psychological investigator assumes an indifferent (unbiased) attitude toward the objects of his observations. In contrast, Eastern psychology contends that the human being and nature are inseparable. We cannot stand apart from nature in such a way as to objectively observe. In other words, each of us comes to know the world, Eastern psychology tells us, by the unfolding of the world within us.

The reasons, of course, are complex and many. However, the Eastern concept of *maya* may be the single best explanation. *Maya* pertains to our tendency in the West to make distinctions in our consciousness based upon false dualisms. Examples are the separations we make of subject and object, self and nonself, life and death, day and night, good and bad. Our dualistic illusions can be explained as follows:

> We cannot escape the fact that the world we know is construed in order (and thus in such a way as to be able) to see itself. This is indeed amazing. Not so much in view of what it sees—but in respect of the fact that it sees at all. But in order to do so, evidently it must cut itself up into at least one state that sees, and at least one other that is seen. In this severed and mutilated condi-

tion, whatever it sees is only partially itself. We may take it that the world undoubtedly is itself—but, in any attempt to see itself as an object, it must, equally undoubtedly, act to make itself distinct from, and therefore, false to, itself. (Brown, 1972, p. 104)

In making itself-as-subject distinct from itself-as-object, our Western style of individuality is born—resulting in a "skin-encapsulated ego," with ourselves as isolated containers of consciousness distinct from the external environment and other beings (Watts, 1961). Simultaneously, it also creates space. So, as soon as a person experiences an inexorable space between himself and others, the problem of being and nonbeing is created. Experiencing himself separate from the cosmos, a person becomes conscious that there are things that exist independent of him, to whom his existence is viewed indifferently. At this moment the harbinger of death becomes his unremitting fear (Benoit, 1955). Moreover, according to Eastern observers, the division between the observer and the observed creates human conflict. Indeed, the Indian philosopher Krishnamurti (1972) tells us, it is the source of all human strife.

It is hardly surprising then that psychologies that fail to recognize the *mayas* in consciousness promote the individuation of people in such a way that each of us is potentially at war with every other person for the scarce material and emotional resources of the cosmos. In this worldview, the weak, the limited, and the disabled are given uncompassionate, detached assistance by those better equipped for competitive struggles. Critics contend that psychoanalysis and psychotherapy are two such psychologies.

These critics tell us that we need to recognize that the notion that we are encapsulated selves, trapped in a world in which everything is indifferent to our flight and fate, was not a part of the early Western intellectual tradition. This state of affairs, they contend, is due to an unwitting progression through the centuries in Western society that separated self-examination from the seeker's social and moral responsibility to community and the natural world.

The prescribed ethos of self-examination as a guide to the well-lived life first began during the time before Socrates and flowered during the era of Socrates and his close followers. The accord given to self-examination during these eras was built upon the notion that we are a product of our continuous *dialogic relationship* with other people. Indeed, in the Socratic tradition personal enlightenment is a dialectic process between two or more individuals keenly curious about their relationships with other people. This is why Plato's Socratic dialogues are always couched in terms of social concerns, such as: What is justice? What is responsibility? What is virtue and courage in regard to one's responsibility to one's community?

Within the context of psychoanalysis and psychotherapy, its critics contend, self-examination has completely shed its social and moral concern. It has become an article of psychoanalytic faith to assume that moral probing hinders the analysand from a free inquiry of his mental life. Consequently, the psychoanalyst must extricate himself from all moral inquiries except the recognition that an examination of the unconscious motivation for one's behavior is the highest aim of human conduct. A serious scrutiny of a client's lack of social and moral sense is unlikely to take place with an analyst or therapist who believes that the realm of the mind is far more significant than is the world of other people.

Of course, I am not suggesting the elimination of self-examination as such. What I am saying is that an unending search for one's personal identity is at best insufficient. Self-examination must be wedded to authentic dialogues with other people if we are to actually know ourselves. In other words, if you want to truly know yourself, then you need to examine your interactions and transactions with other people; they exemplify precisely who one is. Consequently, for psychoanalytic and psychotherapeutic practice to return self-examination to its social and moral moorings, their critics insist, practitioners must relinquish their claim that the cause of human happiness is solely dependent upon the resolution of intrapsychic issues.

Psychotherapists must help their clients recognize a simple fact of human nature: None of us can live satisfying and meaningful lives in the midst of others' suffering. All who have tried have failed. Because none of us exists alone, a life lived well is concerned with helping to foster the conditions that extend justice and concern to every member of society. Wise philosophers and theologians have pointed out that there is a basic question to which each of us must respond in summing up our lives: Have I been idle for the most part, unconcerned with the lives of others, a greedy opportunist, or someone who cared and made a difference?

Martin Buber's Notion of Dialogue

The great error of psychoanalysis—as a product of Western psychology—Buber (1999) indicates, is its attempt to understand a person primarily as a solitary unit, separate from other people. This *maya* prevents us from recognizing that the development of our personality is less influenced by our unconscious fantasies than by disingenuous interpersonal relations.

Because our personalities are twofold, rather than solitary, Buber (1965) tells us, dialogue is essential to our nature. In other words, we are captive to the verbal concepts our language provides us to shape the parameters in which we define and come to know ourselves and other people. It is articulate language, after all, that enables us to be sentient, that is to say, capable of understanding and creating a caring relationship with others. Because each of us carries within us the seeds of our wholeness, it is our fundamental task as human beings to strive through the vicissitudes of our lives to fulfill this potential. Buber's notion of authentic dialogue is best fulfilled in friendship and in intimacy.

THE UNDISCOVERED SELF

Self-inquiry is in an important sense an attempt to reach our *undiscovered self*. To reach our undiscovered self means, in effect, to recognize aspects of ourselves that we have not fully considered or of which we were previously unaware. Finding a path to our undiscovered self enables us to answer the *fundamental question of human existence: How shall I actually live my life?* All Western psychological systems seem to have in common the ethos that each of us has a right to an enlightened, cohesive self. An access to this self, however, is not provided us ready-made. It is tested, the Western intellectual tradition informs us, by our willingness to enter the shadows of *the greatest mystery* that any of us will ever face: *Who am I as a human being?* By entering the venues of our undiscovered self, we are told, we gain the ability to create beauty, know profound love, engage in compassionate and trusting relationships, and explore all the other facets of living fully and well—implicit in the question of how we should live our lives.

From what I discussed about the basic assumptions of the original self-inquiry project of the ancient Greeks, one needs to recognize that professional guides are asking the wrong questions about our undiscovered self because they have too narrow a focus. I contend that it is in genuine friendship that this arena is more likely to be broadened.

Actually, Socrates was a close friend of many with whom he had dialogue. But more importantly, remember that Socrates wasn't a professional anything; he didn't receive a fee. He claimed that he was questioning others for his own edification. In contrast, how would one go about a mutual friendship of benefit to both participants in a paid relationship, such as psychoanalysis or psychotherapy—that is to say, who should pay? One simply cannot buy or sell genuine friendship.

FRIENDSHIP AND INNER TRUTH

For many the journey of self-discovery is solitary and lonely. We live as we dream, alone, claims the British novelist Joseph Conrad in his autobiography *A Personal Record.* Apparently this was the case for Sigmund Freud. Freud, according to New York analyst Michael Eigen (1993), felt that his creative work was the only pursuit that made life worthwhile. By creative work, Freud was referring to the solitary journey in search of inner truths. He viewed friendship as adaptive—making life manageable—but if held too highly, he believed, friendship may diminish one's chances for profound psychic transformation.

In contrast to Freud's view, it can be reasonably argued that both friendship and the pursuit of inner truth are of compatible value. Friedrich Nietzsche certainly bonded the two together on the grounds that only the truthful are capable of deep friendship. But for Freud, his obsession with inner truth was all consuming. Consequently, it is a solipsistic foreclosure of human potential to adopt Freud's seriously myopic vision: the belief that the intrapsychic world holds more wisdom and truth than does the world of other people. Whereas it is mandatory that we search our inner depths in seeking our personal identities, it is nevertheless in the world we share with others that personal awareness is best achieved in an open-sharing and trusting relationship in which both partners are present and involved in seeking an increased awareness of their own identities. In other words, within a trusting friendship each of us is enabled to explore, experience, and redefine the contradictory attitudes, assumptions, and ways of being that each of us unwittingly has up until then allowed others in their defining of our selfhood.

THE STRUGGLE TO BE REAL

Because our personality is not solitary (encapsulated consciousness) but dual, the goodwill and exchange of friendship contributes influentially to an understanding and enhancement of our personal identity. In other words, it takes another's perspective of us to enable us to more fully know ourselves. Consequently, unless genuine friendship is allowed to develop in our endeavors at self-discovery, our self-awareness is mitigated. For this to occur, we must allow others to have a deep emotional impact upon us.

Intimate relationship has in it an existential question: "How do I use my relationship with myself and with others to become the person I intend to become?" In responding to this question the seeker gains possibility by *valu-*

ing immediate engagement. Because the dialectic process in this arena involves a balance between *self-awareness* and *peer influence,* there is a need for dialogue with both self and others. Each of these dialogues involves a *letting go* to permit that which the self is experiencing at that moment to emerge—in terms of the seeker's values, wants, and vulnerabilities. The letting go requires a caring for oneself without the defensive stance of constraining other selves or one's own probing self. In other words, letting go is the preferred stance of the passionate seeker in being open to experiencing his avoidances rather than seeking reassurances and certainties about his basic assumptions about himself and the world. The seeker, as I indicated in chapter 3, receives caring from another by sharing his preferences and concerns, freeing the other to relate to the seeker as the other experiences the seeker. When the seeker directly and courageously addresses interpretations of himself by others that are constricting or inauthentic definitions of what the seeker intends for himself, the seeker is enabled to constitute himself in a constructive way. This leads me to the issue of emotional intimacy.

Emotional intimacy, as a crucible for self-discovery, involves the struggle to be real. There is always a struggle in intimate relations about how each agent shall make himself or herself known to the other. The more openly we can share our feelings and concerns about how we are making ourselves known to the other, the more we can appreciate what we currently are sharing together and the preciousness of the present moment. In other words, each of us is a separate person and may someday go his or her own way. Therefore, although we don't fully understand or always agree with each other, this is the best we can do. And, most importantly, the effort has been worth making if we recognize and respond with friendship to the humanity of the other. Here we see the interrelationship of emotional intimacy and communion.

ALBERT CAMUS' NOTION OF SOCIAL AND MORAL RESPONSIBILITY

Algerian born writer Albert Camus' literary work enables us to examine significant moral concerns raised by self-examination as practiced by psychotherapists. I will confine my discussion to his novels *The Stranger* (1942) and *The Plague* (1948) (see H. Lottman, 1980).

We find in all cultures from earliest times that the well-told story is the essence of captivating literature, as well as the crucible for insights about human nature. The lessons of life have always come best from story, legend, and myth. Concepts important to a life lived well—love, caring, compassion, decency, responsibility, creativity, as well as the dark side of the human psyche—are understood more lucidly from tales of particular individuals (real or fictionalized) rather than from generalizations based on scientific investigation of single traits of a large number of people. Let me demonstrate.

M. Meursault, Camus' protagonist in *The Stranger,* has been condemned to execution for having killed a man he has not seen up close until just before he shot him. Meursault is an alienated man, presented by Camus as out of sorts with the mores of his French Algerian society. He tells us, "I have never been able to regret anything in all my life. I've always been far too much absorbed in the present moment, or the immediate future, to think back" (Lottman, 1980, p. 119), and of the event of the shooting, he recalls, "And just then it crossed my mind that one might fire, or not fire—and it would come to absolutely the same thing" (Lottman, 1980, p. 121).

At Meursault's trial, the most damaging charges the prosecutor brings against him is that his lack of strong emotion and his indifference to social convention are indicative of his insensitivity to other peoples' feelings; and so he is an unredeemable criminal who doesn't deserve to live. During his trial Meursault remarks, "For the first time I realized how all these people loathed me" (Lottman, 1980, p. 126). But this is only a passing thought. The most significant of Meursault's personality proclivities is a sheer lack of curiosity about himself and the world in which finds himself. Nowhere in the novel do we find him more than superficially concerned with the implications of his behavior or with other options available to him. His tepid affectivity parallels his lack of curiosity. Asked by his girlfriend to marry her, he replies to her request, "It had no importance really, but if it would give [you] pleasure, we could be married right away" (Lottman, 1980, p. 110).

Believing that life lacks an inherent meaning, Meursault's view of existence posits that acting one way rather than another is immaterial. He wishes no binding commitment to anyone. His sole existential principle is to live with as minimal an effort as he can manage. He tolerates the demands that other people put on his life without question or protest.

In the diary Camus used to structure his novel, he refers to Meursault as a man who doesn't want to explain himself or to ask questions (Lottman, 1980). He is as much a stranger to himself as he is to others. Unaware of what is important to him until it is too late—already condemned to death—he gets caught up in a destructive act without knowing how he arrived there. "His crime is actually the *murder of himself*" (Lottman, 1980).

Dr. Rieux, the hero of *The Plague,* is presented by Camus as a very different type of person from Meursault. A knowledgeable, able, and deeply caring physician, Rieux continually puts his life at risk trying to assist and comfort those who have become afflicted by a bubonic plague in the quarantined, isolated Algerian city of Oran. Rieux does his duty conscientiously and tirelessly, but like Meursault, he can't explain his behavior. While we are not surprised by the existential minimalist Meursault's lack of introspection, we are by the keenly intelligent Rieux. It is the reason to ask: Is the lack of curiosity of the two most important characters in Camus' fiction a mere coincidence, or is Camus trying to convey some important insight about human behavior? To answer this question we need to review the philosophical assumptions of Camus' work.

Camus' fictional characters are presented to address important social and moral questions, that is to say, the problem of guilt and innocence, the ability to act or not in dire times, responsibility or nihilistic indifference. Throughout his work he asks how an ordinary person should live in a tentative and precarious world. His answer begins with the recognition that we cannot depend alone on self-reflection. In *The Stranger* and in *The Plague* he seeks to show us that there is something radically amiss with curiosity—or more properly, something morally wrong with the type of self-inquiry that distances itself from concerns about other people, by reflecting dispassionately on the human condition. Indeed, he shows us that curiosity has a dark side: The pursuit of unceasing introspection inflicts the seeker with inexorable despair, accompanied by a lack of interest in his or her social and moral responsibilities.

Camus recognizes that simple and comfortable categories of good and evil, guilty or innocent rarely apply to most life situations. Especially during times of uncertainty, where reason fails us, Camus underscores our responsibility to other people as a guiding ethical principle, as exemplified in such statements as the following:

> Rieux pulled himself together. There lie certitude; there, in the daily [his medical] rounds; All the rest hung on mere threads and trivial contingencies; you couldn't waste your time on it. The thing was to do your job as it should be done. (Lottman, 1980, p. 130)

> He'd try to relieve human suffering before trying to point out its excellence. (Lottman, 1980, p. 131)

> [T]here are sick people and they need curing. Later, perhaps, [I shall] think things over. (Lottman, 1980, p. 130)

In short, Rieux indicates by his refusal to self-reflect on his caring and altruistic behavior that often it is better to cure than to know: "A man can't cure and know at the same time" (Lottman, 1980, p. 131), he tells us.

It seems to me that Camus is asking a rhetorical question: Does it really matter what are one's actual motives—deep within one's unconscious (even if they could be accurately determined)—for one's virtuous behavior? What is important is that one's expression of these admirable values makes the world a better place to live for all of us. Allen Wheelis, of whom I spoke earlier, in reviewing his life and practice of five decades, admits that relentlessly analyzing life, he and his analysands may have kept themselves from important social and moral obligations.

Camus wrote from the conviction that because we are all bound together under the same sentence of death, the only worthwhile human achievements are those that are socially just. A moral ethic can develop only from a sense of reciprocal justice: a social philosophy in which concerns about the injustices done to others are as significant as the wrongs to oneself. Camus wrote, "[M]an must resolve to act, in order to exist" (Lottman, 1980, p. 132). He knew from his personal experience as a member of a socially and politically suppressed society that a predominance of our societal problems appear insoluble (Lottman, 1980) due to entrenched social philosophies that justify the maximizing of profit at the expense of the safety, health, and happiness of those who lack social, political, and economic power. But his courageous characters such as Rieux and the mysterious Tarrou—another character in *The Plague* who compassionately helps those inflicted with the plague in Oran—resist resignation. They become involved in an endless rebellion in the service of life to "increase the sum of freedom and responsibility to be found in every man" and under no circumstances to "reduce or suppress that freedom, even temporarily" (Lottman, 1980, p. 134).

When it is pointed out that whatever success he will have against the plague is only temporary, Rieux answers, "But that is no reason for giving up the struggle" (Lottman, 1980, p. 136). For Camus, a person is alive only in his struggle, only in his defiant engagement with a world he never made but in which he must live (Lottman, 1980).

Camus believed that only from a compassionate commitment to community—to actively fight against all forms of human suffering and evil—can an individual transcend the limitations and demise of a singular life, and in so doing, create a meaningful identity as a human being. Rightly or not, Camus seemed to believe that this transcendence from egoism to concern with community was best done intuitively, from the heart, not from an endless scrutiny of one's supposed base motives.

Of course, Camus' social philosophy has implications for an appropriate role for self-examination in psychotherapy. There is a need first for the therapist to take seriously the notion that the *mayas* in human consciousness are the fundamental basis of his clients' sense of separation from other people as well as their alienation from the cosmos. The therapist, therefore, should help his or her clients recognize that their experienced impotence as existential beings is not an inherent product of human finitude, but caused by their lack of commitment to social and moral responsibility. Acting on these responsibilities holds the prospect of human wholeness and fulfillment.

The ideas of Buber and Camus suggest to me that *living fully and well comes from a composite of balanced relationships,* that is to say, an overall sense that one has given sufficiently of oneself to balance the care and goodwill one has received from others.

My clinical experience has shown that for this to happen, *three crucial roles* must be competently assumed. These roles are those which one might call *patient, student,* and *helper.* The *patient* role is based on the awareness that without the emotional recognition of dysfunctional aspects of our behavior we cannot ameliorate problem areas in our lives. Equity and balance theory asserts that those who are deficient in some important area of their functioning deserve to be given to by those who are abundant in these areas. The *student* role is based on the understanding that without utilizing the cognitive skills of the learner we could not generalize from one situation to another or gain from other people's experience. Equity and balance theory assumes that the student is pursuing normal psychosocial development: As a learner she acquires knowledge; later she will teach others what she has learned. Finally, the *helper* role indicates that without the experience of being of assistance to others and recognized and appreciated for these efforts, our lives would remain sterile and unsatisfying. Equity and balance theory claims that the helper should give because he has himself been accorded and now is overabundant in some important areas of function in which others are in need of his help.

All three roles are essential to healthy psychological and social functioning at appropriate times. People who are not living fully and well are those who have rigidly maintained one or two roles in neglect of all. Psychotherapy and psychoanalysis focus almost exclusively on the development of skills in recouping what one has failed to gain earlier in life (the *patient* role); it totally eschews the role of *helper.* To enable it to broaden its vision in helping people live fully and well, therapists must redefine their premises. Essential to this endeavor, I have sought to show here, is an understanding of the crucial role of equity and balance in human existence.

LOOK AHEAD

The problem of impeded self-inquiry is usually exacerbated in people with more serious emotional disturbances. My position is that in studying the conditions that militate against curiosity in a severely troubled person, we are given access to an enlarged version of the curiosity problems of less-troubled people. In the next chapter we gain some perspective about why curiosity is impeded in people, from my work with a highly intelligent and seriously destructive young man.

Chapter 6

THE DARK SIDE OF CURIOSITY: A VIOLENT CLIENT WHO READ CAMUS

O my soul, do not aspire to immortal life, but exhaust the limits of the possible.
—Pindar (523–443 B.C.E., Greek lyric poet)

Curiosity is a crucial factor in the development of morality. Here the absence of curiosity is shown to be a decisive factor in destructive behavior.

CASE STUDY

Early in my career I was the psychology consultant to the back wards of a division in a large federal psychiatric hospital, Saint Elizabeths, in Washington, DC. Most of the patients in the division had been hospitalized for decades; some, I later found out, for 40 or 50 years. Indeed, examining the very thick clinical files of these long-term patients, I discovered in one file a note from the eminent psychiatrist William A. White, who at the time was serving as the superintendent of the hospital. The note informed the patient—then a young sailor fresh from naval battles in the First World War and a recipient of a court-martial for striking an officer on his battleship while he was intoxicated—that he would never have to leave the hospital; here he would always have a home, protection, and friends. This note was 50 years old at the time I read it. This patient, like most of the other long-term patients, spent only fleeting moments each day (for some, only a few minutes each week or two) in contact with reality.

During my first consultation with the nursing staff of the division, the head nurse expressed serious concern about an energetic patient. This patient, in his early thirties, whom I will call Davis Harrington, had carried out a series of brutal attacks on elderly patients. He would calmly walk up to another patient who could not defend himself and pound him with his fists. On occasion, he approached patients from the back, pushed them out of their wheelchairs, and then kicked them.

"What do you think is the reason for Harrington's violence?" I asked. The head nurse shrugged her shoulders; neither she nor any other staff person present offered a better explanation than citing Harrington's history of getting into fights with other patients.

"How long has the recent series of assaults been going?"

"Several weeks," I was told.

"Why hasn't this patient been transferred to another division that houses young and active men?"

A nurse replied, "In the past Harrington had been sent to another division. He was returned because the younger, stronger patients there kept beating up on him. You need to be told one important fact: His mother is a politically active society woman downtown. She has close friends on the city council. She is up here at the hospital at least four times a week. And she has told the hospital superintendent that her son must be placed on a ward in which he is safe from attack. Dr. Rendel (the division administrator) doesn't want to antagonize Mrs. Harrington or the hospital administration by permitting Harrington to be beat up again. Nor does he want to be chewed out by her again for isolating her son from other patients by being put into a quiet room (a padded room with no movable objects)."

Given Harrington's political situation, apparently neither Dr. Rendel nor his staff knew how to protect the vulnerable patients in the division from Harrington's rage. I needed to quickly evaluate Davis Harrington and help the staff formulate an effective way to control him. For the time being I could spend only a few minutes scanning his clinical file. My cursory perusal revealed that Harrington had been hospitalized at this hospital for almost 10 years. At the time of his admission, he was a literature major at an Ivy League university in New England. He reported to a psychologist at the school's counseling center that he was hearing voices that told him that he must not go to class anymore because his instructors were homosexuals who would try to make him queer. Advised by university officials to seek private psychiatric help, he was asked by his mother where he would like to be treated. He chose this venerable psychiatric hospital in his hometown.

Asked why, he said that as a child he had always been fascinated by the odd patients walking on the hospital grounds he had observed through the iron gates. Now he was impressed that the hospital had such patients as Ezra Pound and "Axis Sally"—people convicted of collaborating with the enemy during the Second World War. Harrington's admission note to the hospital quoted him as saying that "while at (the hospital) I would like to spend some time with Ezra Pound. Perhaps, I can learn to write as brilliantly as him, or at least find out how I can become the son-of-a-bitch he is."

The Interview

Davis Harrington had close-cropped blonde hair, blue eyes, a wiry medium build, and for considerable periods of time was in an almost continual state of agitated motion. At his mother's insistence, his file reported, he was given only moderate doses of medication. Physically, he would be no match for most patients his age, but to elderly patients who had poor contact with reality, he posed a deadly threat.

When I attempted to interview him in the nurse's station on his ward to get some idea why he was assaulting other patients, he refused to sit down and speak with me; instead, he picked up an ashtray off the desk and flung it at me, followed by a notebook, pencils, and various other objects. Two psychiatric aides, watching through the window, rushed in and subdued him.

"What do you want to do now?" one of the aides asked me.

"Lock the two of us in a quiet room," I replied.

"Do you know what you are doing? He is dangerous," pointed out the head nurse, who joined us in the station.

"Just be sure to unlock the door in exactly 15 minutes," I told her as casually as I could, to give Harrington the impression that I was in control of the situation.

Almost immediately after the quiet room door was locked, Harrington came after me, swinging away with his fists. I was his age and in far better physical condition and was easily able to push him away. But I had no wish to parry his fists for 15 minutes; and of course, that was not my intention in being in seclusion with him.

To properly interview Harrington, I had to gain control of the situation. To do so required me to transform the situation from that of violent physical altercation to one of meaningful dialogue. I used *paradoxical intent* to initiate this endeavor. In other words, I congratulated Harrington for the volume of noise and commotion he regularly provided to the ward. I said,

As you well know, Davis, this ward has a deadly quiet to it. The other patients live in their own world most of the time. What they desperately need is to return to this world. Therefore, I sincerely appreciate your past help in keeping things lively on the ward. The staff on the ward may have been relieved when you have finally quieted down. But they were mistaken. You serve an important therapeutic function here. In fact, I was ready to ask Dr. Rendel to buy and have installed in the ward a sound system that plays lively music all day—to keep the patients awake and alert. But if you keep the noise and commotion going you will save the hospital money. With you around we won't need a sound system.

Harrington, again jabbing with his fists, came at me in a fury. I pushed him back again. He went to the far corner of the room and sat down. He did not look at me; his head down, he stared at his hands and feet.

I sat down in the opposite corner. After a long moment I said, "I see that you attended an Ivy League school for four years. You must be intelligent. You must have some idea why you hit other people."

I waited. Harrington did not look up or speak. "Are you, then, a person that has no curiosity about himself and the reasons he behaves the way he does?" I asked.

Harrington pulled up his head and said, "Maybe I am bored with life. Maybe I have life all figured out. Maybe there is something poisonous in me that I don't want to look at. You might as well ask M. Meursault why he shot the Arab."

Well acquainted with the writings of the French existentialist Albert Camus, I assumed that Harrington was referring to one of Camus' fictional characters. A few moments of reflection suggested to me that he might have provided me—probably without his conscious awareness—with some important clue to the problem of impeded curiosity. However, I was not surprised by Davis Harrington's lucidity, despite his bizarre social behavior. In four decades of treating patients diagnosed as psychotic, I have found that many bright paranoid schizophrenic patients are rational, logical, and persuasive—up until their systematic delusion is broached.

Assuming that Harrington was unwittingly providing me with clues about the factors that had blocked his own self-inquiry, I asked him, "So who do you regard as the more realistic figure: Meursault or Rieux?"

DH: "Meursault, of course!"

CG: "Why do you say Meursault?" He despised the old men he abused, I inferred, because seeing them painfully confronted him with his own limitations and finitude. Undoubtedly, impotent rage from oedipal issues were involved as well.

DH: "He knows too well that life is meaningless, so why try?"

CG: "Come on! Rieux's life is hardly meaningless. He cares deeply about other people and they care about him. And of course by his efforts he alleviates much suffering."

DH: "But isn't that Camus' irony! He makes quite clear that despite Rieux's heroic struggles the plague might win out in the end and obliterate all that Rieux has done."

CG: "How do you apply this to your own life?"

DH: "Why try when whatever I do will likely be erased? It is too unpleasant to keep being reminded of my limitations and finitude. And isn't that what you want me to do when you ask me to be self-introspective? I'd rather make noise, commotion, even pretend that I'm strong and have some control over what happens to me."

Harrington's allusion to the fear of erasure I took to mean the recognition that the busywork of our daily endeavors can somewhat decrease our sense of vulnerability. But at certain moments, such as when we or a loved one comes down with a life-threatening illness, we are baldly forced to confront the impermanence of our existence. These moments (as discussed in the previous chapter) evoke more than mere anxiety; often they unleash sheer terror.

Some experience this particular terror more acutely than others; Harrington seems to have felt it profoundly. The continual terror most *floridly psychotic people experience,* in its ultimate sense, is *an inability to defend against the prospect of total loss of meaning of themselves as a person.* Ernest Becker contends that the psychotic feels more keenly overwhelmed by life, more conscious of finitude, more fearful of death, than others. These people have "not been able to build the confident defenses that a person normally uses to deny them. [His] misfortune is that he has been burdened with extra anxiety, extra guilt, extra helplessness, an even more unpredictable and unsupportive environment. [As a result, he cannot] *confidently deny* man's real situation on this planet" (Becker, 1973, p. 63).

This underbelly of terror, experienced by us all in at least a subliminal way, is the basis for mitigated curiosity. Harrington's candor in revealing his deepest fear to me—which caught me by surprise considering his earlier hostility—started for me an existential exploration of the dark side of curiosity in my own life and those of my patients I discussed in the previous chapter.

THE GREAT METAPSYCHOLOGICAL ERROR

The great error of the Western psychology worldview, contends Martin Buber (1999), as I pointed out in the previous chapter, is its attempt to understand a person primarily as a solitary unit, separate from other beings. This *maya* prevents us from recognizing that the development of our personality is less influenced by our unconscious than by hostile and competitive interpersonal relations.

Psychologies that fail to recognize the *mayas* in human consciousness promote the individuation of people in such a way that each is viewed as being at war with every other person for the scarce material and emotional resources of the cosmos. In regard to seriously destructive people such as Harrington, the terror of finitude may be even greater than for other people; there seems to be more conflict and emotional separation between the seriously destructive person and his caretakers early in life than for less-destructive people. As a result, Washington, DC, criminologists Samuel Yochelson and Stanton Samenow (1993) report that "the fear of death is very strong, persistent, and pervasive in the criminal's mental life. He lives every day as though it were his last" (p. 259).

After my interview with him I returned to Harrington's clinical folder to carefully read his psychiatric history. I found that there were numerous violent fights in the Harrington household. Drunk and abusive, his father regularly abused his mother, frequently threatening her with death. When as a youngster Harrington ran to his mother's side to try to protect her, his father would slap him across his face, shove him aside, and call him "Mamma's little fairy, who is trying to act brave."

There were also clear indications of Harrington's growing despondency during his adolescence in his history. Either his family did not recognize his depression or else they responded to it in practical and convenient ways. For example, his mother reports that she ripped up his initial essay for college admission. He had been asked to write on the subject of his anticipated future after college. He entitled his essay, "Winning Friends and Influencing People as a Drunken Corporate Lawyer Like My Father."

I suspect that Harrington refused to self-explore because he feared he would find only the despised, cruel, and manipulative encapsulated self he inherited from his family and of which he believed he was a permanent prisoner. As an immutable self, separate and isolated from the care and compassion he undoubtedly craved, he experienced no meaningful future.

Is there any viable escape from an accentuated sense of limitation and finitude that mitigates against self-exploration? The writings of both

Camus and Buber suggest that there is: curiosity that is concerned w
common ground that each of us has with other people—*a curiosi
seeks to recognize our social and moral responsibilities.*

THE MORAL PHILOSOPHY OF ALBERT CAMUS

Camus was a psychologically astute writer; even his severest critics—
such as those at *Temps Modernes* magazine in Paris, including Jean-Paul
Sartre, Simone de Beauvoir, and Francois Jeanson—never accused him of
psychological naivete, but of moral innocence. Camus was first and foremost a moralist (Judt, 1998). The extraordinary appeal of Camus' writings,
according to the American writer Susan Sontag (1966), is derived from its
quality of moral beauty which most 20th century writers ignore. "If the
world were clear," Camus claims, "art would not exist" (Lottman, 1980,
336–40). His fictional characters are presented to answer important social
and moral questions—that is, the problem of guilt and innocence, the ability to act or not act, responsibility or nihilistic indifference.

Throughout his work he asks: How should an ordinary person live in a
tentative and precarious world? His answer begins with the recognition
that we cannot depend on self-reflection. In *The Stranger* and in *The
Plague* he tries to show us that there is something radically wrong with
curiosity—or more properly, something deficient with the type of inquiry
that distances itself from concerns about other people, by reflecting dispassionately on the human condition. This was the philosophic style of the
cosmopolitan French intellectuals he so despised for their disdain for the
problems of ordinary people. These intellectuals showed Camus that
curiosity has a dark side: The pursuit of unceasing introspection leaves the
seeker plagued with inexorable despair accompanied by a lack of compassion for other people.

Curiosity and Compassion

In his writings Camus tries to show us that people cannot live in har-
mony and contentment in the midst of others' deprivation and suffering.
Those who have tried have failed. Camus' social philosophy has implications for an appropriate role for self-examination in psychotherapy. There
is a need first for the therapist to take seriously the notion that *mayas* in
human consciousness are the fundamental basis of his clients' sense of
separation from other people as well as their alienation from the cosmos.
The therapist, therefore, should help his clients recognize that their expe-

rienced impotence as existential beings is not an inherent product of human finitude and is rather a function of their lack of commitment to authentic dialogue and curiosity about other people. It is Buber (1999) to whom we now best turn to understand authentic dialogue.

THE SOCIAL PHILOSOPHY OF MARTIN BUBER

According to Buber (1999), because our personalities are twofold rather than solitary, dialogue is essential to our nature. Buber contends that

> Man exists anthropologically not in isolation, but in the completeness of the relation between man and man; what humanity is can be properly grasped only in vital reciprocity...there resides in every man the possibility of attaining authentic human existence in the special way peculiar to him. [But] it would be mistaken to speak here of individuation alone. Individuation is only the indispensable personal stamp of all realization of human existence. The self as such is not ultimately the essential.... The help that men give each other in becoming a self leads the life between men to its height. (p. 85)

In other words, according to Buber, as I indicated in the previous chapter, human wholeness requires an authentic dialogue with another person who also seeks wholeness. As a whole person, one must enter into primary relations that Buber calls *I–Thou*. Here the totality of what constitutes a human being is revealed. In Buber's words, "I requires a Thou to become; becoming I, I say Thou. By evoking Thou the composite of my being is revealed; I am no longer restricted to a predictable, ordered world, for the I–Thou has no bounds" (Buber, 1970, p. 62).

It is in the I–It world that we perceive a space of restricted boundaries, limitations, and finitude. The events of this world are measured, ordered, and predictable; its relations are distant, manipulated, and objectified.

These contrasting spheres of human existence—*I–Thou, I–It*—show the importance of genuine curiosity in the healing process. The disturbed, suffering person, Buber (1965) indicates, seeks to escape the world of distancing, manipulation, and objectification. But she is caught up in a mendacious assumption. She, together with her significant others, finds it convenient to pretend that her conflicts with others do not derive from their lack of understanding and genuine concern for one another, but because each is *compelled* to act dysfunctionally with the other as a condition of their essential personality. (This description is in close accord with what I inferred was Davis Harrington's view of himself.)

To dissolve these egregious relationships and find wholeness requires that the sufferer experience a *radical discovery*—a moment of surprise. What Buber means by this is that in the healing encounter, the sufferer needs to be taken off guard by the freedom she experiences to be as she intends in the presence of the other, rather than as how others in the past have demanded she be. As a twofold process, the healer also needs to be surprised by the strengthening of his creative capacities as he experiences himself in dialogue with the other (Buber, 1965). In fact, the depth of healing is a product of the healer's capacity to sustain the unexpected—to remain curious and surprised by what he learns about himself in relation to the other. Responding courageously and compassionately to this curiosity and surprise holds the prospect of human wholeness and fulfillment.

If there is a significant difference between me and the destructive people I have treated, it is in how we have responded to feelings of shame. People like Harrington *deny their identification* with people they unwittingly sense share similar vulnerabilities and hurts—by running away and making intimacy and interpersonal cooperation impossible; or else they treat the vulnerable other they encounter in hurtful and destructive ways— so as to deny their painful identification with the other. These destructive people's interpersonal failures as well as their destructiveness is derived from their *refusal to stay with* and *self-reflect* on their shameful feelings. When I experience shame, in contrast, I have been willing (at least, some of the time) to closely examine my feelings, and as a result, I have often been able to constructively respond to those aspects of myself that have caused me to feel bad about myself. I have come to recognize that not all experiences of shame are deleterious. Quite the contrary! In different manifestations and contexts shame may be toxic, restraining, or even constructive. Whereas toxic shame is the harbinger of hopelessness, healthy shame—the recognition that which we require to feel pride and self-esteem are realistically attainable although yet not achieved—provide the crucible of human freedom. In other words, in small doses, shame is a prod to self-improvement by providing a means for penetrating self-discovery.

Destructive people such as Davis Harrington, in contrast, shy away from self-examination because their internal world and its undiscovered self are far more frightening to them than the social world they inhabit with others. In the external world, due to their own superior physical, social, or intellectual skills, they play a dominant role. Moreover, they have developed an accentuated capacity for denial and rationalization of their insensitivity and unkind behavior. Ironically, their lack of self-monitoring provides them with the means of taking advantage of or controlling others. For example, most of us would pause to reconsider any impulse to harm seriously someone else, no matter how justified we experience our anger; but the Davis Harringtons don't. The rationalizations they have used for their previous cruel behavior—untempered by a curious concern about the reasons for their strong emotions—facilitate continuous impulsive acts of destructiveness and social dominance.

I wish I could say that I engaged Davis Harrington in an authentic dialogue and that both of us were better people for having done so. The reality is that I was only a consultant to Harrington's psychiatric division, not his psychotherapist. Appalled by the psychopolitics that exposed vulnerable patients to serious risk, I tried to convince Dr. Rendel that arousing the ire of Mrs. Harrington was the least of his worries because if any patient was killed by Harrington, Rendel should be prepared for professional liability. He did not seem concerned. However, the situation changed radically when I asked a reporter/friend on the city desk of the newspaper to call Dr. Rendel and inquire about the situation. I had described the situation to the reporter without divulging Davis Harrington's identity.

Harrington, soon after the reporter's phone call, was transferred to a more appropriate psychiatric division. I referred him to one of the division's psychologists for psychotherapy. I indicated in the referral note that I believed that he would probably be a difficult and challenging, but at the same time a fascinating and insightful, candidate for therapy.

What I learned about the importance of curiosity in human development from my encounter with Harrington has been of immense help to me in my career as a psychoanalyst and social theorist, as the chapters to follow reveal.

LOOK AHEAD

In the next chapter, by recalling and coming to terms with a painful childhood experience of my own, I was able to help a troubled young client recognize the hurtful impact of his parents' marital conflicts on his own impeded curiosity—so that he could overcome his fears about self-examination and become his own healer.

Chapter 7

AN EXPLORATION OF IMPEDED CURIOSITY: THE BOY WHO WAS HIS OWN THERAPIST

The first and simplest emotion which we discover in the human mind is curiosity.
—Edmund Burke (1729–1799, English statesman)

Every vocational career has its limitations and its own particular perils. For psychotherapists, boredom is one of the most ubiquitous and untoward. Yet the vast volume of material examining clinical practice has largely ignored boredom. Those who write about psychotherapy appear to have made the tacit assumption that once a therapist has acquired clinical skills he or she should be able to remain attentive and curious over a lifetime of practice. Those who have made this judgment have poorly served their colleagues. Severe ennui seriously afflicts a considerable number of practitioners, if not every therapist at some point in a full-time practice.

In that people who are drawn to practicing psychotherapy are generally highly stimulated by and responsive to the inner life, a state of boredom stands in sharp contrast to their usual way of being in the world. It usually indicates that they have lost touch with the goals, purposes, and directions with which they entered their career, such as gaining important realizations about themselves by learning from clients. As such, boredom represents the externalization of personal satisfactions that formerly the practitioner sought *within* himself or herself and from an exploration of the inner promptings of other people whom the therapist came to know intimately.

BOREDOM AS A DEFENSE AGAINST CURIOSITY

Curiosity, as well as boredom, has been a neglected subject in the psychotherapy and psychoanalytic literature. Freud, for example, never addressed the issue of curiosity systematically (Nersessian, 1995). His interest (Freud, 1905, 1909) was in trying to account for children's sexual questions (Aronoff, 1962). Nevertheless, hindrance to internal curiosity—that which intimidates and abates the appetite for an exploration of one's motives—is part and parcel of psychotherapeutic inquiry. And, arguably, there is no greater clinical challenge for the therapist than trying to treat a client who appears to lack an interest in the underlying causes of his unhappiness.

Psychoanalytic clinical theory (Fenichel, 1945; Greenson, 1953) enables us to recognize that boredom is not actually the absence of sufficient stimulation to remain alert, but rather a defense against a threat that the clinical situation unwittingly fosters, an evocation—as a case study I present here shows—that can be so unbearable that the practitioner unwittingly feels the need to deny its presence. Thus, during moments of ennui the practitioner may abandon his usual attitude of curiosity and attentiveness to his own promptings and those of the client; instead he distracts himself from that which is conflicting him by dozing, answering his telephone, reading (if sitting behind the analytic couch), or fantasizing that he is somewhere else, with someone else.

For some psychotherapists boredom is not confined to circumscribed areas of unresolved personal conflict; it is more pervasive. Because of their lack of fantasy, boredom always involves intersubjective factors—an interaction of factors from the personalities of that particular client and therapist—the increasing number of clients in recent years who have impeded fantasy life and lack of curiosity about themselves increases the possibility of a countertransference reaction of boredom in the therapist (Inner-Smith, 1987).

WILLIAM STONE

The case study I will present shortly is concerned with my untoward shame reaction to a client's reticence in revealing his hurt and suffering. A therapist cannot directly enable a client to be curious by instruction, of course. But his behavior can be paradigmatic. The case study I will present explores my adverse response to a child client, whom I call Leon. In struggling to find a way to open the painful secret from my own childhood unleashed by my work with Leon, I modeled a means for Leon's own personal exploration. Before examining my clinical encounters with Leon, a patient, whom I call William Stone—involved in Leon's story—is discussed.

William Stone had been a highly successful attorney and well-regarded law professor in Washington, DC prior to the Second World War. But after the tragic death of his wife and child in a car accident in which he was the driver, he spent a considerable amount of his time standing in Lafayette Park—across from the White House—giving long, rambling speeches on the evils of modern technology. Due to the high regard he had earned as a law professor, the park police largely ignored him, even when he shook his cane at passersby. However, when he began to actually strike his detractors in the park, he was brought to the federal psychiatric hospital in southwest Washington. His violent behavior quickly proliferated during his early days at the hospital. There he refused to speak with anyone. The science of psychopharmacology was not yet sophisticated. To contain his potentially dangerous behavior, for most of the years he spent at the hospital, he was kept in a locked seclusion room—his only interactions were with psychiatric aides who took him in a straitjacket out of his room twice a day for exercise and reasons of hygiene.

Twenty-five years later, I joined the staff of the hospital and was asked to be the psychology consultant to a psychiatric unit for long-term, seriously disturbed patients—the unit in which Mr. Stone was housed. Another patient on the unit—a fellow patient of Stone—had the annoying habit of roaring like a lion. Neither I nor the psychiatric staff understood him. As a result, we didn't know how to help him. In reading over the clinical files of the unit's inpatients, I found Stone's background intriguing. Obviously, for 25 years, his intelligence and education had been wasted. I approached him cautiously on one of his forays out of his cell, asking him whether he would be willing to help me understand the patient on the unit who roared like a lion. He replied with a smile. "Of course, I will help. I am pleased that someone recognizes me. It has been a very long time since anyone has asked me for help."

Stone told me that he had observed through the small window of his cell the patient who roared like a lion walking past his cell for almost 20 years. Whenever he approached someone on the unit, that patient or staff member would pull his arms quickly upward, cover his ears with his hands, and turn away. No one ever seemed to look at him directly or was concerned with what might be bothering the man.

"What is bothering him?" I asked.

"Since I've never been able to speak with him I don't know. But clearly he is shouting because no one would notice him if he was quiet and rocking back and forth all day in a chair, like the other nondescript old-timers on this God-forsaken ward."

The psychiatric staff and I made toy trumpets from the folded-over pages of a large newspaper, and when the patient walked by, roaring, we picked up our trumpets and held them to our ears. Our message was that although he was shouting we could not understand him, but we wanted to inform him that we were trying to reach him.

The Case Study of Leon

A number of years later, while in private practice, I was asked by a colleague whether I would consult with the family of an 11-year-old child at a private school in which my colleague was the school psychologist. Leon, a bright and usually energetic child, had become unaccountably depressed and uninterested in his schoolwork. After interviewing the child's family, my colleague suspected that spouse abuse was taking place in the family.

I held twice-weekly psychotherapy sessions with Leon and once-a-week sessions with his parents and younger brother and sister. Leon was extremely reticent, responding to my inquiries with a shrug of his shoulders or unenthusiastic single-word replies.

Because I wasn't able to elicit the information I needed directly, I asked Leon whether he would do some pencil drawings for me—from which I could attempt to make an interpretive assessment of the psychodynamics that were preventing Leon from trusting his hurt and suffering with me. Twice he flatly refused to do so.

I had always enjoyed working with children. But my work with Leon failed to gain my usual curiosity and attentiveness. As importantly, in my efforts to reach Leon I was suddenly aware one session that my face was flushed, wet with perspiration, although this was a cool autumn afternoon. I also felt gripped by a sense of a slow, if not unmoving, passage of time. I gradually realized that there was something about being with Leon that posed a threat to some part of me that I had suppressed and that something had unsealed an emotional envelope that held a painful secret. I judged the precipitant to be the therapeutic mirror.

Analysts use therapeutic mirrors to help their clients see themselves more clearly. I am alluding to the therapist empathically reflecting to the client those disavowed aspects of self that have been frustrated and denied in his mothering relationship that I discussed in chapter 2. The therapeutic mirror is reversible, however; it forces the therapist to perceive himself without guise. In other words, confronted by Leon's unspoken hurt, I was compelled to see shameful aspects of myself at an age close to his own. I had suppressed these painful memories; they never came up in my own personal therapies.

When I was 9 or 10 years old, a loud, foulmouthed great-uncle who showed up for a family gathering asked me to bring out my collection of about a dozen foreign coins. Their cash value was negligible, but I prized these coins more than any other possession. Their lettering, symbols, and some of their unusual shapes sparked daydreams of faraway places I someday hoped to visit. When I handed my treasure to my uncle, he put half of them in his pocket, shoved back the rest, grinned at my dismay, and refused to return what he had taken. In short, this boorish older man had found a way of ruining my good feelings about my hobby and replaced them with anguish.

I ran to tell my mother what had happened. For a puzzling long moment she was silent, and then she snapped, "You should be ashamed of yourself for being so selfish. After all," she pointed out sternly, "he didn't take them *all*...and he *is* your uncle."

I dropped the matter. Even so, I continued to feel miserable for months, though I was too young and psychologically unsophisticated to associate my unhappiness with the incident and my mother's scolding.

The most damaging thing about the whole affair, of course, was not my uncle's theft but my mother's response; her reproach undermined my trust in other people. Suddenly, the external world was no longer safe. It was a place where people didn't deal fairly with me. By taking my uncle's part, as in earlier incidents in which she had undermined my belief in fairness, my mother had invalidated the values that I had been led to believe by her were sacrosanct. As a result, I felt confused about what was right and wrong, indeed, whether much of what I had been taught or had found by way of my own experience was valid. In other words, at the age of 9 or 10 my sense of reality underwent a process of sudden psychological decompensation.

Only much later as an adult was I able to understand that my anguish was a result of intersubjective shame. I had been accused of selfishness by my mother because of her unwillingness to cause conflict with my grand-mother's sister and her brother-in-law, while at the same time she tried to avoid confronting her own sense of shame in failing to protect me from the cruelties of the world.

As a child I was vulnerable to the shame of being called "selfish." I felt compelled to "shut up" and bear my hurt alone. As a result, I felt unable to have fair exchanges with other people based upon mutual respect and compassion. I tried to hide these feelings from everyone, including myself.

Happily, one of my schoolteachers detected my shame-imbued depression. She knew that despondency was not my usual demeanor. With caring and understanding she drew out the story that I had forgotten and explained that I was in no way to blame for how my uncle and my mother had treated me.

Following my self-reflection about the coin incident, a kaleidoscope of memories flashed through my mind of all the passive-dependent therapy and analytic clients I have seen through the years who behaved as if they had chosen not to exist for themselves or for anyone else. With the vivid memory of so many dreary hours spent with these clients, I had to ask myself, why did I continue to practice?

Reflecting upon my apprenticeship years as a practitioner, during my difficulties with Leon, it was obvious that I had been drawn to the profession of psychological healing from an intense interest in learning about myself. Practitioners who believe they know themselves well enough from their own personal analysis and introspection will find their work dull and mechanical. Unless a seasoned practitioner is still available for further self-understanding, he will feel restive and bored. Did I know myself sufficiently well that it would be unlikely that I would learn something important about myself from the people with whom I clinically worked? I asked myself. Of course not!

Further self-reflection revealed that I was trying to deny my identification with many of the shadowy clients I had treated. Might I have been one of them if it had not been for the wise and compassionate intervention of my teacher and if these experiences had been a regular pattern of my developmental years? I had hoped, my introspection suggested, that by becoming an analyst my vulnerability to shame—that had imprisoned me following the coin incident and other events that had similar meaning for me—would dissipate and be overthrown; apparently, it hadn't. Further reflection enabled me to recognize that my feelings of boredom early in my time with Leon were a defense against my curiosity, that is to say, seeing myself earlier in life—moments when I felt totally alone, supported in guidance by no one, and unable to ask for help. In short, Leon posed a threat to me because I unwittingly feared that spending time with this deeply shamed lad would compel me to re-experience the terrible feelings of confusion and helplessness of my own childhood.

But then it struck me that Leon could become one of those shadowy people unless I or some other therapist was able to create a climate of trust in which he felt sufficiently safe to share his hurt and suffering. I remembered the teacher whose sensitivity and intelligence saved me. It gave me a clue to how to help Leon.

In an inspired moment I told Leon about my experience with Mr. Stone. After hearing the story of my patient/consultant at the federal hospital, his eyes widened, his mouth agape for a long moment. He finally said,

"You mean...mean that a crazy guy could help...could understand other crazy guys!"

"Do you ever think that you might be crazy?"

"Aren't I crazy?"

"What does crazy mean to you?"

"I don't know! Maybe, doing weird things that can't be explained—like how those homeless people in the street behave."

I related an aphoristic story about emotional disturbance to Leon that I had been told by a clinical supervisor during my clinical psychology internship:

A man is driving down a road deep into a rural area. He has seen few other automobiles in the past hour. His car suddenly jolts violently, veering to the side of the road. He stops and gets out of his car. He checks the wheels of his automobile. One of them has fallen off and slid down the road. On inspection, after retrieving the wheel, he sees that all four of the adhesion bolts are missing. He is perplexed and doesn't know what to do.

"Hey mister, come over here!" a voice calls out. He looks up and sees a long, high fence in front of him, with large buildings in the background. There is a man of about 70 years of age standing behind the fence, his fingers wrapped around the wire, watching his dilemma. He walks over to the fence. The man tells him, "Your problem is easy to solve. Just take off one of the bolts from the other three wheels and attach them to the wheel that fell off."

"That is an excellent suggestion," the driver replies. "Say, what is this place you're in?" The man behind the fence points to a large sign farther up the road that indicates that the buildings behind the fence are those of a state hospital for the mentally ill.

I paused for a moment and then added, "Because a person is troubled with emotional conflicts doesn't mean that he is not intelligent, sensitive, or caring about other people."

Leon looked up sharply, his words excited, his movements more animated than I had seen before. "If you give me a pencil and some paper, I am now ready to draw those pictures for you." He drew a picture of a boy of his own age, whom he referred to as Peter. I asked him to tell me about

Peter. He described a deeply troubled lad who had serious psychological concerns that I suspected mirrored those of Leon himself.

"What should Peter do about his problems?" I asked.

"He should go to see Dr. Goldberg."

I was taken off guard by Leon's response. But to catch the moment, I asked, "Why should he go to see Dr. Goldberg?"

I nearly fell out of my chair when Leon said, "He can help him. He is a very good doctor."

Leon became my consultant in helping to understand Peter (Leon). I agree with the New York psychoanalyst Herbert Strean (1988) that a client cannot meaningfully be involved in therapy if he is not regarded as a respected consultant about his own treatment.

In working with Leon, it became clear that he felt that he had become the scapegoat for all of his family's problems and would continue to feel that way if my work with him focused only on the problems his teachers and his parents had identified about him. What he most desired, he told me, was to regain the sense of enthusiasm and curiosity that he had lost and which his young brother still exuded.

"You say that your brother is always asking a lot of questions. Why do you think he does that?"

"He is a little kid and he is curious about everything."

"Were you like that once?"

"Yeah! I guess I was!"

"How was it for you to be filled with wonderment and curiosity?"

He paused a while and said, "I guess it made me feel like the world was a special, interesting place."

"What happened?"

Leon spoke about his father's angry comments about everything he said and did. His father's behavior indicated that there was something threatening to his father when Leon reached out to try to learn and know. On these occasions, his father would yell at him, "No! Don't do that!" or "Why do you ask so many questions? What's wrong with you?" Leon didn't feel it was safe to explore his own psyche, either. His mother's depression gave him the sense that the inner world of the self was a dreadful place, so there was no hope for things ever getting better by one's looking inward.

"Are you going to allow your parents to influence you in feeling that the world is not an exciting place to be? After all, you aren't going to be living with them forever. And if you don't practice being curious now, you may forever forget how. So why don't we practice being curious about ourselves in our sessions here. Okay?"

Only after Leon was able to again foster in himself a sense of excitement about his life and the world around him was he willing to explore his concerns about his parents' conflicted relationship and the effect it had on him and his siblings.

CONCLUSION

Natural curiosity is what keeps us alive and well. A common characteristic of people in psychotherapy and psychoanalysis—regardless of their symptoms and their backgrounds—is the paralysis of their curiosity about who they are, where they are headed, and what other people represent to them. Clients take on self-curative attitudes and get in touch with their own natural rhythms in how they intend living their lives by regaining curiosity about themselves and their place in the world. Therapists cannot directly teach or enable their clients to become curious; rather, it is their curiosity about themselves that frees clients for their own self-exploration. Obviously, for the bored therapist the first issue to explore is the analyst's identification denial with the client.

Now I am hardly contending that every boring person a therapist encounters carries a Pandora's box of extraordinary suppressed secrets from the therapist's background. But I do believe it is incumbent for the therapist to determine which of his identifications with the client is fostering his boredom.

LOOK AHEAD

The case study presented in the next chapter shows that by coming to terms with our mutual shaming by means of a candid exploration of our personal fears and ambitions, a highly destructive client, who had spent more than half his life in psychiatric and forensic institutions, and I were able to escape the imprisonment of a futureless present encounter and find a constructive perspective for guiding our lives.

Chapter 8

EXISTENTIAL ANGUISH: THE WOULD-BE RAPIST TRAPPED IN THE PRESENT

We cannot do evil to others without doing it to ourselves.
—Joseph Francis Desmahis (1722–1745, French poet)

Inevitably, the psychoanalyst's office is a place of shame. On the one hand, the client seeking treatment is ashamed, perceiving her visit as an indication of her incompetence as a person, and this shame is magnified by the very presence of the therapist, which forces her to reflect upon unworthy and mortifying aspects of herself as she reveals her secrets.

On the other hand, the client's shame is capable of humiliating the therapist. Unable to reach and heal a suffering patient, any caring practitioner is also vulnerable to feeling shame. This inexorable shaming will awaken the therapist's personal concerns and conflicts as well.

When Roy came to me for treatment, he was 35 years old. The youngest of five siblings in a working-class family, he exhibited some of the classic Lombroso characteristics of criminal physiognomy: thick neck, barrel chest, powerful torso.[1] Well over six feet tall, square-chinned, with piercing pale blue eyes, he wore his blond hair cropped short and had a tattoo on his left forearm.

When Roy was five years old, his father deserted the family. Starting at age seven, the boy spent half his life in psychiatric and forensic institutions. Usually, the incidents that led to his detention involved the sadistic intimidation of women, stopping just short of rape.

Although he was a high-school dropout, Roy was a facile conversation-alist with an exceptionally large vocabulary. He was also cannily obser-vant of other people and could analyze their motivations quite plausibly.

He had come to me, he said, because he sincerely wanted to straighten out his life. Fair enough—but the route he had taken was bizarre. Some time before, I had helped train the paraprofessional staff of a county hot-line crisis service. Afterward, I continued to be available as a consultant for unusually difficult or risky situations. One evening, Roy called the ser-vice to say that he was worried because he had been making obscene tele-phone calls for years and couldn't force himself to stop. The obscenities he repeated, together with his frequent allusions to violence, alarmed the vol-unteer who took his call. She asked him to hold for a moment while she spoke with her professional consultant.

Roy shot back, "You can't help me, kid? Just give me the doctor's num-ber!" She tried to put him off, but he became insistent. "Little girl, I know who you are. I'll have no trouble finding out where you are. And when I do, I'll come over there and rape you again and again."

She promptly gave him my home number.

Roy called me for an appointment, explaining that his finances were limited, even though he was a skilled cabinetmaker, but he would find a way to pay my standard fee. We met several times in preliminary ses-sions—with more than a little misgiving on my part about his motiva-tions—before I agreed to work with him. In the first place, despite his claim that he wanted to examine his life closely, his history was checkered with numerous short-lived forays into various treatment programs. Sec-ond, my office was in my home, so it was possible that Roy might be using the pretext of visiting me to case the neighborhood for targets of theft or even rape.

Why, then, was I willing to risk treating such an intimidating person in my home? Even today, I'm not entirely certain, but it had something to do with my need for an intensive challenge. For some time, I realized then, I'd been feeling apathetic toward almost all areas of my life other than psycho-logical work and intellectual activity. This situation was at odds with the person I had been in adolescence, a jock so deeply absorbed in sports that I had entered college expecting to become a professional athlete.

Now I was recognizing in myself the very malady I was struggling to help my patients transcend: the foreboding sense that I might never actu-ally live my life well. This existential malaise demanded some means of resolution, and practicing psychotherapy was one of the few areas in my life that had recently given me some sense of actual accomplishment.

Roy was evidently a very difficult person, but it seemed likely that dealing with him would generate a resurgence of my vital energies. In addition, I felt a partial identification with him because we had both played highly competitive football. Fantasizing a physical as well as a psychological combat with him recalled the days when I matched my youthful daring against intimidating opponents on the field.

To my dismay, however, Roy did not cooperate with my need for accomplishment. On the contrary, he was resistant to an exploration of his motivations and threatened my overvalued persona as a highly competent practitioner. He laughed at me whenever I tried to relate his present conflicts, such as being frequently fired from jobs because of his violent confrontations with supervisors, to events and feelings in his early life. His brutal snicker conveyed unmitigated contempt for my technique and me, but his words were hardly less upsetting.

"Who are you trying to kid, Doc?" he would say. "You're no better than me. If I stay around long enough, maybe I can help you. But what can you do for me?"

These frequent attacks made me feel embarrassed and exposed. I began to wonder what he suspected about me. Surely, I thought, he had not been able to detect my own personal dissatisfactions.

Finally, about six months into Roy's therapy, we encountered a serious crisis. For about a year, a serial rapist had been loose in the county, luring women out of their cars at night by pretending to be a police officer. I started to worry that Roy might be this rapist, though I didn't want to confront him directly because he'd be likely to suspect, despite my pledge of confidentiality, that I'd go to the police. Suspicion alone could cause him to mask, distort, and lie about his past behavior—as well as about the feelings attached to those harmful events in which he remained pathologically mired. I felt that my main therapeutic responsibility was to work with his *neurotic guilt,* not the possibility of his actual guilt as a rapist.

One afternoon session, contrary to my usual practice, I spoke first. Referring to his menacing conversation with the young woman volunteer on the hot line, I asked Roy whether he had ever raped anyone. I felt that he would probably be less reluctant to admit more remote crimes than the current attacks. And because serial violence rarely begins as such, there would most likely have been previous sexual crimes if he were the Beltway rapist.

To my great surprise, the usually glib Roy sat for a long moment with his eyes downcast, and for the first time, I realized that my willingness to accept him as a client meant a great deal to him. Until then, I had assumed that therapy gave him the so-called psychopathic or secondary gain of securing, and temporarily savoring, the exclusive attention of someone he believed to be a successful professional. Consequently, the real pain in his reply took me aback.

Looking up, he said, "I think you're afraid I'm the Beltway rapist." In a troubled tone, he continued, "If I was that mug I would tell you so. Why do you keep trying to make me have a guilty conscience? I don't! That's not what's bothering me!"

He went on to say that he'd already been punished for many things he had done that most people would regard as immoral. He felt no resentment.

"That's the way the game of life is played," he said.

What was bothering him, he continued, was more difficult to confess than any crime.

"Look," he said, "I'm a real big, powerful guy. People are scared of me. And I've never been afraid of anyone or any situation, but inside, I'm scared shitless, lonely and sad, all the time. It's strange; because I can have just about any woman I want and get her to do what I want. Like, for example, getting the woman I hang around with to pay my bill to you when I run out of money. But what bothers me most is that I'm going to die, I'm going to leave without having really been here. I'm more ashamed to admit that I don't know how to live than of anything immoral I've done. I don't know what's missing in me. That's why I keep coming here. And I've trusted you. Why the hell can't you trust me?"

At that moment, I felt unprepared to address his anguish. My professional training had emphasized that unconscious neurotic guilt—usually of an incestuous nature—is the major cause of human unhappiness. But I suddenly realized that there was a real difference between Roy and my other clients, who harbored identifiable feelings of guilt.

I recalled Washington, DC, psychoanalyst Harold Searles's (1961) poignant article, "Schizophrenia and the Inevitability of Death," which argues that psychosis is the defensive strategy of fictitiousness. In other words, the psychotic pretends that he is neither alive nor dead, for to be alive is to be launched down the pathway to death. To someone like Roy, convinced that he has not yet fully lived and will never live well, the prospect of death is especially terrifying.

But I also saw that the dread of death Searles describes is undoubtedly true of all of us, an identification I would have to closely examine in terms of myself if I expected to reach my client effectively. And yet there was something shameful about trying to become more fully identified with the unsavory Roy. As long as I continued to work with him, it would be impossible for me to find refuge from the self-doubts and concerns we had in common.

Fortunately, clinical experience had taught me to recognize when my reactions were being *induced* by clients. In this case, therefore, my feeling shameful with Roy indicated that he probably was feeling shameful with me. Once again, I was encountering a case of unrecognized shame. Until this critical session, I had not given either his shame or mine its proper due.

The Boston psychoanalyst Erik Erikson (1950) asserted that shame is produced by a crisis of trust between mother and child. In order to ascertain whether or not conflictual aspects of Roy's relationship with his mother were deeply implicated in his shame, I needed his *personal story*. That is to say, I could not effectively treat his despair (and other psychological conditions) without understanding how he saw himself and his experience of being in his world. For this exercise to be meaningful, he needed to describe himself with personal statements drawn from the deep recesses of his psyche rather than as someone might perceive him from the outside.

Not surprisingly, many clients find it very difficult to reveal their personal stories. Otherwise articulate, highly thoughtful people are suddenly at a loss for words when asked point-blank to convey a full, coherent sense of themselves. One of Freud's most important discoveries, to reiterate, is that the fear of what we might learn if we take an intimate look at ourselves is the single greatest cause of emotional disturbance. It follows that despairing, shame-afflicted clients want to hide their sense of incompetence not only from me but also from themselves. To deal with this problem, I suggest that clients draw upon the thoughts and feelings they form early in childhood and then continually revise throughout their lives.

We are, after all, meaning-oriented beings. We create our personal identity in the *stories we tell ourselves* about what has happened to us. We may not have one favorite story that says it all, but we can each tell stories that reveal a paradigm of how we see ourselves in relation to the world, its opportunities, and its obstacles. Because we cannot empirically discover any absolute truths, we derive our stories from a wide variety of sources—the events, legends, and myths of family and society—in order to create a reliable guide for living.

In fact, these myths succinctly show just how my clients navigate through life's straits and vicissitudes. At least as a working hypothesis, they help me clarify what my clients want from life, which obstacles they fear, and which resources they can use to attain their desired selves. I begin by asking for a story that best represents what life has been for them. When they come to the end, I ask them to go over the events again, describing as much as they can about the thoughts, feelings, and actions of the other people involved. Finally, I ask for the moral, or significant message, exemplified by the tale (a detailed discussion of this approach is found in chapter 13).

When I asked Roy for his personal story in the structured way I have just described, he spoke more openly about his mother than he had about her or any other person during previous sessions. He seemed to be seething with resentment, claiming that his violent temper came from being "done in" by women like her and his sister.

As a very young child, he recalled, he always looked forward to seeing his mother; he felt safe with her. But she died when he was only seven, and his sense of security vanished. His circumstances forced him to live with an older sister, who did not want him around; she was having enough trouble raising her own brood after her husband deserted her. Forever afterward, Roy felt alone, unguided, and severely shaken. Naively, like most children, he had believed that his mother could keep his world safe, predictable, and just, as long as he returned her love with unquestioning devotion. When she died, he was left feeling bitter and betrayed, by her and, indeed, by the entire world.

Trust in ourselves usually develops together with trust in our physical surroundings. If we fail to perceive or predict correctly the events of the external world, we can lose trust—often permanently—in ourselves and in those who have cared for us. Roy's feeling of self-worth was overthrown when he found out that his confidence in his mother had been misplaced.

Life is not always reasonable and fair. In each child's life there will inevitably be disappointments and misunderstandings. Nevertheless, the child must be protected from experiencing too-frequent and too-prolonged emotional pain. On the other hand, if there is too little stimulation in the child's life because he has been thrown on his own when he is still too immature to care for himself, he may develop an unrelenting hunger for excitement. Children who develop precocious restlessness, fed by a craving for stimulation, rarely form the appropriate sensitivities to the subtleties and nuances of life. They can perceive the world only in bold black or white dimensions. These children are compelled by an unrelenting obsession: "I've been cheated. I won't stand for it! I must have my own way! If not, others won't have their way with me again!"

I refer to the emotional unavailability of parents and caretakers—depriving the child of attention, vigilance, guidance, and compassionate concern—as *benign neglect.* It is a factor no less lethal in the development of the malevolent personality than are physical and sexual abuse.

Benign neglect thinly conceals the parents' ambivalence about being parents and adults as well as their rage and hostility toward each other.

When young children have to create their own morality because their parents have left them to their own devices, the result is usually children who are out of control. This is the theme of British writer William Golding's provocative novel *Lord of the Flies.*

Roy's story was an important revelation to me: For the first time, I saw that the shame ordinarily at work in our lives does not necessarily arise from malevolence, intentional cruelty, or even the ill wishes of another person. Roy's shame had its origins in his mother's love; for the more fervently we have believed in the benevolent qualities of love, the more grievous are our pangs of shame and despair when we are disappointed (Lynd, 1958). Roy's mother tried to shield him by keeping her fatal illness a secret. As she lay dying, he was not even allowed to help her in the small but important ways available to young children. Consequently, he felt betrayed by what seemed to be her lack of confidence in his ability to care for her. Roy's expressions of intense anger toward others as an adult were actually unsuccessful attempts to expunge the morbid impotence he had felt as a child after this traumatic event.

His hurtful shame, therefore, derived to no small extent from his inability to protect the person he loved most, and the loss of his loving bond with her crushed any yearning for loving or caring for anyone else ever again. In short, his shame was caused by his separation from loving relations and his feeling inadequate to carry on by himself.

Until this session, Roy had never been willing to examine the hurt, resentment, and contempt that arose from his painful experiences with his mother and sister. Instead, he angrily and brutally acted upon his agitation, deftly rationalizing his contemptuous behavior toward women and his violence toward men.

"I have the balls to do what other men just fantasize about," he would boast.

All of his adversaries were displacements for the people who had hurt him in the past. Understanding *displacement*—a psychological defense set up when someone who has hurt us is no longer available or too powerful to confront—is essential to understanding malevolence. Roy and other wounded people, who are at least partly aware of what they are doing, choose to harm victims whose suffering resembles their own original hurt. Seen from this perspective, the malevolent person can be intimate with himself—at least, with the hurt self he disavows—only during these acts of displacement. At all other times, he keeps in place a callous defense that denies any identification with the hurt and pain of others.

"Since life is cruel and mean," Roy frequently said, "I'll be cruel and mean, too."

In other words, he had transformed himself from abandoned child—a victim—into the victor of an ongoing struggle with others for dominance. At the same time, by becoming a master manipulator of women, he subtly flaunted his sense of superiority over his father, who in Roy's view was *not man enough* to handle women because he allowed his wife to die and had abandoned his own son.

Roy and I shared a common bond. If betrayal was the symbol of shame and anguish in Roy's life, it was in mine as well. My despair was the product of feeling betrayed by my professional life. Many therapists develop a sense of fraudulence about the examined life. They feel that their commitment to analytic understanding of themselves has not harvested the savory fruit of the well-lived existence that their faith in psychotherapy had promised. This is a subject that few therapists are willing to talk about publicly, instead deferring their nihilistic feelings for conversations with close trusted colleagues or for their return to the analytic couch.

Meaningfulness does not wane categorically for the therapist who is in despair. Confidence and the sense of well-being depart bit by bit (Wheelis, 1960). Therefore, through the skills and tricks of the trade, the seasoned practitioner may still carry out his professional duties almost competently, even when his convictions about the theories he subscribes to and the illusory benefits of pursuing the examined life trouble him. For the seasoned practitioner, these disturbing effects may first reveal themselves in a crippling manner for his private life. For me, the experience of being a seasoned therapist undoubtedly gave me skills in enhancing my relationships outside my clinical work. On the other hand, preoccupation with clinical problems gave me a legitimate excuse to avoid responsibilities to my family and my marriage. Inevitably, of course, these effects of disturbed meaning will manifest themselves in clinical practice.

If I had dared then to look back honestly over my career, I would have had to admit that the years did not seem well spent. But like other disillusioned practitioners, I thought it was too late to recover what was lost. Why did I feel such despair? I had come to realize that analytic expertise and insight into human affairs are not always finely attuned, dependably rational tools. Originally, I had believed that I could rely upon the wisdom of the examined life to succeed in both my professional and my personal affairs. But by the time of this vignette I had become convinced that knowledge and analysis had not actually done much to help me live any more fully and satisfyingly than someone who was less self-examined. Moreover, I had similar doubts about the significance of my professional work.

This existential malaise, as I suggested earlier, had grown over the years as I shifted from being an active participant in life to spending most of my time observing it. I had hoped that my scholarship in books and articles would provide lasting meaning in my life. By contrast, of course, clinical work is written on the wind because it is largely unobserved and subjected to the mercurial nature of my clients' lives.

In short, my writing was an attempt to deny my own vulnerability and mortality, but we cannot continuously fool ourselves about the truth of impermanence, as I was reminded when I interviewed for an administrative position at a large teaching hospital. The process of meeting with various staff members went well until the end of the day, when the director of the outpatient clinic looked up from my resume and stared at me quizzically.

"What is this all about?" he asked. Since I clearly had no idea what he meant, he pointed to the list of my 50 or so publications. "Why do you need to write so much?"

Of course, I felt immediate resentment because he seemed to be reducing my publications to little more than some unresolved childhood conflict. Then I became considerably anxious, instantly recognizing once again, as most of us do from time to time, that the conditions upon which our hopes and aspirations depend are fundamentally and terribly fragile. At such moments, we also realize how quickly and easily our apparent achievements can be taken from us and how our desires, even when they seem satisfied, may prove to be empty.

One force motivating my writing, although I had not consciously acknowledged it until then, was my shame in regard to my father. This was evident in one particularly vivid memory.

While still in analytic training, I wrote a book about my clinical work. It was well received professionally, and I proudly gave my parents a mint-new copy the next time I visited them. My mother opened it excitedly, glanced over practically every page, and said that she was impressed that I could write about such a difficult subject. My father gave my book a brief look and shrugged.

"You should write a novel instead," he said. "People like to read about ideas in a story rather than an academic book." Then: "Are you making any money yet?"

I nodded (untruthfully, of course, since I had only just begun to practice).

"Good! Good!" He walked off to watch television.

The shame I then felt about wasting time writing a book recalled my shame about athletic and literary activities I pursued in my teens, while both of my parents worked overtime at strenuous jobs to give me a first-class education at a boarding school. Because I did not want my father to feel that his years of toil and sacrifice had come to nothing, I decided to write a better book next time, one that would show him at last who I was and why I had chosen my career. I was never able to write that book, though I wrote many others, before he died.

It was in that boarding school, with its German accent and the conveyance of the love of books, Mozart, and the outdoors, that I first heard mention of psychoanalysis. Also, there I first experienced the capacity of the psychoanalytic mind-set to reach the inner recesses of the psyche. My teachers, non-Jews who had fled the Nazi Holocaust, were well educated and trained in psychoanalysis and Gestalt psychology. They conveyed an understanding of human behavior that was for me mysteriously powerful. They seemed able to put into articulate words the intrapsychic messages that sustained periods of silence for my classmates and me.

My experience with these European teachers is related to my reasons for becoming a psychotherapist. At some subliminal level, psychological knowledge presented to me a means of both understanding and escaping the confusing conflicts of my nuclear family. In other words, studying psychology led me to a career in which I found the financial and psychological means to separate successfully from my family.

Because psychology had such a salubrious effect on me, I was, as a beginning therapist, somewhat uncomfortable about being paid. My most gratifying clinical year was my internship. I assumed that the clinical skills I was developing would enable me to experience the world in a way that ordinary people could not. The fact that I was paid a minimal wage, less than half of what I had made the year before and so low that I was actually eligible for welfare benefits, was no problem for me; my sacrifice was my investment in the future.

Contrasting how I experienced myself in my twenties, a beginner having an unforeclosed future, with my perspective of midlife, its future more limited, I felt betrayed by myself and by those mentors I had trusted.

Accepting my malaise, or in effect dealing with my tragic sense of the existential condition, is no less onerous for me or any other practitioner than for our clients. Session after session, I have to face aspects of myself that I would rather deny or evade. But it is necessary for me to use myself as a mirror to help my patients learn to integrate themselves, even though the mirror, as I already suggested, is dangerously reversible, a potential threat to bearer and gazer alike. That is, I may encounter my own sense of vulnerability in the eyes of my clients, and this bold sight of my frailties evokes the discomfort of shame.

But no matter how deeply the therapist suffers in these circumstances, he must continue to try to help the client work toward healing. In essence, this is the agonizing existential dilemma for the shameful practitioner: the therapist–patient bond requires that she help someone whom she might resent for bearing witness to her own vulnerabilities.

During the most difficult moments of my critically important session with Roy, I felt myself losing connection with what was familiar and safe. I could neither escape nor control my shame; there was no place to hide. Time seemed frozen, endless.

Even so, my shameful awareness was strangely illuminating, and I began to see that the key to my impasse with Roy lay in the *untranscendable* sense of shame. I realized that we were struggling with shame in *existential time*. In other words, the shameful feeling that we are incompetent to find purpose in life is important to us only because our time is limited and we will one day cease to exist. Our most disturbing experiences are those that threaten our relation to time; the most painful aspect of them, as in Roy's case, is the inability to imagine a future moment when we will be free of our anxiety or depression. I also became aware that our most profound human experiences—joys and dejections, ecstasies and fears—are heavily influenced by differing dimensions of time (May, Angel, & Ellenberger, 1959). To my knowledge, no theorist has yet described the crucial phenomenological distinctions among the three existential anxieties: guilt, anticipatory anxiety, and shame.

Guilt is experienced as an act already committed, an event in the past. The culpable person experiences his guilty deed as one that he has *chosen*. Moreover, he may haggle or negotiate with the internal representatives of authority within himself as to when he will address his culpability. The victim of neurotic guilt, for example, chooses to remain in the past.

Anticipatory anxiety, by contrast, is stuck in *uncertainty about some future moment*. Obsessive concerns about what may lie ahead prevent the person from concentrating on life's immediate demands.

But in my impasse with Roy, I was suddenly, startlingly aware that my feeling of vulnerability was occurring in the immediate moment: There was no sense of passing time. I had no choice but to be whom and where I was. I was the shame. And I could not transcend myself. Time had stopped and I felt engulfed by the prospect of the pervasive shaming moment remaining everlasting (further discussion of the relationship of time and disturbances of the self are found in the next chapter).

Shame ensues when we try to avoid the present because the constructive role of shame is to teach us the reality of time, how to enhance our lives in the present because our time is implacably limited, and how to release the past in order to stop harming our present and our future. Too much emphasis on guilt, therefore, compels the client to discuss superficial, often irrelevant material. The result is that he and the practitioner will evade the profound concerns they both harbor about the conditions of their own self-worth in the present moment.

With Roy, I had the option: Would I, or would I not, keep my vulnerabilities concealed from him? To the extent that I ceased concealment, I realized, I would be free to explore the factors crucial in having a meaningful alliance with my client. Most important, we needed to examine how each of us was allowing the other to be perceived. I asked Roy how he experienced my treatment of him.

"You've always used the word *discount* to explain how people put me on the defensive when I was a kid," he answered. "But that's what you do to me."

He was hurt, in other words, that I had not confirmed his feelings as legitimate and real. Evidently, I had allowed my own shame to stand in the way of responding to him in the present, preferring to keep our therapeutic encounters focused on the remote shadows of his past. By working with his transferential distortion—how Roy might be confusing me with conflictual people in his background—I was denying my participation in the present and giving no importance to what he needed right now. In the same vein, I had been relating to him as if I were an objective, detached scientist on an archaeological quest rather than a fellow traveler suffering similar despair over not having lived fully and well. I had been ignoring the mutual shaming that existed between us because I seemed to have denied my common humanity and shared human fate with Roy.

Roy needed me to bear witness to the unfairness of a life ravaged by shame. I recognized that my feelings of shame in the presence of my clients were not only a manifestation of my own unresolved issues. They were also a testimony to my conviction of *what ought not to be* in my clients' lives. At the same time, as a professional guardian of *what can be,* I recognized that I had to remain actively alert to the constructive aspects of Roy's shame.

To reach the deeper sources of our existence, we need to have a dialogue with a responsive other. Sharing shame experiences, though painful because they produce a disturbingly accentuated self-consciousness, are moments in which we become aware, however fleetingly, of the ambitions, longings, and sentiments that are valuable to our sense of who we are. By providing a mirror to reflect aspects of ourselves that are usually hidden, shame confronts us with the reality of our tenuous existence, as opposed to the "vital lie" described by Ernest Becker (1973) (discussed in chapter 2).

Any practitioner who chooses to acknowledge both his own and his client's shame clears the way for discovering important options for living one's life. Experiencing my shame with Roy taught me that I have a personal as well as a therapeutic obligation to take an active role in my encounters with other people. Those of us who become psychotherapists typically share our clients' exquisite sensitivity to suffering, but we also differ from someone like Roy, for example, in having found that human conflict can be successfully handled by psychological means.

Quite to the contrary, Roy had felt deceived and betrayed by the many regimes of psychological treatment he endured. He was especially bitter about the electroconvulsive therapy forced upon him at one institution. Having spent most of his life in one form of psychological treatment or another, he well knew that ECT was clinically contraindicated in his case and therefore constituted abusive psychiatric treatment. Because of this and other incidents, Roy had severed his empathic identification with others in order to develop a characterological shamelessness toward his own feelings, thus shielding himself from his psychological vulnerabilities.

I needed to offer him some existential choices based upon the constructive influence of psychological examination, but paradoxically, in my malaise I now found the examined life deficient. And yet, as I have indicated, my growing understanding of shame showed me that sharing my own feelings of impotence, vulnerability, and transparency might be the critical sine qua non of healing Roy's devastating despair. Furthermore, if I could not feel compassion for myself, how could I genuinely feel compassion for my clients? Rather, by regarding my own emotional struggles during a session as the pangs of caring and concern, not as weakness, I might be able to provide a significant therapeutic experience. In short, I concluded, only when a practitioner and a client share their common humanity can they actually begin traveling down the road to finding meaning in human existence. Until they trust each other in the present, they cannot deal effectively with the shame and guilt of the past. This suggested a reversal of the usual psychotherapeutic procedure, but my consideration of the role of shame left me no other reasonable conclusion.

And so my therapeutic task with Roy was beginning to become clear. First, I had to demonstrate that each one of us should work toward emotional maturity by engaging in psychological examination and then using this psychic data as signposts in our struggle with the unbecoming aspects of our selves. Second, I had to acknowledge to him that I had just as much investment as he did in making us known to each other. Third, I had to offer a psychological scrutiny of myself as a means of repairing our therapeutic alliance.

I told Roy about my experience at the job interview, explaining that from subsequent self-examination I had come to realize that my sudden anger had sprung from the painful recognition that I was living a lie. In other words, my frantic efforts to give my life permanence had been futile; for me, as for everyone else, such attempts were illusory sand castles in the dunes of time. On the other hand, I went on, I could now recognize that my life is given meaning by my relations with other people, albeit a kind of meaning that is always shifting, mercurial, and subject to the whims of circumstance. I said that I was willing to offer this understanding of myself as a means to help him make sense of his own life.

Eyes are the windows of the psyche, we've been told. We avert our eyes to conceal the desolate domain of our inner self or, similarly, to avoid having to concern ourselves with the tribulations in the psyche of the other.

It was not until I allowed my eyes to meet and lock with Roy's that I knew that the shaming between us was indeed the key to his healing. When we looked frankly at each other, I sensed his wish to assure me that I need not feel ashamed of what I had just revealed. Then I asked, to be sure, and he nodded. In return, he said that he wanted to feel he was an acceptable person in my eyes, even though he had never contributed anything of value to anyone.

A couple of weeks later, I had to leave town for a month or so. When I returned home, there was a message from Roy on my answering machine. He had decided to turn himself in to the police for a criminal act he had committed some weeks before beginning his treatment with me. Because he had always felt the need to impress others with his mature sexual prowess, he had been ashamed to tell me about an incident that involved exposing himself to two young adolescent girls sitting in a parked car. From our sessions, he said, he had come to recognize that the only thing to be ashamed of was not living his life openly and to the best of his capacity. He had decided to confess his behavior with the two girls and take his punishment, then get on fearlessly with the rest of his life. The last sentence of his message sounded like a quiet resolve.

LOOK AHEAD

By means of a case study I show in the next chapter that the experience of abject loneliness is dependent upon a disturbed consciousness of time. This time disturbance diminishes the person's capacity for personal agency.

NOTE

1. In 1864, Cesare Lombroso, a young Jewish physician in the Italian army, conducted informal studies during his leisure in order to compare "honest" with "vicious companion" soldiers. When he returned to civilian life, he studied criminals in the general population, eventually concluding that he had discovered the origins of criminality. In his book *L'Uomo Delinquente,* published in 1899, Lombroso claimed that he had identified the "born criminal," recognizable by such characteristics as "enormous jaws, high cheekbones, prominent superciliary arches, solitary lines in the palms, extreme size of the orbits, handle-shaped or sessile ears," as well as by "insensitivity to pain, irresistible craving for evil for its own sake, the desire not only to extinguish life in the victim, but to mutilate" (Hibbert, 1963, p. 186).

Chapter 9

LONELINESS AND DREAD: THE WOMAN WHO TRIED TO ESCAPE TIME

The time is out of joint; O cursed spite that ever I was born to
set it right!
—William Shakespeare (1564–1616, English playwright)

All doctors soon learn that their patients consult them far less often for specific illnesses than because they are unhappy and seek relief from their loneliness and despair. Countless numbers of people find themselves entrenched in lives that are barren of intimate, trusting companionship. For them, the search for wise, caring, and trusted friends to support and inspire them has been long and futile. Self-esteem and a sense of living fully and well are dependent upon being desired, understood, appreciated by others; a sense of security is bolstered by the knowledge that there are concerned others to whom one can turn in times of need. The failure to foster caring from others leads directly to feelings of inadequacy, depression, and intense loneliness.

One would assume by the ubiquity of the problem that behavioral scientists have given considerable attention to an explanation of why so many people lack the facility for emotional connectedness with others that would avert extreme states of loneliness and despair. But in fact few contemporary behavioral scientists have attempted penetrating examinations into the problem of loneliness. Rarely is it even mentioned in psychiatric textbooks (Fromm-Reichman, 1959).

The French philosopher Henri Bergson has pointed out that "time is the heart of existence." I, too, am struck by the observation that our most profound human experiences occur more in relation to time than in the dimension of space. They fall somewhere in the continuum of "I wish that this experience would go on forever!" to "I cannot stand another moment of this!"

To recapitulate what I discussed earlier, there are three temporalities of ontological disturbance: guilt (past); shame (present); and anticipatory anxiety (future). Guilt is experienced as behavior already chosen and committed; what is unclear is when the subject will deal with the guilt. Shame is felt as the loss of the safe and familiar; time seems frozen, endless, with no place to hide and contain one's vulnerable feelings. The subject feels engulfed by the prospect that the pervasive shame will remain everlasting. Anticipatory anxiety is teleological—the person's sense of purpose is obsessed with what he or she regards as decisive-to-be moments in the future.

The experience of abject loneliness is dependent upon a disturbed consciousness of time (Hartocollis, 1983). *Loneliness,* as I seek to show here, *is the denial of the present moment—its possibilities and its demands.* As such, loneliness poses an existential dilemma. During the normal course of our lives we find that our existence is slipping quickly away. When we are joyous we wish to halt time, to suspend it, to cherish every aspect of it. But most of us find that we don't know how. In contrast, when we are imprisoned, suffer, and are in pain, time seems slow; its unwelcome confinement hangs heavily upon us. We feel engulfed by the prospect that the pervasive feeling of shame and helplessness that we must bear alone will continue everlasting. The sense of solitary shameful helplessness is the full measure of loneliness. The writings of two interpersonal psychoanalysts, H. S. Sullivan (1953) and Frieda Fromm-Reichman (1959) underscore that loneliness is such a devastating experience that people will do virtually anything to avoid its confinement, even resorting to anxiety-arousing experiences, which in themselves most people try arduously to avoid.

The propensity for loneliness is a derivative, as British humanistic psychologist John Cohen (1962) indicates, of a series of unmet reciprocities of a person in relationship to his or her significant others:

> The infant is lonely if he lacks tenderness and contact with the mother. The child is lonely without parental participation in play and conversation. The juvenile is lonely if...rejected by his fellows. A more poignant loneliness comes during preadolescence with its intense need for intimacy with a single other person. Any companion is better than none, because loneliness is worse than anxiety. We prefer to be tied to someone we hate rather than be left in isolation.... The bitter fruit of loneliness is a distorted picture of one-

self and therefore also of other people; and at the end is a warped person incapable of living amicably with his fellows. (p. 56)

A client, whom I shall call Christine, fulfilled each of these developmental phases in the fostering of the lonely person. Indeed, her feelings of being forsaken were sufficiently desperate that they constituted what I show to be *dread.*

CASE STUDY

Christine was in her early thirties when I saw her for psychological consultation. Her family physician referred her because of her severe depression. He told me in a phone conversation that she was deeply dependent on her husband for the will to live from day to day. He was concerned that if her philandering husband were to leave her, Christine would be a strong suicide risk.

Fair-skinned and blue-eyed, Christine was a tall, slim, serious-looking woman, who in my presence never smiled or wore any cosmetics. She taught structural engineering in the department of physics at a local university.

Childhood

Christine was the only child of a German-born father and an American mother. Her father, considerably older than his wife, had been an eminent chemical engineer before he fled his country to escape involvement in the Nazi scientific-industrial war machinery prior to Germany's invasion of Poland in 1939.

Her relationship with her father had been close. He was chronically depressed, her mother emotionally unavailable to him. Christine, since childhood, had been her father's caretaker as well as his confidant and companion. The same was not true of her relationship with her mother. Christine described her as a very pretty, vain, socially busy woman who claimed that she didn't understand her daughter. Christine believed that her mother was intimidated by Christine's intelligence and resentful of the closeness Christine had with her father. Moreover, unlike her athletic mother, Christine was shy and physically awkward; despite her natural prettiness, she attracted little interest from boys except in scholastic matters.

Her mother was continually upset at Christine's lack of social skill and popularity with her classmates. In a rage over one or another of Christine's social faux pas, she would lock Christine in her room, telling her: "If you don't need or want other people's company then you can stay in your room until you are old, gray, and lonely—maybe then you will have realized what you missed out on in life."

More than once Christine was forced to remain in her room for two entire days. Only the beginning of a school day freed her to leave her room and the house. But sometimes not even school allowed her to escape her imprisonment. Her passage to freedom resided entirely in her mother's mood.

Her bedroom and bath were located in the attic of the house. Neither had a window to allow contact with or even observation of another living being. The only person available to her was her own reflection in her bedroom and bath mirrors: languished eyes, pleading for liberation from her confinement, with the look of despair. She could not bear to view her image for more than an instant.

Despite the severity of her confinements she could remember no moments in which she felt hurt or angry with her mother. What she could recall was tremors of terror she felt at realizing that her tenuous hold on life was dependent on her parents' goodwill toward her.

Christine's isolation was informed by her misconception that she was alone in her shame and despair. "Loneliness," Fromm-Reichman (1959) indicates, "in its quintessential form is of such a nature that it is incommunicable by one who suffers from it." Unsurprisingly, then, Christine saw herself as a social and emotional cripple, unable to recognize her *pluralistic ignorance—the unquestioning belief commonly held by the lonely person that she is unique in her state of aloneness and despair.*

Christine's passivity in regard to her isolation—that is to say, her unwillingness or inability to secure the company and concern of others—came from what seems an almost sheer inarticulateness in communicating her needs—common to the desperate lonely (Mendelson, 1990). The willingness to strive for our wants is derived from our passions. Our passions induce us to become involved in our existence. However, Christine's emotional language was limited. She spoke matter-of-factly about her most intimate experiences. I could only ascertain the possible pleasure or aversion she had experienced by assembling the contents of her factual descriptions and then asking myself what I might have experienced if I had been in her place.

Christine's emotional inarticulateness is a product of her feelings of shameful helplessness. As I indicated in chapter 1, psychotherapists have been too often confused about the meaning of human suffering, attributing many of their most complex and difficult cases—like that of Christine—to problems with guilt (such as her libidinous relationship with her father) rather than to shame because of the sonority of guilt. Guilt usually has a vociferous voice, while generally shame is a muffled cry. There are words and agreed-upon language to express one's guilt (Lynd, 1958), which enables the sufferer to confess and redeem herself, temporarily closing the lid on her hidden terrors and uncertainties. The same cannot be said of the experience of shame. Shame will not allow our painful nakedness, namely the cast of who we are and who we seek to be, an articulate voice. For most people shameful experience is regarded as impossible to communicate and to share with another human being. Few need persuasion that our most terrifying moments are those that cannot be shared with others. They cause us flight and secrecy, leaving us feeling frightened and isolated. In short, in the throes of shame the sufferer feels transparent, empty, lacking in power and legitimate entitlement. Given these denigrating feelings, when confronted by environmental oppression a person abnegates his prerogative to protest or try to prevent unfair treatment and abuse by others. Instead he attempts to hide in order to cover the opprobrium that follows the disturbing perception that he is disintegrating as a person and has no recognized capacity to alter or even articulate his frightening sense of loss and dissolution. In turn, the sense of dissolution severely impairs a person's emotional sanguinity.

In terms of emotional maturation Christine was a child: in a primitive state of being in which emotions happened to her in relation to pleasant or averse events in which she found herself. She experienced herself as if looking at herself as an object, as happy, sad, or whatever. Her typical moods—of terror or relief—were abrupt and extreme. Most of the time, however, Christine's demeanor was one of indifference or subtle discomfort.

She suffered from what humanist psychologist Rollo May and his associates (1959) refer to as epistemological loneliness, a problem they describe as not simply one of a lack of interpersonal relations and communication with other people. "Its roots reach below the social levels to an alienation from the natural world as well" (p. 57). Thus, when Christine discussed a film or play she attended, a book that she read, she found it difficult to render a subjective reaction: to say whether she liked it or not. Instead she regarded its technological attributes, that is to say, whether it appropriately met cinematic, dramatic, literary, or some other such standard.

Adulthood

Christine was one of only three women in her Ivy League university engineering class. Her husband, whom I call Jim, was a classmate. The first time she saw him in class, flirting with her other two female classmates, she felt nauseated at both his behavior and his edge-of-the-city outlandish clothes. But his attention slowly turned toward her during their freshman year. It was her intelligence, he had told her, that attracted him. Although she regarded him as at least as bright as she, he was too busy chasing skirts to give much time to his studies. He depended on Christine to help him pass class exams. He never needed to exhort her to write his class papers. "I would have done anything he asked of me," she said. Throughout her life, Christine was most comfortable when she actively was of help to others—without asking or expecting anything in return. Correspondingly, when in the presence of others during events that didn't require her helpful involvement, Christine tended to drift off into her private world.

Christine started a sexual relationship with Jim the first week they spent time together. It was the first and only intimate relationship she has ever had. Her menses began during the second week of their relationship. They had abruptly stopped when she was 14 for about 4 years. Her medical exams were inconclusive. I suspect that her unusual condition was a way of denying her femininity and that it was related to her relationship with her father. She had fantasies about sexual union with her father that had badly frightened her, and I believe this caused a hormonal imbalance.

Her present life centered on her marriage. Her major satisfaction was her sexual experiences with Jim. It wasn't her own orgasms that were most important to her, although she took immense pleasure in them, but that Jim so frequently wanted sex with her even after a 15-year-old relationship. She claimed that their actual intercourse lasted two to three hours in which he stayed erect in her for the entire duration.

Initially, when Christine asked Jim to attend conjoint sessions with her, he cited numerous problems with his business to which he first needed to attend. When I called him, he said he would come in a few times to speak only with me about his take on his wife's problems. With Christine's approval, I saw him alone for three sessions.

Jim was slim, slightly over six feet, with straight, combed-back blonde hair and a thin mustache. He wore dark shirts with light colored ties and the types of shoes those cast as gamblers or hustlers in theater productions of *Porgy and Bess* and *Guys and Dolls* wear. Jim's hustler appearance was somewhat muted by his thick eyeglasses.

Jim was no more conscientious as a professional engineer than he had been as a student. He frequently was laid off from his engineering positions. For income he ran a number of profitable massage parlors. Christine claimed that these parlors were legitimate. Jim's story was different. He bragged to me of his sexual exploits with his workers, who were prostitutes, and any other woman he could manage to corner.

During one of these conversations, I casually asked him what he estimated was the longest duration he had stayed erect in a woman. He studied me for a moment and said, "I guess I am better at that than most men. But hell, why go to all that trouble? Twenty minutes, tops! I'm finished then and they'd better be, too!"

I asked Jim whether he knew of any instances at home or in her professional life in which Christine experienced difficulty in estimating time. He laughed and said he had no idea what I was referring to, because Christine was a very precise, well-organized person.

Although Christine was reticent in revealing her inner being, I had been impressed that everything she had told me was direct and, I surmised, the full content of her awareness. Clearly, there was something amiss in her judgment of time, but it wasn't a pervasive temporal disturbance. Her difficulty seemed confined to emotional experiences—both those that were painfully untoward and those that were essential to her self-regard.

The incident that compelled Christine to drop her denial of Jim's extramarital behavior occurred shortly before she discussed her marital problems with her physician. Jim had been apprehended by an undercover sting operation for having tried to solicit sex from a police officer disguised as a female prostitute. Christine had been called to the district jail to bail out Jim. Getting him out of jail forced Christine to recognize that in centering her life on Jim, she had given him implicit permission to pursue quick sexual interactions and affairs without his need even to keep these behaviors out of her awareness.

Because of the deprivation and lack of reliability of her important childhood caretakers, Christine had turned to Jim, a person she regarded as powerful and resourceful, as her protector. His main preoccupation was in carnal sexuality; as such, she regarded his sexual interest in her as the strength of their bond. To deny the frightening recognition of how fragile the bond actually was, Christine had tried to disavow—by greatly overestimating the duration of their sexual encounters—her awareness that his sexual interest was not confined to her alone.

No longer able to ignore the prospect that he might leave her and she would be confined to a permanent aloneness, Christine became preoccupied with suicidal thoughts.

MOTHER–CHILD INTIMACY

Ideally, the mother teaches her child not only how to love and establish intimacy with another person, but also as important, how to be intimate with herself. The mother's caring responsiveness, as discussed in chapter 2, especially as communicated through her eyes and facial expressions, symbolically gives the child access to the mysteries of her mother's psyche. The child, in turn, feels the permission to enjoy her own company. Lacking this emotional nurture, children such as Christine regard their innate longing for intimate connection as troublesome and painful.

BENIGN NEGLECT

Benign neglect, by which I mean *the deprivation of parental attention, guidance, and compassionate concern for the child,* can be as devastating as physical abuse. The extensive empirical research inspired by well-respected attachment theory indicates that not having caretakers emotionally available impedes the security and well-being necessary for a child's constructive sense of personal identity (Ainsworth, 1962; Bowlby, 1953). In an important sense, Christine suffered more deeply from her father's benign neglect than she did from her mother's overt abusiveness.

Accordingly, a recent study sought to separate the effects of five types of maltreatment: sexual abuse, physical abuse, verbal abuse, emotional neglect, and physical neglect. The study found that the most damaging of these is emotional neglect (Acocella, 1998).

Christine's father would often tell her after a confinement incident that her mother was treating her badly, but not to judge her too harshly because she was a frustrated and unhappy woman. Christine's mother had expected her husband—as a result of his early eminence in Europe—to be affluent and successful. He wasn't. He was employed as a low-level inspector of government buildings for the General Accounting Office.

Christine anxiously waited each time she was locked up for her father to come to her room and free her. By the time she reached high school she finally realized that her romantic fantasy of her father rescuing her would not happen; he, too, was so compromised by the travails of his harrowing experiences to escape the Nazis and reach the United States that he hadn't the resolve to confront his angry, strong-willed wife.

It was her father's statements to Christine that her mother was treating her unfairly and his failure to stop the abuse that fostered in her the recognition that there was no remedy for her unjust suffering. In other words, since he conveyed that he could be neither of direct help nor guidance in overthrowing her continual unjust treatment, he taught Christine that her suffering must be endured. This is an operational description of *dread*.

RECIPROCATION OF TIME AND BEING

To understand Christine's dread during her lockups, we need to examine the reciprocation of time and being in the ideas of eminent twentieth-century philosophers Søren Kierkegaard and Martin Heidegger. "In possibility everything is possible," writes Kierkegaard (1999, p. 153). But every possibility is experienced in *time*. It is time, Heidegger (1962) tells us, that contains the possibility of *care*. In other words, painful feelings of loneliness and longing are fostered from an acute awareness of unmet needs over the passage of time. Similarly, our consciousness of time is a temporal crucible created by our longing over time for the care of a nurturing other (Hartocollis, 1983).

In Christine's case, *care* was a derivative of her fervent wish that either her mother would cease to imprison her or, if she would not stop, that her father would rescue her. The possibilities for Christine's wish for caring, according to Kierkegaard's formulation (1999) can take two forms: "One form is the wishful yearning form, the other is the melancholy fantastic—on the one hand hope; on the other, fear or anguished dread" (p. 153).

Throughout her childhood, Christine continually and anxiously awaited these caring behaviors to occur; they never did. Their deprivation had a profound affect on Christine's sense of time.

"Time itself," Heidegger (1972) indicates, "passes away. But by passing away constantly, time remains as time. To remain means: not to disappear, thus to presence. This time is determined by a kind of Being" (p. 3). For Christine this state of being was the negation of future possibility that her parents would ever be caring parents. The loss of future possibility fostered in Christine the sense that the present moment had stopped—was virtually endless—because the present moment had no future toward which to intend. It was *the apprehension of an unending, aimless present moment that portended the oppressive dread* from which Christine suffered.

THE LOSS OF PERSONAL AGENCY DURING LONELINESS

German American theologian Paul Tillich (1952) tells us that loneliness is never absolute because the content of the universal is within each of us.

To take possession of these resources Christine would have needed to focus on actively seeking possibility in the present moment. But her disturbed sense of time diminished her capacity to actively attend the present moment and by doing so to control her own *personal agency—the experience of freedom of choice based on the felt sense that she is capable of behaving as she intends.* Her personal agency, in this regard, was severely impeded by her exclusionary conjunctive speech.

EXCLUSIONARY CONJUNCTIVE SPEECH

Christine's story illustrates for us the power of the spoken word (or in this case, more specifically, the power of silence) to shape how an individual experiences herself. In other words, spoken words or their absence lead to self-narratives and interpretive readings of the world in which we live. These self-narratives are experienced in regard to the sense of *time* and *space.* In regard to Christine, her response to her disturbed time sense can be detected in the *conjunctive* inner speech of her phenomenological experience in the dimension of her life space (the confinement of her small room).

Conjunctive words are those parts of speech that connect phrases, clauses, and sentences: words such as *and, but, however, unless. But,* when used in regard to one's own experience, is *an exclusionary conjunctive term* that *recognizes that the possibility for a desirable human experience exists for other people; however, the speaker himself is excluded from this existential possibility.*

Exclusionary conjunctive speech played a crucial role in Christine's desperate loneliness. Rare was it that she felt lost, empty, or desperate during the first moments of being alone. She had books, records, and hobbies to occupy the time. *But* she never knew how long her mother's anger at her would persist; thus, she had no sense of the duration in which she would be condemned to her aloneness.

Her inability to anticipate the temporal confines of her imprisonment led her to such exclusionary conjunctive statements to herself as, "I am not with anyone at this moment, which is all right, *but* I fear that this condition will continue. I will always be alone. I cannot bear that thought!"

In short, in her confinement Christine experienced time stopping, engulfed as she was by the prospect that her loneliness and dread might be everlasting, and she would be alone forever in her private prison—seen and cared for by not another living being.

LOOK AHEAD

A case study is presented in the next chapter of a client involved in business dealings and personal relationships with members of organized crime. A rationale is offered for the therapist's role as mentor for those who lack early and present experiences with role models of constructive behavior.

Chapter 10

A MIRROR OF THE SOUL: REFLECTIONS OF A VIRTUOUS STALKER

No man was ever so much deceived by another, as by himself.
—Lord Greville (English poet, 1554–1628)

The psychotherapy literature is amiss in its dearth of discussion of constructive human behavior. A case study is presented here in order to examine the therapeutic need to foster in clients a sense of personal goodness.

Nick, my client, sitting across from me in my consulting room, told me that one morning about six months past, he looked into his bathroom mirror. Overnight, it seemed, his hairline had widened and there was pudginess around his neck and chin. He found permanent creases across his forehead. This was the moment in which he recognized for the first time that his life was slipping quickly by. In the past, he acted from the conviction that all obstacles and conflicts in his life were removable by his abundant willpower and persuasive personality. Now, he feared, it would not matter whatever he tried to do about the rapid progression of his mortality. Every remedy, cosmetic, or willful effort would be futile. The bald truth stared him in the mirror. His looks, his vitality, his physical and sexual virility—that had impressed others since adolescence—suddenly had surrendered to time. He sensed that from this moment to his last breath, life would no longer be enjoyed, but feared. To live meant to anticipate the painful awareness of the increasing shadow of his physical decay and imminent demise. The latter was captured in an image of a tombstone with his name imprinted, together with the inscription: "He lived. He made money. He ate well. He died."

In the days following, he found all aspects of his life—that had been challenging but usually successful—took on a hard-edged desperation. The warm comradeship he had with friends since childhood in South Boston was deemed to have vanished like stars on a moonlit night. His buddies no longer called. When he was able to reach them, they were elusive and off putting.

As a man in a legitimate business with people involved in organized crime—he sold them casino equipment for their nightclubs and disco bars—Nick had reason to be cautious of his associates' behavior. Nevertheless, he believed himself to be a realistically trusting person. He now realized that he had become in a brief period of time suspicious of virtually everyone's motives—especially the friends who were no longer attentive.

His sexual moments with Debby, his long-time girlfriend, had lost their joyful and liberating qualities; sexual activity had transformed itself into a frantic effort to persuade himself that he was still virile and attractive.

Unless he broke free, he decided, by doing something bold and outrageous—in the style of his free-spirited and often violent youth in an immigrant Greek working-class neighborhood—he was doomed to a depressive existence for the remainder of his days.

The first time I saw Nick, he was sitting halfway up the rows in an ascending-style lecture hall classroom. I was teaching a continuing education class in understanding human behavior. Although the class consisted of students from all walks of life and from virtually every part of the world, Nick's presence seemed out of place here: middle-aged, with a gray shading to his dark hair, wearing a carmine shirt, a white tie, a tan corduroy sports coat, and sunglasses perched atop his head. On this first class of the semester, everyone was taking notes except the man in the bright shirt. He seemed to be staring intently at me throughout my presentation. The gist of my talk was as follows:

I have been frequently asked by students what I believe is the best way to describe what a psychologist does. Every psychologist, of course, has his or her favorite metaphor. Mine is the psychologist as detective.

Behind every serious psychological conflict lies a painful mystery—namely, why the sufferer has behaved in important arenas of her life in ways that seem pernicious to her best interests. The psychologist as detective, in examining the stories told by those who are suffering, soon learns that in order to solve these mysteries a series of secrets harbored by his clients needs to be uncovered and their contents understood by someone compassionate and wise. In other words, to uncover baffling and disabling mysteries in his clients' lives, the psychologist must possess the skills of a relentless psychic explorer—fitting together psychological clues in such a way that they tell a coherent story about the other's needs, desires, and intentions that adequately explains why that person seems to behave in such a way that defies living fully and well. At the same time, he must be able to relate to his clients as a fellow sojourner in the pursuit of human adventure.

Psychology, at its best, is a creative and compassionate art. It has yet to achieve reliability and validity as the science that practitioners have striven for through the past century. The only dependable instrument available to the psychologist is his own humanity, utilized wisely and caringly in an endeavor to understand and inspire his clients. I routinely compare myself with each of my clients. In so doing, there are three questions that I cannot easily avoid: What are other people like inside themselves? That is, are they like me? Second, if not, then, why not? And finally, what can I learn about myself by investigating this other person?

I imagine many of you, I said to the students, wonder whether the notion of a psychologist as detective is a recent metaphor, or whether it had been conceptualized prior to the advent of modern psychology—which is about a century old. And you would be right to ask this question. There has been a cadre of writers, whom I refer to as literary psychologists, who pioneered the practice of psychological detective work long before modern psychology. They include most notably: William Shakespeare, Fydor Dostoevsky, Nathaniel Hawthorne, Edgar Allan Poe, Mark Twain, Joseph Conrad, and Arthur Conan Doyle.

Freud (1908) held that fictional characters of these writers have provided psychologists with unmatched insights in understanding human behavior. But is it possible that some or even most of these brilliant psychologists, while having considerable fascination for what happens in the psyche of others, confined their psychological exploration only to others because of their inordinate fears about what lurked in their own psyches? Edgar Allan Poe, for example, is generally regarded as the inventor of the detective story. American literary critic Joseph Wood Krutch (1926), in his renowned psychological study of Poe, claims that Poe invented this literary genre to serve as a fortification against the madness he suspected lurked within himself. Poe studied the most advanced scientific and theoretical tracts of his day in trying to understand his own intrapsychic foe (Smith, 1973). Based on these studies, he linked up madness, secrets, and shame.

The helpless despair that shame breeds is one of the most unbearable of human experiences. For many people shame is not an occasional single, isolated event in their lives; it is part and parcel of a persistent set of emotions, preventing them from pursuing their lives fully and well. As such, it leads to a lifetime of secrecy and cover-ups of their vulnerable sense of self. I believe that this was particularly true of Poe.

Poe's stories brilliantly evince the paradox of shameful secrets; more than the substance of a secret, he seemed to believe, secret-keeping itself insulates those who harbor self-incrimination from other people—fostering isolation and madness.

Writing, for many, serves as a mirror to the writer's inner psyche. Mirrors hold great fascination for most of us as an inseparable part of our endeavor to make sense of who we are. A crucial aspect of this exploration is magical: the assumption that the mirror has the capacity to transcend or even supplant physical veracity—reflecting back not how we actually appear, but rather what is hidden beyond our ostensible image. For Poe, it seems, it was the reflection of a troubled and despairing soul.

Poe was a writer of undoubted superior intellect. But he seemed involved for most of his short life trying to demonstrate his superiority (Walsh, 1968). In creating the character of his literary detective, C. Auguste Dupin, Poe projects an idealization of himself as he desired to be—a cool, infallible thinking machine who brings the powers of reason to bear fully on life's complex problems and triumphantly and skillfully solves them (Walsh, 1968). However, the shameful feelings he harbored about his own sexual difficulties (Krutch, 1926) resulted in his literary doppelganger, Dupin, going through the motions of trying to solve an actual sex and murder crime (the Mary Rogers case) with uncharacteristic blunders in logic (Walsh, 1968).

As I was ready to leave the lecture hall, after discussions with students who waited for me after class, I noticed the man in the carmine-colored shirt standing by the classroom door. He stepped toward me and asked:

"I wonder if it would be all right if I spoke with you sometime?"

I inquired about what he wished to speak with me.

"What you said about that writer Poe and his keeping secrets making him crazy—or something like that. It made me think that maybe you can help me. You see: I've been having very troubling dreams."

In our first consultation Nick informed me: "What you said about the detective and mysteries hit my problem right on the head. I've been dreaming about a murder. In the dream:

A heavyset, cloaked man is stalking a beautiful young woman, a socialite, during a dark, freezing evening. The man, remaining in the shadows, fol-

lows her as she stops under a worn-out motel sign—some of the bulbs illuminating the sign are burnt out. She opens her small black purse, takes out
a long, thin key, and then walks into the concrete motel yard. Fugitively,
scrolling the yard and beyond, the stalker sees only his prey. He rushes the
motel cabin door just as she has turned the lock and is pushing open the
door. Slamming the door closed with the sole of his heavy foot, he roughly
cloaks her mouth with his large hand. Still gagging her, he carries her to the
bed. While strangling her, he has his way with her.

Nick's recital complete, he looked across at me, with what appeared to
be a sheepish look of discomfort. I inquired. He answered: "There are two
things I should tell you: The first is that the dream is not entirely original."

"What do you mean by 'not original'?"

"There was a murder of a very beautiful socialite in a motel in western
Canada about six months ago. She was married to a prominent attorney
and member of the Canadian Parliament—a lying, corrupt man, much
older than her. Of course, I know plenty of guys who have 'whacked' people—I grew up with them. I supply their casinos and off-hour clubs with
my roulette wheels and video games. They tell me their stories because
I'm 'family.' But I never think about these stories afterwards. Why should
I? But I can't stop thinking about this Canadian murder. I even buy every
week the local newspapers from the city in which the murder took place.
I'm sure I know who killed her. I also sense that the police know the killer
but won't arrest him because they're involved in a cover-up. The journalists, who write stories about the murder, have to be lousy investigators.
They don't seem to recognize that there is a cover-up. But why am I so
caught up with this case?"

"What is the second matter that you alluded to about which I need to be
informed?"

"I didn't know until I started to tell you about the dream.... I mean I just
recognized myself in the dream."

"What part do you play?"

"I'm him—I mean I'm the stalker/killer. What's going on with me? I
mean its not that I actually killed that Canadian woman and forgot about
it. I have never been north of Massachusetts, let alone to Canada."

"Had any startling or unusual things happened to you just prior to your
first having this dream?"

It was then that Nick told me about the frightening experience with his
mirror. It seemed evident that his mirror encounter had reflected his apprehension that he was no longer in control of his own life.

My assessment of Nick was that he was a reasonably intelligent person, but not someone for whom a probing search for childhood shames and trauma would be long and well tolerated, or even propitiously pursued. So I said to him:

"You claim that the journalists who wrote the stories about the murder case don't know what they're doing."

"Yeah, so what?"

"Why don't you rewrite the story of the murder the way you believe it should be written, and in so doing show me how the story should be properly investigated."

Nick's face turned crimson; he drew his face and neck toward his chest, away from my direct view of his face. "I can't write. I'm dyslexic," he finally articulated. "That is why I dropped out of high school."

"I have a friend who also is dyslexic," I told him. "She found a way around her reading difficulties. She is now a Ph.D. psychologist. So why don't you try writing the story anyway. You may surprise yourself!"

After discussion about the embarrassment he accrued growing up with reading and writing difficulties, Nick did set about writing his true crime story, as he believed it should have been investigated. He brought revised versions of the story to our twice-weekly sessions. In listening to these versions I was puzzled. He was not a reader of novels. Indeed, he had attempted to read few books since leaving school. Yet, his stories were not attempts at newspaper journalism, but that of the novelist, in which details knowable only to the killer—his innermost thoughts and feelings—were described. How could Nick have this information unless he was the killer or had personally interviewed him? I inquired.

"You remember my telling you about my shock in looking into the mirror one morning and seeing someone I had never seen before. I knew that I had to do something outrageous to break free of my constant...what's that word you use?...obsession...with my life's end. So I stopped working at my business. I receive a substantial revenue from the lease of my machines. I don't have to stay around to collect. I told my customers I would be on an extended vacation. With considerable time on my hands, I started to take adult education classes in psychology, to figure out what is going on in my mirror. I also began to spend much time wandering around the city at night. I was shagging a series of women. I didn't care if they were attractive or not. I have had my fill of attractive women. I was looking for something different."

"Different how?"

"Someone alone. Someone who doesn't have a clue about what's coming off."

"What do you mean?"

"Someone who is not young, but still doesn't have a clue about how to take care of herself."

"What interests you about such women?"

"I was angry at them. I don't know why. But that anger made them sexually exciting to me. But I'm not a rapist. I just followed them without any of them—I'm sure—knowing that I was around and was shadowing her. What did I want with them—how should I know! If that writer Poe, who you said was such a smart detective, and even he didn't understand himself, then what do you expect of me?"

"Let me ask you about any fantasies you might have had about those women."

Nick dispassionately discussed his fantasies about controlling and raping the women he was stalking. In finishing his report, he shrugged his shoulders, adding:

"So what is the big deal with me having these thoughts? Every guy I know has them also."

"However, some men certainly do act on their rape fantasies. And you were capable of easily overpowering the women and taking advantage of them. But you didn't."

"Hey, look! I've done a lot of violent things when I was younger. I still do on occasion when some guy tries to muscle in on my business. But women, mistreat them—never! That's not the kind of people I come from. If I even lifted a hand to hit a woman, I'd have the cursed eyes of my mother, my aunts, my sisters on me—even my old man's unblinking stare, as he sucked on his pipe. I can only get away with thoughts in my head of about taking advantage of women."

I was again puzzled by Nick's behavior, until I thought about the numerous indictments I had read about Edgar Allan Poe's considerable perfidy in his writings (for example, Walsh, 1968)—suggestive that Poe's behavior was impelled from his sense of impeded virtue. Pride and shame are the monitors of our personal identity. When a person can feel pride in his competence and knows that he has won the esteem of others, he forms a positive identity. But if instead he is disregarded and mistreated, and indeed subjected to a pattern of humiliation and shame (as Poe's history clearly shows him to have been), he will acquire a sense of badness. He will lie and cheat in trying to compete with others he feels are more advantaged in the attention they have received from significant others. Undoubtedly, Poe's sense of vulnerability to others' disregard played a decisive role in his macabre stories. I indicated to Nick that the fact that his disturbing dreams came closely on the heels of his stalking behavior, following his resolve to initiate outrageous behavior, strongly suggested to me that it was a warning from some part of his virtuous self that acting in the predatory way in which he had embarked was not in keeping with his sense of rightful behavior that he had told me was a legacy of his upbringing.

"What do you mean by 'rightful behavior'?"

"Your sense of your personal goodness."

Nick indicated that he knew what virtue meant—he had it preached to him in church as a child: "Acting devotedly to God and charitably to other people were the keys to Heaven." His parents and his older brothers forcefully impressed upon him that it was a wise policy to keep a decent reputation and stay out of trouble with the police—because people from his background and neighborhood have two strikes against them in competing with the more privileged people outside of South Boston. But personal goodness, he didn't know what that was—unless I was referring to the behavior of saints and maybe some priests. He added:

"Look! I've lived a selfish life, no doubt about it. But what am I going to do at this stage of my life—become a saint? And then why—because some priests and teachers I had in school said that's the way a person should behave?"

As a psychologist I strongly hold that one does not respond wisely to the dilemmas and opportunities in another's life—even if well-intended—simply by possessing theoretical and factual knowledge about the reasons the other has become fearful and why his yearnings have gone unsatisfied. The able psychologist guides by the maturity of his own tested self, and in so doing, teaching the other how to temper the hard realities of life with passionate and romantic dreams. Psychotherapists are not only listeners of their clients' tales; they also live in the same world. It is the psychotherapist's enlightened presence in their shared world that gives the client the hope and inspiration for a more optimistic life. Consequently, I believe that genuine healing requires more than knowledgeable understanding. If the psychotherapist has lived an empty life, what can he offer those who seek a guide to life but an inane and illusory expertise? Therefore, psychological healing demands that the psychotherapist extend to his client the goodwill and friendship that are derived from his firm place in the world outside the consulting room. In other words, one ably guides another over similar terrain. Those psychological guides who have cowered in the underbrush of their own personal journeys have neither a compass for the brave nor a sturdy walking stick to bolster the unsteady gait of the fearful.

Accordingly, I responded to Nick's concern: "Nick, I am certainly not a priest, or a rabbi. Virtue holds no importance to me because of any religious connotations. I would not even suggest that you concern yourself with it because acting virtuously is the right thing to do. In my own life a concern with virtue is a *functional* issue. That is to say, my own experiences have strongly suggested that none of us can live satisfying and meaningful lives in the midst of other people's suffering. All who have tried, I believe, have failed."

"But that's your take on life, Doc! What does that have to do with me?"

During the past four decades my clinical experiences have reinforced a conviction I formed during my clinical apprenticeship that psychotherapy cannot meaningfully survive in a moral vacuum. Psychological inquiry that does not support constructive human values because its practitioners believe that they should not influence their clients' moral choices is not only unrealistic, but shallow and rootless as well. Most life situations contain moral issues—whether or not we recognize or choose to attend to them. Clinical concerns are extensions of this reality. Moral concerns are attempts to find principles and rationales for how to deal with the complex and difficult dilemmas that confront human dignity and purpose. With this as my compass, I said to Nick:

"What I have said to you should concern you because it seems to me that your sense of your own unworthiness has impelled you to live vicariously through someone else's life—an existence of sex, intrigue, and violence. But you haven't yet given in to that existence because I believe that your suppressed sense of goodness somewhere in you is trying to impress upon you, in a way you cannot easily ignore, that there is a basic question to which each of us must respond in summing up our lives: Have I been idle for the most part, unconcerned with the lives of others, a greedy opportunist, or someone who cared and made a difference? So by a sense of personal goodness I mean a faith in human possibility in which one takes an active and constructive role."

Nick was unusually quiet. Finally he said quietly, "How can I find out if what you are telling me is your bullshit or if it also applies to me?"

"That's not difficult! You can become your own psychological detective. You've tried the selfish way for 50-plus years. It hasn't led you to a satisfying, fulfilling life. Try another way and see whether it fits you better than what you have been doing; that is, see how you feel and what you are able to do acting in a very different way from your usual pattern of behavior. If you are willing to try this, then I have some specific suggestions for you."

I discussed with Nick various options that I recognized as available for his endeavors as his own psychological detective. Nick responded with impatience:

"Come on, Doc! I have no time to waste. Tell me which is the best method."

I told him that although psychotherapists have spent the past century arguing that their preferred method of psychotherapy is the best, what is actually the best can be determined only by the client: by what he is willing to do in order to gain what he claims to want for himself.

Nick eschewed the psychodynamic methods I described to him that would probe his childhood for traumatic experiences and/or would focus on his and my relationship in our sessions in order to locate unresolved interpersonal conflicts.

"I don't need the 'whats' and 'whys' about why something is something. I want the most straightforward way to experience my life differently."

I reviewed with him our previous discussions about his life, stopping at his telling me of his fondness and devotion to his many nieces and nephews. I also recalled out loud his youthful career as a consummate athlete and his continuing interest in sporting events. I discussed with him my notions of the importance of equity in how one lives one's life (described in chapter 5): giving back to others because one has benefited from being accorded by other people in the past.

"There are many children out there without fathers, without mentors or guidance." I pointed out, "You have plenty of money, lots of time available, compassion for children, athletic skill, and worldly experience. You can use them all in a constructive way. Personal goodness has its roots in *doing*—feeling and intending benevolently are not sufficient."

In our next session, having done some research, I handed Nick the names and telephone numbers of some community leaders who were in need of Nick's resources. Nick first spoke to a priest in his neighborhood about children in the parish who were having difficulties at home, at school, or with the police. He decided to spend time with three of them, acting as a "big brother": taking them to movies and ball games as well as speaking with them about the problems they were having with other people. In a couple of months time he brought these boys and several others from his neighborhood together and started a baseball team—Nick furnishing the uniforms, equipment, and whatever else they needed. He then enlisted several neighborhood merchants to sponsor teams. They began a youth baseball league in the neighborhood.

Nick scheduled sessions with me whenever he felt the need to discuss his work with the youth group or some aspect of his life that was troubling him. We also had sessions in which he explored what he was learning about himself by involving himself differently than he had in the past with people. Moreover, by my teaching him how to reflect on his feelings of shame and closely observing how shame influenced his behavior, Nick was able to become his own psychological detective:

"I realize now that I was following those sad women because I identified with them without recognizing it. But, I guess part of me understood that, and that side of me that was ashamed and angry at the vulnerabilities I shared with them. By taking control of them in my fantasies, I must have been trying to show myself that I wasn't like them at all. And the woman in the murder case: she was educated and sophisticated—the type of woman who never gave me a second look. By seeking to point out her killer, I suppose, I was trying to show in some far-fetched way that I could be of service and was worthy of a woman like her. But my anger toward women who have humiliated me confused in my mind whether I wanted to be her rescuer or her assailant."

"That was then," I said. "And now?"

"I am beginning to be able to trust my own gut. What I mean is that I am willing to act on my urges unless I feel a hesitation. When I do, I respect the hesitation, and stop and reflect about some secret I haven't spelled out loud to myself. In the past I wasn't aware of how the information and events contained in some secret of mine was affecting me. I should also tell you that my image in the mirror is no longer so bad. I now see a 55-year-old man in the mirror that is doing the best he can in living his life more meaningfully than he did in the past. Also, I haven't followed any women since I started this project with you. And, as you probably suspect, I don't dream any longer about the murder case."

Case studies reported in professional journals are by necessity highly condensed and selective. In this chapter, I have focused on the more unconventional aspects of my work with Nick—the *rebuilding* rather than analytic aspects of my work with him. In this regard I believe I part company with many of my colleagues. There are, of course, many analytic theorists who, like me, emphasize the importance of relational and existential issues in psychotherapeutic situations—they notably include Carl Jung, Harry Stack Sullivan, Karen Horney, Alfred Adler, Erich Fromm, Stephen Mitchell, and Jay Greenberg. Nevertheless, I believe that these theorists focus more on analyzing (examining) their clients' lives than they do in rebuilding them. I make this claim because not one of them devotes any attention in their writings to a client's social and moral responsibility to others. As I have already indicated, psychotherapy is potentially the most knowledgeable discipline in seeking out the motivations that encourage cooperative and altruistic endeavors. Only when a client recognizes that his personal worth is no less predicated on his compassion and responsibility to others than it is on his individual concerns can he meaningfully rebuild his life.

However, in investigating Nick's dreams and fantasies I did conduct the conventional psychodynamic probes, and I made numerous attempts to have Nick find his own path in how he should live his life. These efforts proved futile until Nick inquired how other clients like him had gained a constructive perspective in how to live their lives. I made the decision that it would be more authentic for me to share my own personal experiences with Nick rather than to discuss other clients with whom I had worked. In doing so, I supplemented the conventional psychodynamic approach to healing toxic shame and despair.

My modification was based upon my clinical experience that people who have led highly destructive lives need their therapist to be a *mentor* as well as a therapist. It was quite obvious that Nick lacked positive role models in his early developmental and present life. What I have selected to focus on here are the mentoring aspects of my work with Nick. This work can be summarized as follows:

What is required in addition to a psychodynamic probe in working with clients such as Nick is an orientation that regards the client's reports as a life story that must be retold as a *better story*—a story that includes developmentally appropriate responses from the client to the existential, social, and moral issues that he heretofore has not recognized or has ignored. In other words, the therapist enables the client to address denied conflicts in his life story—conflicts that have prevented him from responding authentically (directly) to such questions as:

1. What am I actually experiencing?
2. What does my experience mean in terms of the person I intend to become—that is to say, what is the relation of my experiences to my core values?
3. What fears and conditions are interfering with my ability to experience my existence authentically?
4. How can I re-experience my experience, bringing it into fuller and more authentic awareness—that is, what insights, experiments, and ways of being will help me complete my experiences—to give my existence a sense of living fully and well?
5. Having experienced and completed my experiences, I should have a more lucid conception of who I intend to be. How do I put these values into action—in terms of myself and in regard to others?

LOOK AHEAD

In the next chapter a case study is presented of a hospitalized patient who claimed to have been abducted by aliens from a distant planet. Four levels of meaning for the patient's belief that he—and other contactees—have been abducted is provided. These explanations are related to the search of each of us for personal significance.

Chapter 11

THE INVENTED SELF: THE GENERAL'S ABDUCTION BY ALIENS FROM A UFO

Though this be madness, yet there is method in't.
    —William Shakespeare (1564–1616, English playwright)

James J. Crawford, III was a scion of a New Hampshire family. The Crawford boys served in the army as far back as the French and Indian War. At age seven each was sent to military school. During his junior year of upper class Crawford was accused of leading a gang of cadets in the theft of swords, medals, and uniforms held in the school museum that once belonged to illustrious alumni. Despite his plea of innocence and a lack of proof, he was sent home. Bewildered and ashamed by the alleged theft, without interviewing him, his parents shipped him off to an elite prep school in Connecticut. His father, Colonel James J. Crawford, II (retired Army), chairman of a New England railroad, severed contact with his son the day that Junior left for prep school. Only his mother, a brother, and a sister kept in touch with him—surreptitiously.

For two years Crawford planned revenge against what he referred to as the "scholastic establishment." He focused exclusively on his grades, achieved an excellent academic record, and was selected class valedictorian. He chose as the topic of his speech the federal government's theft following the Revolutionary War of a large tract of land in New Hampshire that belonged to his family. The evidence he marshalled to support his claim was so carefully and convincingly presented that those in the audience—including his mother—were not certain whether or not Crawford's claim was valid. However, the embarrassment of making family matters public cut the last thread Crawford had with his family. They enrolled him in a southern military college. Upon arrival, after a long car ride from home with his brother, in which no issue of substance was broached, the brother angrily told him, "You are not wanted at home. Find other arrangements for holidays and vacations!"

Upon graduation at the outset of the Korean War, Crawford was commissioned as an officer in the Army Engineer Corps and sent directly to the war front. His accusation of the federal government's crime against his family again erupted during his station there. His claim, systematic and persistent, earned him an evaluation in an army medical facility in Japan. The psychiatrist who interviewed him strongly recommended his discharge from the army as psychologically unfit.

THE WHITE HOUSE UNIT

In the mid- to late 1960s, I was the psychology consultant to the so-called White House unit at Saint Elizabeths Hospital (SEH), a large federal psychiatric hospital in southeast Washington, DC. The unit held patients who were stopped in what police and security officials regarded as bizarre attempts to reach the president or some other important official of the federal or the district government. In order to advise on the treatment of these patients, I supervised their psychological evaluations administrated by the clinical psychology interns assigned to the unit. On occasion I conducted an evaluation myself.

Appropriate immediate treatment for the patients on the unit was necessary—all were highly disturbed, yet the hospital administration was trying to have them returned to their home states. This is to say, most of the patients were from out of state. So if the mental-health worker from the patient's home state who was summoned to transport the patient concluded that the patient was too disturbed to travel, the worker might refuse the transfer—leaving the patient at SEH.

William Crawford, III had been stopped at the gate of the White House by the executive branch security guards. Politely, but firmly and expertly, two officers questioned him in the small sentry house three steps beyond the gate. He insisted that he had to see President Johnson immediately—the nation was at peril if there was a delay.

"What is the problem?" he was asked.

"I have vital intelligence about national security."

"How did you come by this information?"

"The message—which can only be delivered to President Johnson—was given to me by people from a distant planet, who have chosen me to represent them on their crucial mission to save the earth."

"How did you get together with people from another planet?"

"I was abducted and brought into their spacecraft above Washington."

The guards glanced at each other with a weary look that acknowledged that they'd heard this story before. With a straight face, one of them reassured Crawford that they understood the importance of his mission. But they were not authorized to listen to more of his story. Since President Johnson was currently out of town, he had left in charge a special agent to evaluate matters of national security for him. They would promptly bring Crawford to speak with the agent. Crawford was soon transported to the White House unit at SEH and evaluated by the unit's intake psychiatrist. In keeping with psychiatric beliefs of the time (Grinspan & Persky, 1972; Meerloo, 1968; Warren, 1970), that anyone who claims to have been abducted by aliens is psychotic, Crawford was admitted to the unit.

A few days later I began my employment at SEH. I was pleased to be starting my professional career there—a venerable hospital in the history of American psychiatry, in the forefront of psychiatric research and innovative clinical practice. As the largest and most important federal psychiatric hospital in the country, many leading psychiatrists and psychologists have been at SEH on staff or in training. In addition to housing important political forensic patients such as Ezra Pound and Axis Sally, one could see at any given time a number of patients with the same unusual histories and psychopathies that elsewhere a clinician might see only once in a lifetime of practice.

On my first day on the unit, I walked into the patient lounge and observed a close knot of patients surrounding a tall, slim man with blue eyes and a blond crew cut. He appeared to be about 40. He spoke with animated cadence. In grammatically precise sentences, he was regaling them with his experiences on an alien spaceship. The audience, made up of patients who earlier in the day were walking the halls of the unit conversing with their hallucinated companions, or seated in the lounge rocking back and forth aimlessly, were now alert and quiet—apparently captivated by the way Crawford told his story.

At the point at which I reached the circle of patients, Crawford had told the others that the hospital staff did not want him to inform President Johnson that unless the United States stopped the violence in Vietnam, the aliens would destroy major cities in the United States. The hospital superintendent and his clinical director, he indicated, had direct ties to the CEOs of the giant munitions companies that supplied the army with its weapons. Of course, they didn't want the war stopped! As a professional soldier and a combat officer, he said that he had indisputable evidence of his allegations. He referred to the suppressing attempts by the hospital staff as a prima facie example of psychopolitics: keeping people who hold political opinions contrary to those of the establishment in psychiatric institutions. His audience nodded in agreement: "Right on, General!" they shouted at him, "You said a mouthful. You should be leading us in Vietnam, not that moron General Westmoreland!"

I must point out that assuming that his audience agreed with him cannot be simply be dismissed as a product of their collective psychoses. The country was in a social and political turmoil. There was unrest and open rebellion against the government from all segments of American society.

As I listened, I became aware that there was something familiar about Crawford. I had seen him before. But where and when? Then in mid-sentence, he sniffled in an unusual way—sucking his upper lip into his mouth—and I recalled my previous meeting with him. I had traveled to Washington three weeks before my starting assignment at SEH to find an apartment and to attend the practical matters involved in moving to a new city. A friend from back home was visiting me. It was a beautiful August day—clear skies and low humidity. The city was replete with marchers protesting the Vietnam war. The newspaper reported that the marchers were going to surround the White House—on the Mall in back and in Lafayette Park in front. We chose to observe from the park. Many of those we saw in the park were strangely garbed. The most unusual of them was a man in a World War II Army officer's dress uniform whose resplendent medals General MacArthur would have been proud to wear. It was as if the bearer had fought in every campaign in every one of America's wars. He was handing out pamphlets and talking to those who reached out for his information. As he spoke he sniffled in an odd way. My friend turned to me and said that she had a feeling I would see this man with the grandiose display of medals at SEH someday. I agreed. But I didn't realize how soon that would be. Dressed in his drab hospital clothes, and without an army cap, I had not initially recognized Crawford.

The next day I found in my mailbox on the unit a psychological evaluation request. It was taken for granted that Crawford had not been abducted by aliens. Either he was a paranoid schizophrenic or was suffering from severe anxiety and stress that had impaired his ability to reason. The unit psychiatrist wished me to determine which; he also sought treatment guidelines.

Behavioral scientists then held skeptical attitudes toward UFO stories for obvious reasons: the accounts were so outside of reality as we believe it to be that they assumed that these stories, like those of the visitations of guests from the heavens in past centuries, were the products of some sort of odd delusional system. None of us then had any idea about the very large number of people who believed that they have been victims of alien abductions.

We are now better informed. We have access to studies that indicate that most of the people who have reported encounters with aliens and who have been psychologically tested have been found to possess no marked psychological disturbance—apart from the possible mistaken belief that such visitations actually happened to them (Bloecher, Clammar, & Hopkins, 1985; Mack, 1994; Spanos, Cross, Dickerson, & DuBreuil, 1991). However, I'm suspicious of the studies that report that UFO contactees for the most part have no marked tendency toward psychological abnormality. John Mack (1994), for example, reports that he has done the most extensive psychological and psychiatric examination of UFO contactees of any investigator. Let's look at the assessment of one of these contactees. Peter Faust tells Mack that his abductions by aliens starting at the "age of nineteen or twenty in which sperm samples were taken" (p. 295) were intensely traumatic. Despite this harrowing experience—in which "I felt out of control, inferior, powerless, and enraged. I'm paralyzed. I want to kill it, and I can't do anything. (I have) no will for they shut me down" (p. 296)—both Mack and the Harvard University psychologist who examined Faust for many hours found him to be "highly functional, alert, focused, intelligent, well-spoken and without any visible anxiety (or) organic neurological dysfunctioning" (Mack, 1994, p. 314). How could this be? Can anyone remain an ordinary person—his personality substantially unchanged—after actually having had such unusual and traumatic experiences?

ALIEN ABDUCTION REPORTS

The term *flying saucer* was first coined on June 24, 1947. An American businessman was flying alone on a routine flight in his own private airplane when he sighted what he reported was a chain of nine saucerlike things at least five miles long, flat like a pie pan, and reflecting the sun like a mirror (Vallee, 1991). His story was widely publicized, and the assumption was made that the objects were spaceships from another planet. More reports quickly followed. Since the end of the Second World War accounts of UFOs have dramatically proliferated (Sheaffer, 1986)—some as fascinating as they were difficult to believe. Starting with the Betty and Barney Hill story in 1961 (Fuller, 1966), they reported abductions. These stories have become more detailed and complex over the years. In the 1950s contactees (as those abducted are called) had friendly chats with cozy aliens, but later it turned to grief and doom about the earth and/or hybrid program. The subjective status of these experiences may be noted from the fact that some investigators consistently find that their subjects have had an overall positive experience from their abductions (Mack, 1994; Sprinkle, 1976), whereas others find the subjects to have had overall negative experiences (Hopkins, 1981; Jacobs, 1992).

Over the past few decades thousands of reports have saturated the media of people who have reported that they were abducted by aliens. The Roper Study conducted in 1991—presenting the combined data from three national surveys of about 6,000 adult respondents—"suggests that hundreds of thousands, if not millions, of American men, women and children may have experienced UFO abductions, or abductions related phenomena" (Bigelow, 1992).

There is supposedly some physical evidence of the landings of spacecraft from alien planets that cannot be readily explained, such as burn marks on the soil where these craft were reported to have landed, crop circles, crashed saucers, animal mutilations, photos of UFOs, federal government secrecy about Area 51 in the New Mexico desert, and so forth. Moreover, there are a number of reports of those who have claimed independently of one another to have seen the corpses or photos of the bodies of the aliens who crashed in Roswell, New Mexico at the end of World War II. The case for believers is perhaps best summarized by what John Mack calls the "five dimensions" of the abduction experience—evidence that he claims is not easily explained away:

1. The high degree of consistency in a recurrent feeling of being watched, followed, and tracked by aliens. Unlike people with delusional systems, those who report this tracking provide a highly descriptive account of their experiences.

2. Some of the reported contactees have unusual red marks, small cuts, and scars appearing on their bodies for no apparent reason.

3. The contactees have no known psychological disturbance or other emotional conditions that could readily explain their unusual stories.

4. Children as young as two or three years of age have reported abductions by aliens. Budd Hopkins, who has worked with young children for a

couple of decades, has found that many of his original subjects were born in 1941/1942—suggesting that the alleged abduction program was begun then (Randle, 1994).

5. There seems to be common collaboration of description by people who independently witnessed an abduction. In other words, so many of these stories have similar core elements—as if many different people experienced the same unusual events.

Nevertheless, one of the more telling criticisms of Mack's evidence and that of other UFO believers is lodged by J. Allen Hynek (1972), who points out a suspicious feature of the contactees' reports is that until the late 1950s, when it was still believed that the planets in our solar system were likely to support intelligent life, most of the reported visitors came from Mars, Jupiter, and Venus. But once scientists had the means for space probes—and later built satellites—this idea was shown to be unlikely. Correspondingly, visitors began to hail from planets outside our solar system. Moreover, the reported advanced technologies of these aliens are so superior to our own to strongly suggest that these civilizations would have perfected space travel as far back as the dawn of humankind. Yet historical records indicate few UFO reports, and even those are quite ambiguous. On the other hand, there are multitudes of reports of sights and experiences of God, the devil, and other supernatural spirits that no longer appear to be around. Why? A plausible explanation is that reports of supernatural events correspond to prevailing cultural myths. In other words, the words and concepts for God and the devil were in the public domain from earliest time; obviously, those for interstellar travel were not. The ability of ordinary people to describe unusual events depends upon the availability of linguistic concepts to articulate these events. People in personal crisis use those existent concepts to metaphorically express their turmoil.

Moreover, professional magician and investigator of unexplained phenomenon Randi (1982) points out that "despite 10,000s of reported UFO sightings...nary a nut or bolt (of one of these craft)" has been found by anyone. This is explained by believers in UFOs variously as the aliens being too careful and sophisticated to leave evidence, the federal government having sufficient evidence to confirm the reality of aliens visiting the Earth but having withheld the information, or that the aliens don't come from another planet but rather are from another state of consciousness from that with which we are familiar. In other words, they operate in a reality that has physical laws and properties different from those based upon Newtonian/Cartesian notions of the universe. Mack (1994) contends that alien abductions offer a new way of understanding reality and our own connection to the universe.

THE PSYCHOLOGICAL EVALUATION OF THE GENERAL

Crawford was meticulous in manner and dress—even in hospital-issued clothes. At first he remained mute, turning his head away from me during our initial interview. I needed to establish a basis for rapport. I told him:

"I've seen you before. It was in Lafayette Park on a Sunday, apparently before your strange experience."

"I am relieved by what you are saying: seeing me outside the hospital and prior to the time I was abducted. It proves that I am credible and sane. I am also gratified that you believe in UFOs."

"I need to correct you. I'm agnostic about most things that I don't myself directly experience." Crawford looked downcast as I spoke—as if he had lost his last ally and his remaining hope. His despairing countenance suggested that he felt doomed to being regarded as mad. I commented on his look. He replied:

"How can you help me if you don't believe what I said actually happened? For if it didn't, then I am mad and belong in a lunatic asylum."

To indicate that I was not closed to his story, I said:

"I too have had an unusual and disturbing experience when I was 12—an event witnessed alongside of me by a classmate, who later denied that he had seen what I had."

Recognizing that I had his close attention, I continued: "I was attending a summer camp in rural western New Jersey. One starless night, I was standing inside my group's unlit cabin, staring out a window into the still, pitch-black sky; another camper, somewhat older than I, was also looking out the window. Suddenly, an eerie blue-white light blazed across the sky, pulsating and cascading like a luminescent waterfall. I shot a glance at the other guy, who looked back at me, and although neither of us said a word, our eyes acknowledged that we were sharing something uncanny. A few days later, on an overnight hike with our group, I started to talk about what I had seen and turned to my co-observer for confirmation. A look of fear distorted his features. 'I don't know what you are talking about,' he responded."

Crawford told me about his upbringing (the information found at the beginning of this chapter). He spoke with irony, biting wit, and sharp allusion. Yet he acted as if what he was saying was simple, plain, and direct—

for example, he seemed surprised that I needed to question him from time to time as to what he meant and that I asked for examples.

Nevertheless, after a few moments' pause he went step by step through his abduction experience. He had sleep problems for many years. He was restless, tossing and turning in bed in his hotel in Washington. Finally, he fell into a deep and strange slumber:

"It is as if I was in two places at the same time: lying still on the bed and hovering in the room above myself."

"Has this ever happened to you before?"

"Yes, a number of times, but never the same as what happened that night."

"Which was?"

"As I was floating above myself, I saw two shadowy figures that gave off a silvery light—without themselves being illuminated. They seem to have entered the room by passing through the window—although I knew I closed it to turn on the air conditioner earlier in the evening. They passed below me apparently without taking note of me. They drew my prone body on the bed to them as if by magnetic pull. Then all three passed through the window without opening or breaking it. I found myself following them without effort or conscious intent through the window into the open night sky." Crawford stopped, looked straight at me as to assess whether I believed him, took a deep breath, and continued:

"As I approached them I saw a thin, almost invisible rope or line extending toward them. I intuitively knew that the extension was from a flying craft above them. In an instant I found myself in the craft, observing my prone self brought to an upright, still position—as if I was in a trance. Other figures entered the now well-lit chamber. I focused on the leader, a tall, slender being—with pleasant features. He spoke to me—the 'me' that had been in a trance had disappeared—in a voice I heard from within my head. He inquired about my biographical and psychological histories. I found I could not lie, or even hold back information. 'Perfect,' the leader responded, 'We have a special mission for you. We want you to represent us to your American government.' I wondered why they had chosen me. To my unspoken question the leader replied, 'We recognize that you are an exceedingly lonely man, who is misunderstood by his people—especially those who should be closest to you. We believe that you can identify with us: the loneliness we feel away from our homes, feared and misunderstood by earthlings.' 'But how will I know what to tell the American government?' I asked. 'We will give you a special ability.' " Crawford completed his statement with his head in his hands.

"What was this special ability?"

"It is called remote vision," he told me, raising his head. "It is too complex to describe in detail, but in general it is the ability to transcend time and space, and in so doing, communicate with earth people, aliens, or anything that exists in another temporality. I now have this ability. Sometimes I see things that are not there."

"How do you know that?"

"Because other people don't seem to see what I see. To equip me with this power they told me that they had to do medical procedures on me. I saw myself lying on a cot in the aliens' surgery. There were other people there on tables as well. Technicians were working on them with large, crude instruments. I heard screams and pleas for mercy from those lying on the tables as the technicians took scopes of their skin, incurring small painful hemorrhages."

Wait a minute! I said to myself as I listened to Crawford's description of the instruments and procedures in the aliens' surgery: Is this a medical laboratory designed by a race of beings who are so technologically advanced that they defy all known laws of astrophysics, or clandestine anatomists of the early nineteenth century, or is this even a visit to the laboratory of Dr. Frankenstein? There is something all wrong here! Crawford is describing a medical regimen that is actually far inferior to contemporary medicine. Why in the world would a species of beings that supposedly can travel across galaxies in seconds use such painful and primitive medical techniques? Are they a sadistic race of beings, or is Crawford's appalling description due to his lack of a medical knowledge in which to couch his creative delusion?

"Do you believe that the events as you have described to me actually happened to you?"

Crawford looked away and said, "Telling the truth is really a very difficult thing for me to do unless I'm compelled."

To my best knowledge then and now, no abduction has taken place in public view or in a large group of people. Most seem to occur at night in the dark—suggesting that in some important way they are sleep related. With this in mind, I said to the general: "When you go to bed tonight, right before you fall asleep, tell yourself that you have a key that can open the door to the truth. Use your remote vision, if you need to, in order to help you tell the truth."

I interviewed Crawford the next day and asked whether he remembered last night's dreams.

"Yes, of course! The truth is this: On a Friday next year the general will be missing; in his place there will be a burning Washington."

Based on his psychological testing evaluation and an observation of his behavior on the unit, I diagnosed Crawford as suffering from a schizophrenic reaction, paranoid type. His disturbance was characterized by grandiosity and premonition, ideas of reference, weird and peculiar thoughts, accompanied by some cognitive confusion and emotional liability. His report of an alien abduction was attributed to a systematic delusion.

Treatment considerations are always perplexing for patients such as the general. What should the psychologist's recommendation be for a patient who exhibits a severe delusion: to dissuade him from continuing to believe in his delusion by showing him the erroneous nature of his belief? Or to help him see the function his belief serves in how he feels about himself and about his relationship to other people? I recommended that the focus of his treatment be on the latter.

On a Friday the next year, as I was leaving SEH for the weekend, I saw dark black smoke billowing up from the center of the city. I asked the security officer at the hospital gate about the smoke.

"Haven't you heard? Martin Luther King has been assassinated in Memphis. They are looting and rioting here in the Adams-Morgan area."

Using the telephone in the guards' station, I called Crawford's unit. The general had been missing since the night before. During the remainder of my assignment at SEH, he was not found.

CONCLUSION

The bulk of the research on UFOs and alien abductions have attempted to either confirm or disprove their veracity (Spanos, Cross, Dickerson, & DuBreuil, 1993). At the present time we have insufficient proof to do either. On the other hand, we are in a propitious position to study the psychology of people who report these incredible psychic events. We are best served by trying to understand the different levels of meaning the experiences serve those who report unusual experiences. Everyday events usually slip by us without our conscious awareness. Extreme events, in contrast, because they are larger than everyday happenings, force us to stop and concern ourselves with what is happening to us and its meaning. In fact, the most important finding of the Roper Poll on UFO experience is that there is a very large number of people in the United States who have had experiences they don't understand. We can begin to understand these experiences by examining the nature of recalled events.

None of us ever recounts literal truth in our narratives because our mind and our memory don't hold fixed perceptions (as would a static photograph). What we remember is a product of our conspiracy with events. By this I mean the following: Each of our stories was initially prepared by our telling ourselves what was happening to us as it transpired—as if we were speaking to an audience not present. This is why our memories have the features of a story: a beginning, a middle, an end, and a stated or implied moral. In other words, like all good stories, our memories are conceptualized in such a way as to dramatically present our welter of diverse sensory experience in a coherent way to an audience. To understand the intent of a memory we need to know who the audience was in the mind of the experiencer, how he felt about his audience, and what he wanted from them. For example, a person who experiences himself as alienated from his audience is more likely to regard those he encounters in his experiences as more alien to him than will a person who believes he is living a meaningful life. And he will have greater need for security and satisfaction from those he encounters as well as from his audience than will those who experience themselves living fully and well. In short, the experience of having been abducted by aliens speaks to those who have had a great deal of difficulty in feeling themselves fully human and significant. In the following sections I examine this contention from four related levels of meaning.

Historical

There is a great deal of similarity between the reports of those who have been abducted by extraterrestrials and the ancient legends of the devil, angels, succubuses, incubuses, and other alien beings who have had sexual encounters at night with unwilling humans. In short, the alien abduction story is a recurring theme in human history. It reflects the anxiety that has racked humankind from its earliest moments of reflected thought in regard to the recognition that we are finite and limited—our fate ultimately is beyond our control. Those who report alien abductions are likely to experience this threat even more keenly than do other people.

Moral

Every story we tell has a stated or implied moral. One of the most interesting questions in regard to the reported alien abductions is whether those who report their unusual experiences believe that the aliens intend to interact with humankind for their own selfish purposes or instead that the aliens wish to sagely guide us away from impeding calamities on our planet. To answer this question we can not easily separate the investigator's moral philosophy from those of his subjects. John Mack (1994), for example, seems to believe that psychotherapy and postmodern science is bereft of meaningful value because they lack the capacity to teach wisdom. Alien abduction, Mack contends, provides us with deep insight about our serious social problems. Mack's subjects, correspondingly, are initially terrified and helpless. In time, however, they become willing participants in the aliens' efforts to stop political and ecological disasters on Earth. The contactees are assigned responsibility by the aliens to provide a warning to the rest of us. They are also employed to create a race of hybrid beings that are spiritually superior to the present human species.

Metaphoric

Metaphors are not simply the tools for more creative and elaborate conceptualization; in fact, they are the fundamental ingredients of our awareness of ourselves and the world around us. The alien abduction stories that have a constructive moral intent usually contain a common metaphoric theme: the death of an ordinary, stultifying life; the courageous endurance of an unusual ordeal; and following that, the reward of redemption and rebirth. In short, these stories are metaphorical representations of the feelings of desperation, despair, and powerlessness that multitudes of people in the United States feel about their existence on this planet. Figuratively, they have been raped and manipulated by powerful forces they don't understand. In return for their suffering, they expect a better world. These expectations are wish fulfilled during their reported abduction—experienced on a different level of consciousness than ordinary experience. For example, false memories may be false in regard to ordinary experience, but they are valid in terms of their representation of the betrayal, contamination, and loss of hope between the experiencer and a powerful authority figure. Those who report alien abductions have suffered more mistrust than have other people.

Personal

A number of studies have revealed that certain people are particularly vulnerable to a variety of extraordinary encounters. Ring (1992) calls them "encounterprone" people. His research indicates that they have a greater incidence of childhood illness, trauma, and abuse than his control subjects. As a result, they have significantly greater tendency to dissociate reality, and by virtue of their dissociated state, to tune into alternate or nonordinary states of consciousness. These findings are supported by Parnell's (1988) psychological examination of people who claimed communication with extraterrestrials. He found that they harbored more unusual thoughts and feelings and showed more of a tendency toward unconventional thinking than did a group of people who reported UFO sightings but claimed no contact with aliens. In short, no one becomes mad except to inure himself against some great suffering.

But it isn't illness versus health that needs to be examined here—but the way that people differ among themselves in the way that they relate to conflict and use coping strategies. As I read the accounts in Mack's (1994) book, each one of his reported contactees had undergone a personal crisis or a loss of meaning in his or her life prior to the reported abduction. However, Mack indicates that these conflicts were the result of a series of abductions since childhood. But isn't the reverse more likely? People who experienced troubled lives and/or a lack of purpose for their existence desperately seek a way to explain their troubles and give meaning to their lives.

The limited ways that Crawford had confined his life didn't permit him to find definitive purpose in his life. This deficiency led to feelings of shame, loneliness, and alienated anguish. What he and others like him seek is to be part of a serious enterprise that values their help and services.

The general was also a man who didn't know himself very well. His UFO experience was a desperate effort to encounter his undiscovered self.

I understand the case differently today than I did at the time. The now-vast literature of investigations of people who have claimed alien abductions strongly suggests that many of the reported abduction experiences are the product of a sleep disorder (Baker, 1992; Hufford, 1982). I recognize now that Crawford's sleep problem is a disorder known as sleep paralysis. Then it was a little-known medical condition with which I was not familiar.

> Sleep paralysis refers to an episode of total body paralysis that occurs just prior to sleep onset or upon awakening. The paralysis is accompanied by the sensation of a weight pressing on the chest and frequently is accompanied by vivid and frightening hallucinations of a person, animal, or monster. The contents of the hallucinations appear to vary as a function of the sleeper's beliefs and expectations, and in individuals who believe in extraterrestrial visitation the hallucinations may take the form of space aliens (Spanos, Cross, Dickerson, & DuBreuil, 1993). Once thought to be very rare, sleep paralysis is turning out to be increasingly common—affecting nearly half of all people at least once. Today many medical investigators believe that sleep

paralysis may explain many of the claims of alien abductions (Kristof, 1999).

Having said all this, one mystery remains: To this day I have not been able to explain how Crawford was able to foretell the future so precisely. The event doesn't fit into the neat and narrow boxes for which modern science has tried to account for human experience.

LOOK AHEAD

The next chapter is an investigation of terrorist groups. I show that acts of terrorism are carried out by those who regard their inner being as having to be denied—because it is either bad or worthless. By means of projection identification onto a charismatic leader and a strident political and/or religious cause, these fanatics experience their unworthy or evil self as having to be sacrificed so that their good self—now projected onto the leader and the cause—can survive and reign.

Chapter 12

A CLINICAL PERSPECTIVE ON TERRORISM: THE FAILED COURAGE OF THE FANATIC

Goodness is the greatest force in the world.
—W. Somerset Maugham (contemporary English novelist)

Sigmund Freud (1930) was one of many who claimed that religion was born in an endeavor to ease our feelings of helplessness in the face of the powerful forces that direct our fate. In humankind's journey through history, we have erected, dedicated ourselves to, and then subsequently discarded countless images and conceptions of the forces we suppose to govern our destiny. At the same time, in each era, there have been those who have found themselves footloose—unable to identify with, and as a result, unwilling to make firm commitments to the dominant values of their society and its sacred images. These individuals, regarded as marginal, ostracized, and suppressed by the keepers of the overriding ethos of their society, have sought redress of their dissatisfaction with the course of life presented by the dominant values of their society. But alone no man or woman can transform society or create a separate improved world, so they find others who harbor similar strivings for an improved society (Cantril, 1941; Edwards, 1944; King, 1956; Maier, 1942). Accordingly, a religious social movement can be seen as the consequence of the social ferment that arises from the failure of mainstream religious groups and the various segments of the social order to adequately meet the sociopolitical, as well as the spiritual, needs of a segment of the population.

Once the stage is set for a religious movement, the appearance of an inspired and inspiring charismatic leader is required. Otherwise, the movement comes to a temporary halt or may even quickly expire. Centuries after they lived, such enlightened paradigmatic figures as Buddha, Confucius, Jesus, Mohammed, Moses, and Socrates still profoundly influence the lives of others. Many other charismatic leaders, however, have been raging, deluded people who have wreaked havoc on the lives of their followers.

I was sitting at my desk at home, less than two miles directly south from the World Trade Center buildings, when I heard a report of the WTC bombings. I opened the window of my study: I heard the wailing sirens of police cars and ambulances and the incessant bells of fire department trucks, and I saw the billowing black clouds pitched against the early morning sky.

RELIGIOUS DOGMA AS ABSOLUTE TRUTH

Among the many sundry disturbing thoughts that moved like a kaleidoscope through my mind after I turned on the radio and was informed of the suspected identity of the assailants was this: If I could make just one universal law it would be that no one—absolutely no one—would be allowed *to interpret God's will for other people.* Even the most devout people of religious faith must now recognize the serious danger of making claim that one's religious beliefs represent absolute truth, whereas other people's beliefs are false.

We all now need to fully realize that many who experience their inner being as empty and/or evil are drawn to the dogma of religion and use that dogma as an overriding truth—an ideology that demands that nonbelievers bend to the zealots' interpretation of God's will; if not, they must be subjected to damnation and death.

Fanatic acts are carried out, I have found from my four decades of clinical work with seriously destructive clients, by people who experience their inner being as having to be denied because it is unworthy and evil. Those aspects of themselves that they have regarded as virtuous are split off from their own personalities and attributed by means of projective identification to a leader and a strident religious cause—that has powerful political and social implications for every segment of their society. These self-denigrating fanatics, now devoid of any constructive sense of self, other than their identification with an omniscient and omnipotent leader, experience their totally worthless selves as having to be disregarded or sacrificed so that the good self—now part of the leader and the cause—can survive and reign as Absolute Truth: The fulfillment of God's commandments. It is paradise, of course, in which they have been promised that their self-sacrifice will be abundantly rewarded.

THE PERSONALITY OF FANATIC HATRED

The capacity for violence, I believe, is potentially in all of us; yet, undoubtedly, some personalities are more susceptible to its expression than are other types of personalities. Psychoanalytically oriented anthropologist Western La Barre (1980) indicates:

> True believers are authoritarian personalities because they are infantile dependents on the divine authority of the Shaman, not mature assessors of their own judgments. Fundamentalists abjectly depend on part tribal culture, not on their contemporary common sense. Every fundamentalism is an intellectual lobotomy. (p. 52)

Authoritarian personalities are cognitively closed minded and defensive. Their ability to make sense of their lives is largely inflexible. They are people who seem unable or unwilling to withstand high degrees of anxiety in situations that are cognitively complex or ambiguous or that invoke considerable uncertainty of outcome. Because anxiety is easily aroused in such situations, they seek quick, easy, and absolutely correct solutions.

For people from authoritarian backgrounds, high-level psychological functioning is most difficult during periods of *historical dislocation,* such as postmodernity; this is the time in which symbols of long-standing authority are confronted, undermined, and cast away. This is when leaders appear suddenly, recede equally rapidly, and are difficult to believe in when they are around (Lifton, 1993). It is not surprising, then, that people who come from authoritarian backgrounds wish to return to the straightforward virtues of yesteryear in which there were clear-cut heroes and villains. These are the types of people who are ripe for charismatic leaders, such as Osama bin Laden, who appear to hold unswaying convictions in their belief system.

It is understandable, then, that followers in fanatic cults are indoctrinated to believe that they are superior to everyone else, that they alone possess the absolute truth.

ALTERED STATES OF CONSCIOUSNESS

I have suggested why people are drawn to a religious cult leader, but not what keeps them adherents of those who exhort them to carry out terrorist acts in which people are murdered. Religious dogma is usually not sufficient. Programs of psychological monitoring of followers are integral to the regimentation of cult life, membership recruiting, and indoctrination. To ensure obedience to cult doctrine, critical thinking is strongly discouraged by practices that dictate ways of suppressing negative thoughts about the leader and his dogma; in the place of critical thinking an emotional dependency on the cult authority is fostered.

Religious cult leaders appear to be highly adroit in inducing altered states of consciousness in their followers. Modern brain research indicates that each of the brain's hemispheres has separate neurological functions. Moreover, each side of the brain is regarded as having distinctly different ways of apprehending reality. If these were valid contentions, then it would appear that each brain hemisphere participates in a somewhat different reality from the other. In general, the left is rational and analytic; the right speaks the language of movement, imagery, and metaphor. By utilizing such tactics as "loading the language," as American research psychiatrist Robert Lifton (1963) terms it, the cult leader and his lieutenants begin to block out the critical faculties of the left hemisphere. In short, speaking in metaphoric phrases and clichés that relate to the typically unsophisticated, underdeveloped right hemisphere of most individuals, these cult leaders gradually take over the thought processes of their flock.

The leader also relies on psychedelic and mood-altering drugs, nutritionally deficient diets, sleep derivation, and the monotonous repetition of religious rhetoric to control his followers in mind, body, and spirit. Taken together, these practices induce a state of psychological confusion and dependency on the leader and his doctrines. The fanatic follower is caught up in a series of existential paradoxes imposed by the interface of both overstimulation (e.g., repetition of ritual and dogma that seems unending) and understimulation (e.g., intellectual and physical deprivation). In this paradoxical climate, the follower is susceptible to interhemispheric brain conflict. One hemisphere inhibits the other in an attempt to suppress contradictory perceptions. It is as if the follower is not able to ascertain whether he is rejoicing in paradise or suffering in hell.

SOCIAL JUSTICE

One would be naive to contend that terrorist fanaticism is a product of religious dogma and the skillful manipulations of cult leaders alone. Cogent social and political factors must not be underestimated.

Fanatic violence is an attempt to seek *social justice*. This is a statement of explanation, not of justification. The condoning of a destructive person's deadly actions by his fanatic leader and his reference group is crucial to the enactment of violence. No one murders without a belief that that which is being done is justified. The violent fanatic's sense of entitlement in violating society's most entrenched taboos is buttressed by his leader's and his reference group's interpretation of the *social contract*. In other words, whether or not we are inclined to philosophical considerations, we all operate from an intuitive grasp that our humanity is defined by our agreements with other people. The whole fabric of an orderly society resides in an implicit social contract, founded on trust. This trust is based upon the belief "that others will act predictably, in accordance with generally accepted rules of behavior, and that they will not take advantage of the trust" (Silberman, 1978, p. 130).

But what happens to an individual if he believes that his political state or some foreign regime repeatedly has unfairly treated him? U.S. foreign policy, in this regard, far too often supports dictatorships that suppress the rights of their own citizens (indeed, if they regard them as citizens at all!) as well as the means to live decently and well. In short, we support and finance brutal, suppressive foreign regimes, largely because they appear to be anticommunist and procapitalist.

According to eighteenth-century French philosopher Jean-Jacques Rousseau (1954): "In order for an arbitrary government to be a legitimate one, the people of each generation would have to be free to accept or reject it" (p. 10). By this Rousseau intends that the individual who is treated unfairly can legitimately declare his contract with the social order null and void and demand that his natural rights be restored—taking whatever retaliatory actions are necessary to protect his own well-being. Rousseau's interpretation of the social contract seems to be in accordance with the destructive actions of fanatic terrorists. They claim to have been unjustly treated by the United States and demand the right to retaliate.

It is crucial to recognize, however, that a psychoanalytic purview belies the fanatic terrorists' sociopolitical claim to a legitimate recourse to violence. Fanatically violent people are those who are frightened. They experience themselves in danger. Like the children we have all once been, they still expect automatic justice, a spontaneous assuagement of all their feelings of mistreatment. Fanatic hatred is predicated upon the desperate reasoning that holds that those who are denied their humanity by the social order can heal their injured humanity—the shame and self-contempt that is sown by being denied one's humanity—only by forceful assertion. This claim is a product of inner negation.

There is no more unbearable virulence visited upon any of us than unremitting, unrelieved self-contempt that allows no examination. To survive, the sufferers must somehow cast off these terrible feelings of self-hate. They find that regarding other people as sinners and vermin is a quick and automatic way to relieve their self-loathing. In short, self-contempt unexamined becomes effortlessly converted into contempt of the world outside one's own band of true believers.

In short, the history of destructive fanaticism is a long tale of those who, in trying to deny their own self-hatred, were afraid to look inside themselves for guidance and as a result were unable to behave in accordance with the dictates of their compassionate conscience.

COURAGE AND FANATICISM

There is a question that should be raised here: Is fanaticism that involves self-sacrifice an act of courage, or is it instead a desperate flight to avoid intrapsychic turmoil?

A comparison may be useful here: On April 15, 73 c.e., nearly 1,000 Jewish zealots, defenders of the fortress Masada, took their own lives rather than be taken prisoner and submit themselves to the yoke of the besieging Roman legions. Were these zealots courageous or simply fanatic? It seems to me that there is a marked difference between courage and fanaticism. Whereas the source of courage is experienced as an accentuated sense of self, the fanatic identification contributes to a loss of self. In courage there is a feeling of love of self and, when others are involved, love of them is motivation for an act of bravery. By that definition, the zealots were courageous.

In examining the behavior of violent fanatics, it is prudent to differentiate those perpetrators who seek political and social reform from those terrorists who are single-mindedly intent on sheer destructiveness—as I have suggested, in order that others suffer for what they have suffered.

Terrorists have used threats of mass destruction since the Second World War to negotiate the release of comrades from imprisonment, to curb unfair or overly partial treatment of an ethnic or social group, or to extort large amounts of cash. In the World Trade Center, the Pentagon, and the Oklahoma City bombings, in contrast to acts with a liberation cause or for purposes of extortion, no prior warning was given. It appears that the object of the bombing was to foster terror by destroying as massively as could be managed in a single day. This is the deed and the definition of *fanatic hatred.*

Fanatic hatred depletes the self. A follower who identifies with a fanatic leader by despising his human similarities with nonbelievers has an aching need to forgive himself for shameful weaknesses he cannot condone. He tries to distance himself from his own self-hatred by burying it in others and by despising others for what he has projected onto them. In hating others he seeks ways to destroy them. His enemies retaliate. The fanatic finds additional justification from these actions for his hatred of the enemy. He has now prophesy-fulfilled his conviction that whatever brutality he will do to his enemy has been done to him or will be done unless he destroys his enemy. With all-out war exploding in his viscera, there is no room for love, compassion, or tolerance—certainly not for his enemy, indeed, not even for himself!

TRUE PROPHETS

How do today's destructive cult leaders such as bin Laden compare with inspired prophets of antiquity?

Each of the ancient prophets alluded to earlier presented himself as an ordinary being engaged in the constructive development of selfhood. Rather than telling others how to live or leading them into social action, these sages patiently demonstrated by personal example how to live the examined life. They also created a climate in which their disciples could question and reach their own conclusions about how to conduct their lives. Thus, while Jesus believed in the paramount value of life in the hereafter, he apparently did not minimize the importance of the present world or ask his followers to sacrifice their mortal existence.

Above all, the true prophets did not teach their disciples to hate or flee those who opposed them; they all proclaimed that human love is universal and unlimited (Jaspers, 1957). Nor did any of them need the dubious proof of having their followers validate their beliefs by demanding that others die for them; Socrates resolutely chose his own death, and Jesus braved alone fear and doubt on the cross. In contrast, leaders like bin Laden lurk in the shadows, always in hiding, while pressing others to martyrdom.

If I had a second universal wish it would be that, in turning to religion for guidance, lost souls find spiritual leaders who practice love, compassion, and caring for all of humanity. These would be spiritual leaders who, in ministering to the poor, the needy, the ill, and the dying, would do so without the motive of trying to convert nonbelievers to the spiritual leader's faith.

The true prophet, by not presenting himself as omniscient or omnipotent, allows his followers to transform themselves by choosing their own ordeals, rather than suffering trials he imposes upon them. In short, he asks his followers to courageously examine their lives. Courage, as we learned earlier, is to know one's limitations, to accept oneself as less than perfect, to live to the best of one's ability, and to come caringly together with others to heal the wounds of loneliness, shame, and self-hatred.

LOOK AHEAD

The next chapter instructs readers how to listen intelligently and courageously to their own personal stories as well as the accounts of the events and experiences in the lives of those with whom they seek intimate connectedness. The personal story approach provides readers with the armamentarium to recognize and face their own self-deceptions and a constructive means to work them out in seeking personal authenticity.

Chapter 13

THE PERSONAL STORY APPROACH: REACHING A CLIENT WHO DID NOT TRUST

A man is always a teller of stories...he sees everything that happens to him through them; and he tries to live his life as if he were telling a story.

—Jean-Paul Sartre (contemporary French philosopher)

I present here a psychological strategy for addressing the crucial existential question that each of us, unwittingly, tries to answer for himself or herself: How should I actually live my life? I contend that each of us in our own way responds to this challenge by means of personal stories.

Personal stories are the narratives that we tell ourselves and others that arrange the events of our lives in an episodic order—that is to say, our personal tales relate our experiences in a story format with a plot that has a beginning, a middle, and an end, together with an implied moral, that is to say, a personal judgment that evaluates our experience.

We tell stories about ourselves because each of us is a natural-born storyteller. On the basis of considerable empirical evidence, developmental psychologists (Bruner, 1986; Eakin, 1999; Feinstein & Krippner, 1988; McAdam, 1993; Schank, 1990; Singer & Salovey, 1993) contend that the maturation of our sense of self and our narrative capacity constitute the same process of identity formation. Indeed, there even seems to be some evidence that our personal narratives are products of a built-in function that our brain employs to make sense of both our inner and social experiences (Schank, 1990).

Consequently, as meaning-oriented beings that evaluate the events of our lives, our personal identity is constituted in ways shaped by our judgments about our experiences as expressed by the stories we tell ourselves about what happened to us.

Accordingly, we all have, if not a favorite story about ourselves, then certainly several prototypical stories that have direct bearing on how we respond to the world—in regard to its resources, opportunities, and challenges, as well as the scenarios we have composed about the various impediments to the attainment of our desires.

On the basis of my clinical experience it seems to me that to meaningfully respond to the question I posed above—about how we should live our lives—we must discover aspects of our self that we have not fully considered or of which we were previously unaware. We refer to this uncharted domain of our personality as our *undiscovered self.*

THE UNDISCOVERED SELF IN STORY ACCOUNT

As I indicated in chapter 5, each of us has a right to an enlightened, cohesive self. But, of course, this enlightened self is never provided for us ready made. It must be tested by our courage in entering the shadows of the greatest mystery any of us will ever face: Who am I as a human being? Carl Jung (1976) claims that we deny our dark side at extreme risk because that which we do not bring into consciousness appears in our lives as fate. His notion is that a person's past inescapably clings to him or her, and if the shadows of some of these events seem too terrifying to examine, the cast of their shadows become that person's eventual destiny.

Accordingly, since obtaining knowledge about ourselves may be the most difficult task we ever face, the great challenge of self-exploration is finding the *courage* to follow our personal journey in search of our undiscovered self wherever and however it may lead us through the deep venues of our hearts and minds. Consequently, curiosity about ourselves is a crucial concern for each of us—regardless of our level of education or psychological sophistication—who seeks personal enlightenment and an advanced consciousness.

Unfortunately, as the vignettes I have presented in the previous chapters show, our ability and willingness to be curious, for most of us, is seriously impeded. To reverse a mindless journey through life, we must skillfully find a path to our undiscovered self.

I contend that this path is built upon our capacity to tell meaningful stories about ourselves. In other words, if you want to know a person intimately, then listen carefully and compassionately to his personal story. If you want to know yourself more intimately, listen carefully and courageously to your own personal story. In this regard, I have found that the *personal story approach* has helped my clients respond to their innermost intentions by enabling them to listen more skillfully to their own experiences and then to constructively devise the stories they tell about these experiences.

THE TELLING OF THE PERSONAL STORY

Since each of us is a natural-born storyteller, it is hardly surprising that when strangers meet they usually tell stories about themselves. Frequently these stories are poignant expressions of the events and personal experiences of the storyteller. But too often the story fails to convey a clear understanding of the storyteller's inner being because the account is indirect and confusing. By relating a dissonant story, the storyteller says in effect, "Who I am is contained somewhere in my story; but I'm not sure myself. So I will leave it up to you to figure out from what I have told you just who I am."

The *personal story approach* I describe here is intended not only to enable us to tell others—friends, intimates, acquaintances, even strangers—more directly and articulately who they are. No less importantly, because many of us are as much strangers to ourselves as we are to others, this approach is highly valuable for all of us in informing ourselves directly and articulately who we believe ourselves to be and who we seek to become. This endeavor concerns our personal identity.

PERSONAL IDENTITY

One's *personal identity* is complex. It not only consists of one's sense of who one currently is, but it also includes one's beliefs and desires about who one should be and what one can become if one knew oneself better than he does now. From this context, every action and interaction on one's part is judged in terms of the information it provides for either substantiating or disconfirming the kind of person one desires to be. Where a congruent fit exists between the experiences of one's *tested self* (e.g., the import of one's senses about the circumstances of one's life) and the images, fantasies, and intentions of one's *desired self,* a feeling of competence accompanies these experiences.

Harvard University psychologist Robert White (1963) defines *competence* as the ability, fitness, and capacity to live effectively and well. *Neg-*

ative personal identity, in contrast, always involves a sense of incompetence. The potential for experiencing bad (shameful) feelings about oneself is present, therefore, when there is a disparity between the experiences of one's tested self and those of one's desired self. As such, a useful way to view negative personal identity is to regard it as a powerful but unquestioned conviction that in some important way one is flawed and incompetent as a human being. Consequently, it is our negative personal identity that prevents us from telling stories that constructively direct our lives.

THE PERSONAL STORY APPROACH

It has been my experience in using this approach—based on psychiatrist Richard Gardner's (1971) *Mutual Story Telling Technique* for working with children—for the past three decades with people from all walks of life, that this straightforward guide can enable most people to begin to recognize the important themes in their lives and what has up until then stood in their way of reaching their psychological and social goals.

A caution should be noted: Whereas each of us has a host of personal stories, I have found that for my psychotherapy clients some of their stories seem more facile to tell and that they can convey them with more personal authenticity than they do other narratives. Why is this?

Revealing one's personal story openly is usually an elusive and difficult task for those who seek self-discovery. From many years of asking clients during their initial consultation to "tell me how you see yourself," I have discovered that otherwise highly articulate and thoughtful people find themselves at a loss to convey a meaningful sense of who they are.

It is not surprising, then, that those who have consulted with me—because of their sense of themselves as incompetent to live fully and well—have struggled with strong feelings of shame. *Shame* plays a crucial and often disguised role in our lives. Shame, as I have already suggested, is closely implicated in the production of the self-deceptions that prevent us from telling authentic personal stories.

Indeed, it was because of the difficulties many of my clients had in the presentation of a coherent sense of their personal identity that I devised the storytelling approach.

THE SOURCES FOR PERSONAL STORIES

There are no facts, the eighteenth-century German philosopher Friedrich Nietzsche warned us, only interpretations. In other words, because we are meaning-oriented beings, it is our nature to evaluate the events of our lives. These stories derive from a wide plethora of sources.

Because we cannot empirically acquire absolute truth about our world, each of us attempts—by the use of the events, legends, and myths of family and society—to create a reliable guide for living. These family and societal sagas generally undergo considerable elaboration and modification in our personal narratives. Nevertheless, personal myths in story format reveal rather succinctly how we navigate through the straits and vicissitudes of daily life. Consequently, the stories we reveal to ourselves, if carefully examined, can provide us with a working hypothesis for what is directing our sense of personal identity in terms of the forces that are steering our lives—that is to say, they can provide insight into what we want most from life, the obstacles that prevent its happening, and the resources that would enable us to realize and enjoy the intentions of our desired selves.

At this point, I can describe *the personal story approach* as consisting of the following recommended steps: First is that psychotherapists in working with *the personal story approach* use a tape recorder or some other reliable electronic recording device to register the narrative that their clients are formulating. They may instead, of course, ask clients to write down their stories or even simply relate them aloud. But whatever recording method is used, it should be one that requires minimal attention on the part of the psychotherapists and clients so that both can maximize their concentration on the listening to and telling of the story.

Second, for clients to recognize their personal identity, they need to be encouraged to speak directly from their experience of what it is like for them to be in the world as they, themselves, encounter their world: in short, to relate a story that best presents what their life has been for them. In this regard, our personal truths have less to do with the keenness of our intellect than with embracing our experiences with our emotions.

A personal story, therefore, is not simply what has happened to a person, but how that person felt about these experiences while they were happening and how the person feels about them during the recitation of the story in the psychotherapy session.

Third, clients are asked to describe the events in their stories with regard to what each person involved in the story was thinking, feeling, and doing as fully as they are willing to describe these people.

Fourth, like every coherent tale, the personal story should have a plot with beginning, middle, and concluding episodes.

Fifth, in replaying clients' personal stories from a tape recorder (or some other device), I ask them to consider any important components of their story that are missing, seem incomplete, or are simply puzzling in regard to their meaning for the psychotherapist.

Sixth, it is prudent not to interrupt clients' recitations as long as the psychotherapist experiences the spoken account as heartfelt and uncontrived. I do, however, suggest that the therapist stop the recitation to ask clients questions, to make comments connecting aspects of the story, and to underscore his wish to better understand how the clients feel about themselves when he recognizes that clients are presenting themselves as another person might describe them, rather than giving an authentic personal statement from the deep recesses of their psyche.

Authentic personal statements are essential in the process of self-discovery as well as in the establishment of intimate relations with significant people in each of our lives. To reiterate what I discussed earlier: An authentic personal statement is a verbal and/or nonverbal communication in which one conveys one's perceptions and judgments about oneself in a direct and undisguised way. These statements convey the composite of one's regard for oneself (and, in terms of interpersonal interactions, about the other). They are authentic insofar as they are products of one's struggle to self-examine and not deny any aspect of what one has learned about oneself (or the other person). Obviously, people who don't know themselves very well, because they have avoided thorough self-examination, are not capable of authentic personal statements. Consequently, it is expected that clients' initial stories will not be as authentic and personal as they will be once they begin to learn the rules of good storytelling and careful listening.

Finally, the psychotherapist should ask clients what they believe to be the moral, or significant message, contained in their story.

Overall, a thorough review of a client's personal story may require a second, a third, or even more replays. The review usually involves the following seven considerations:

1. What the story tells in regard to what is desirable and meaningful in life for the client;

2. What the client believes should be avoided in his life;

3. His means for obtaining the desirable and avoiding the untoward;

4. What he anticipates will happen if his desired goals are not achieved;

5. What significant ways his story has changed over time and what these changes may tell him about what he has learned about himself and how he seems to have tried to improve his life;

6. Which personal myths he uses to interpret his experiences; and

7. The basic assumptions about the world he has derived from his personal myths.

We have all heard, no doubt, the expression that "He is a guy who is always in the process of reinventing himself." Actually, this enterprise is true for most of us, as suggested above by the fifth consideration. Although there are major components of one's personal story that remain constant over time, we all at the same time seek to improve our lives by reinventing our personal identity. These reinventions are neither useful nor deleterious in themselves. They are constructive in improving our lives only to the extent that the reinvented aspects of our personal story are attempts to make authentic personal statements about our experiences and feelings. Inauthentic reinventions of our self represent the shameful feelings we harbor about our negative personal identity.

I exemplify here the capacity of the personal story to represent the shadows of emotionally laden shaming scenes that have invoked contemptuous inner dialogue and a sense of lack of self-worth by presenting Roger's story.

ROGER'S STORY

Roger is a tall, slender Englishman who wears thick glasses, without which he is nearly blind. This 37-year-old man has a rapid speech and a fidgety manner that initially induced restlessness in me. Although a gifted and highly trained actor and musician, Roger experienced his life as unsuccessful and emotionally empty. He had held a paying job only sporadically in his life. When asked during the initial consultation session to tell a story that closely characterized what his life had been like, he told me that when he was six or seven years of age he took part in a reading comprehension examination with his school class. Long after his classmates went to recess, he remained at his desk, unable to answer one of the questions—which he eventually realized with chagrin was rather simple. He had difficulty finding the answer, he later understood, because he had misread the directions given about the situation in the test question.

Roger was asked what happened next. He replied that his teacher came back to the room and found that he was still at his desk rather than at recess with his classmates. She asked what was wrong. He said that he could not figure out the answer to one of the questions. But once she read out loud the instructions and the question, the answer was readily apparent to him.

I thought to myself that Roger's story appeared to capture in only a few words what I suspected were the primary reasons for Roger's isolation and deep sadness about his life. But how aware was Roger of the basic assumptions he held about the world contained in his personal story? To obtain this information, he was asked what was the moral of his story. Roger indicated that the story vividly demonstrated how he typically fouled up his life by being conceptually confused by problems that he should be intelligent enough to understand and be able to deal with successfully. Notice that Roger focused on his intellectual problems rather than recognizing that there was an interpersonal resource available to him—his teacher.

Roger then indicated that the only reason he was seeking psychotherapy was that he felt that it would be irresponsible on his part not to try to do something about his defective thinking. Again notice his inclination to morally blame himself as irresponsible rather than recognize and express his deficient interpersonal skills—due to his lack of basic trust in other people. When this information was conveyed to Roger, he was able to use it to recognize that his mistrust served to insulate him from what he had experienced throughout his childhood as the unreliability of significant others.

But then Roger claimed that it was too late for him to change his behavior. Everything he had read about psychology and sociology, he claimed, told him that one's cast in life is early set. In other words, in his view, how families treat their young is irreversible. He went on to speak about the embarrassing failures and mistakes he had made throughout his life because of the lack of proper guidance from his parents. Roger is here revealing his *toxic personal myth* about the impossibility of his achieving his desires because of his family background. His immediate family was rather affluent—his father had become a successful building contractor. However, both parents came from poor working-class families, in which many of their kin were hard drinking and dysfunctional. His parents resented their families and had as little do with them as they could manage. Growing up they experienced minimal support and guidance in how to live fully and well. It is hardly surprising, then, that Roger's family saga was replete with toxic messages about trusting other people for help and support.

Toxic Personal Myths

Toxic personal myths are misconceived interpretations that a person uses to explain human experience. They are dysfunctional because they hinder the person from access to her own personal resources and the availability of others' caring and help. As such, they are the generators of our *self-deceptions* that impede our curiosity, preventing access to our undiscovered self. Because toxic personal myths and self-deceptions are major interferences in telling good stories or listening intelligently and courageously to our own personal stories, they are given considerable attention in my clinical work with clients subsequent to the recitation of their personal stories. Here I restrict myself to pointing out how Roger's toxic personal myth kept him in an emotional straitjacket.

As Roger spoke, he conveyed a sense of a person who felt he was isolated and alone in the world because in his mind he was a loser, while other people were proficient. It is not surprising, then, that in discussing the moral of his personal story, Roger had totally ignored the role his teacher had played in helping him solve the problem and by so doing disengaged him from the solitude and humiliation that he felt sitting alone in his seat by himself while his classmates were happily at play.

In working with him I was repeatedly struck with how different my own family saga was from Roger's. Grandparents often serve as important nurturing and mentoring people in their grandchildren's lives, as my maternal grandmother was for me. As a small child I loved to sit by her side at her diminutive chrome-topped kitchen table in her small apartment. Preparing a meal, she would tell me inspiring stories about her life in Europe as a child. I was especially fond of stories about her beloved father. Haskell Felsenstein had been a lover of books and of the human spirit. According to my grandmother, people from all segments of society in their small town came to him for counseling and advice on matters of the heart and family, no less than that of business. Early in life I received the message (my family myth) from my grandmother that, like her father, I could hardly do anything more worthwhile in life than to be a wise and compassionate friend to people in need.

For many people like Roger, with toxic family myths and who are in deep despair, it is their anticipation of their not being able to *cope* that undermines their ability to feel alive and thrive in a purposeful way. Their fearful apprehension is predicated upon the fallacy that a person should operate at full capacity at all times. Consequently, when they become disabled by illness or other human vulnerabilities they unquestionably believe that their suffering is meant to be. The advent of illness or despair indicates to them that the force that controls the universe—God, Providence, fate, or whatever—has decided their fate and no effort on their part can change that destiny. Roger's feeling that he lacked the ability to cope resulted from the personal statements he continually made to himself that if he didn't achieve a state of ideal solution to his conflicts, his lot in life would be one of failure, demoralization, and despair. During his moments of despair, such as the school incident, he heard in the back of his mind what I refer to as a negative inner voice. This voice broadcast in a way that Roger could not ignore that he was an abject and worthless person.

Roger, because of his toxic myth about the reasons for his suffering, like many other shame-bound people, didn't recognize or believe that other people can be trusted to help and care about him. His teacher's behavior, as it was inconsistent with his worldview, was disavowed and ignored.

Roger had not requested help when aware that he didn't seem to be able to solve the test problem by himself. He was asked why. He shrugged his shoulders and said that he had met few people who genuinely cared about him. Roger, like many of my other clients, strives to justify his behavior by selecting those life experiences that are consistent with his personal myth. One of the important utilities of *the personal story approach,* therefore, is that it readily reveals the toxic personal myths that impede clients from fulfilling their intentions. For example, it was only when Roger was asked for the second time what he believed his teacher was thinking and feeling when she went over to his desk that he, with what appeared to be considerable surprise on his part, answered that she must have been concerned and cared about him.

Misery is usually disproportional to our moral sins. Roger had no vocabulary, despite his high intellect, excellent education, and stage training, to express his myth of suffering due to his belief that he was repeatedly betrayed by other people. He simply expected to be verbally misunderstood. At these times, he communicated nonverbally. For example, during the recitation of his personal story he crossed his arms across his chest, pulled his chin over the top of his chest, and grimaced bitterly.

By learning his characteristic style of emotional language by which he unwittingly expressed himself nonverbally—in sessions subsequent to his recitation of his story—Roger acquired the skill to recognize his self-deceptions and, in so doing, was able to modify his personal stories in ways that were more optimistic, flexible, and open to realistic modification than was his original narrative.

To reiterate, personal stories are crucial to the development of our personal identity because of the way our mind functions. This perspective requires our understanding of how our memory operates.

NARRATIVE AND MEMORY

None of us ever recounts literal truth in our personal stories because our mind and our memory don't hold fixed perceptions. Traditionally, psychologists have maintained that our experiences are encoded in our memory like a motion-picture film (except that all the sensory input, not only sight and sound, are captured in memory). Therefore, it is believed by most psychologists that given an appropriate inquiry technique—hypnosis, sodium pentothal, free association, or whatever—a person can bring forth faithfully even the most painful and fearful events. This is a fallacious assumption! Memory is not like a static photograph, a movie, or a videotape, able to capture the event as it actually occurs.

We are language-oriented beings. Our recognition of what we experience and how we understand these events depends upon linguistic concepts; conceptualizations create our sense of reality. It is important to reiterate what I stated in the previous chapter: What we remember is a product of our conspiracy with events. In other words, each of our stories was initially prepared by our telling ourselves what was happening to us as it transpired—as if we were speaking to an audience not present. This is why our memories have the features of a story: a beginning, middle, and end, with a stated or implied moral. In other words, like all good stories, our memories are conceptualized in such a way as to dramatically present our welter of diverse sensory and emotional experiences in a coherent way to an audience. Moreover, not only do we try to explain what happens to us by means of the stories we creatively construct at the time of the event; in fact, we experience what has happened to us as it occurs in terms of a story that has personal meaning for us. Consequently, to understand the intent of a narrative memory we need to know: Who was the audience in the mind of the storyteller? How did he or she feel about the audience? What does he or she want from the audience?

SELF-HELP

The personal story approach need not be confined to the consulting room of the professional psychotherapist. For many people it may be a reasonable alternative to psychoanalysis and psychotherapy. One of the considerable merits of this approach is that it is readily adaptive to a wide range of settings and uses. Using the guidelines I have described in this chapter, it can be an effective means of self-discovery for people in their own solitary contemplations. In still other instances people can use this approach to promote their intimate relationships, and parents, teachers, and other caretakers of children can help their children fulfill their curiosity needs and creative strivings.

LOOK AHEAD

In the next chapter, based upon a case study of a theologian who, while in psychotherapy with me, was given information that he had fathered the child of a parishioner while he was a parish minister 20 years earlier, I examine the issue of moral responsibility.

Chapter 14

THE ADULTEROUS MINISTER: A CLINICAL EXAMINATION OF MORAL RESPONSIBILITY

Responsibility educates.
— Wendell Phillips (1811–1824, American orator)

I am concerned here with investigating how moral responsibility becomes an active agent of moral judgment. *Moral judgment,* according to Washington University developmental psychologist Jane Loevinger (1976), is the cognitive ability to take into consideration another person's perspective in order to understand and resolve moral dilemmas. I define *moral responsibility* as *the willingness to translate moral judgment into constructive and effective social behavior.* It is generally agreed that someone who is morally responsible recognizes that his perception that some behavior ought to be done implies that it can be done. Moreover, he makes the assumption that to claim that something ought to be done makes little sense unless that behavior actually is conducted, as it ought. As such, a morally responsible person is someone who initiates constructive social behavior rather than simply responds to situations in which he is thrust (Gruber, 1985).

Those who have studied moral development have been predominantly concerned with the cognitive attributes that are involved in reasoning about moral issues, but not about what people actually do, based on these factors, to bring about a morally desirable state of affairs (Gruber, 1985). By means of a case study, I suggest here some of the crucial emotional factors at play in moral dilemmas in which a client has difficulty acting in a morally responsible way.

THE GUILT MODEL FOR THE BASIS OF MORAL RESPONSIBILITY

Psychoanalytic theory is the system from which the predominance of psychological theories of morality is predicated. Freud (1905), as I already indicated, mistrusted love as a binding force in mature relationships and, as a consequence, rejected affection as a healthy mainstream of human behavior. Instead, he viewed it as a seductive, repetitive magical wish afflicting everyone. He also did not trust altruistic behavior. In his writings he reduced all human strivings to conflictual drives between fear and aggression; and in so doing, he eschewed altruism and other virtuous behavior as fundamental human attributes. He claimed, instead, that these apparent virtues are actually psychological defenses compelled by feelings of guilt, and/or grandiose fantasies to mask feelings of impotence.

Someone who believes that neither affection nor altruism is genuine is left with only fear and the threat of punishment as moral guardians. Freud (1923), therefore, held that the superego—predicated on fear and threat— is the agent of morality.

But does the fear and threat of punishment adequately explain impeded moral responsibility? I contend here that it does not—because there are strong competing systems of morality within every society (as I have shown throughout this book) that most of us continually struggle to reconcile. It is the seemingly insoluble conflict between these moral imperatives that lies at the core of impeded moral responsibility.

The two major systems of morality I have been concerned with in this book are *righteousness* as a refluent morality (the unreflective enactment of the values of one's society or one's particular reference group) and *compassion* as a reflective consciousness (in which one suspends the certainty of righteous behavior and seeks a more noble and humane vision of proper behavior than one has been taught). Morality based upon reflective consciousness, as discussed in chapter 4, consists of several major components that differentiate it from refluent morality. In investigating moral responsibility, I focus here on one of these crucial factors, *curiosity* about one's common humanity and shared fate with other people that comes from an abiding interest in the other's interiority by identifying there with the other's early (and often continuing) helplessness and vulnerability that one finds all of us as humans are heir to as our common heritage.

CASE STUDY

The client, whom I will refer to as Reverend Miller, was—at the time I saw him in psychotherapy—in his mid-fifties, of slight stature and undistinguished features. He also wore thick glasses. Rev. Miller was then teaching in a religious seminary in Maryland—the state in which I then practiced; previously he been a faculty member of a prestigious Protestant seminary in California. He was referred to me for psychological counseling by a minister who taught with me in a pastoral psychology training program in a federal hospital in Washington, DC. Rev. Miller was referred because as an old and close friend of my colleague, he seemed unable to get over his upset that his parish ministry had been taken away from him a few years before. He lost his position, his friend told me, because the church hierarchy decided that Rev. Miller was unable to concentrate on his ministerial duties—so that several parishioners had left the church in search of a more responsive minister. Rev. Miller seemed unwilling to discuss with his friends or anyone else what was troubling him.

I found Rev. Miller to be a highly intelligent, well-read person who had obtained doctorate degrees in both philosophy and theology. But he wasn't a comfortable client with whom to work. He was reluctant to self-introspect. When I pointed this out to him, he claimed that a concern with one's own self was base; that is to say, it was unfitting for a man of God to focus on his own appetites and their vicissitudes rather than to direct his concerns to his spiritual calling.

Rev. Miller attended our sessions reluctantly—he felt forced to be there by the recognition that if he dropped out of psychotherapy, his church superiors would not allow him to assume again an active ministry. During our initial sessions he was highly secretive, conveying a sense of some considerable mystery that he was unwilling to divulge. On the other hand, he seemed to need to be seen by me as a person who was responsible and earnest, and as such should be restored to active ministry. As a consequence, rather than offering useful material to discuss about his situation, he preferred to answer my questions about his situation, usually without any of the insight one might expect from a man of his intellect and education.

The little that I did learn from him in our early sessions was insufficient for my grasping the cause of his difficulties. It consisted for the most part of his statements that his father, a highly driven businessman, had told him, as the eldest of three siblings, that the more education he received, the dumber he became in regard to practical matters. His father also criticized the time he spent alone writing poetry and reading philosophical books and classical novels. He was told that he should be outside—of his home and the public library—making friends, playing sports, and building contacts with other people so that he could become a successful adult.

His mother, in contrast, suffocated by her husband's criticism and tyrannical control of the family, encouraged his solitary pursuits—quietly urging his intellectual development and his gentility. But she was unwilling to stand up to her husband and, in Rev. Miller's eyes, failed to protect him from his father's assaults upon his character. Not surprisingly, as a child and as an adolescent he had been in severe conflict about the contradictory messages he received from his parents. He came to recognize, he indicated, that his parents were using him covertly to prove who was the better parent/person.

His earliest of numerous attempts to come to terms with his conflictual feelings about himself took place in college. Tormented by his ambivalent feelings about his sexual identity, he sought out psychological help at the university counseling center. A psychologist there with whom he sought help, a man of imposing height and masculinity, had during their sessions, when Miller felt extremely agitated and self-contemptuous, held his hand. For Miller this experience conveyed the sense that one could be at the same time masculine and a compassionate, sensitive person.

It was while he was in counseling that Miller decided upon the ministry as a place where he hoped he could combine the qualities of strength and sensitivity. But he continued to be troubled by the feeling that he lacked the personal qualities necessary to be a compassionate person. Moreover, although he was strongly attracted to several girls while in college, he felt too shy and awkward to approach them for dates or even to engage them in conversation.

REVEREND MILLER'S DILEMMA

In his first position as parish minister Rev. Miller was drawn into a sexual relationship with a parishioner, an unmarried woman of 19. It was his first and only sexual relationship. The affair, he later realized, was a desperate attempt to establish himself as a masculine person, but he had done so without taking responsibility for his endeavor. He had kept secret his relationship with the young woman and insisted that she do so as well. His lack of moral responsibility for his behavior was buttressed by his felt sense of lacking personal agency. He experienced choice only in warding off his conflictual feelings about sexual identity, but not his need to experience himself as sensitive and compassionate. His sense of inadequacy as a compassionate person continued to gnaw in his viscera.

In the second month of therapy with me Rev. Miller took a month's leave to go to California. Following his return, Rev. Miller's demeanor changed from that of a quietly secretive person to that of a highly disturbed one. Upon asking about his agitation, I was told that he had recently learned from the woman with whom he had a sexual affair that he had fathered her child. "At least this is what she claims," he said to me with a look of sheepish uncertainty. "The child," he continued after a long moment to collect his thoughts, "is now a young man of 20 with a criminal record. While trying to steal a car after a failed robbery attempt of a convenience store, the police had apprehended the young man. His mother had informed me that she was able to reach me only after considerable efforts. Now she wants me to intervene with the authorities in order to get her son released."

If he was actually the young man's father, Rev. Miller reasoned, he was probably at least in part responsible for the young man's criminality because he had not been a proper father to the boy—that is to say, he was not the father the boy required in order to live a virtuous life. On the other hand, the lad's mother, who had never married and was occupationally unskilled, also had not given her son the upbringing he needed.

Rev. Miller reasoned that his operative responsibility lay in his having fathered a child in an immoral act with a woman who was not capable of being a proper parent, at least not by herself. But, on the other hand, because he hadn't known of the young man's existence up until then, he wasn't sure that he actually was the father. "Wouldn't she have contacted me before if I were his real father? I cannot rule out that in her desperation to get help for her son she has invented a story that would implicate me in order to get my assistance. I don't know what I should do."

I asked what had he done so far.

He complained, "Isn't it enough that I know that I am guilty—if indeed I am the father? Isn't it sufficient that I have suffered all these years: never allowing myself the fulfillment of my religious mission and my personal ambitions? I have screwed up everything in some sort of repentance!"

My clinical experiences through the years have reinforced my conviction that an exploration of moral judgment is crucial to efficacious psychotherapeutic work. Moral concerns are essential to the well-examined life because they are attempts to find principles and rationality for how to deal with the complex and difficult issues that confront human dignity. Consequently, psychotherapy cannot meaningfully exist in a moral vacuum. Psychological inquiry that disregards important human values because a concern with values does not adhere to science's premise that its investigators be value-neutral, are shallow and rootless. Therefore, in most psychotherapeutic situations it isn't enough for the therapist to simply be there and remain objectively curious about the client. He must have some accentuated recognition of how he is prepared to be there for each particular client. In other words, the therapist must stand for something; he must represent and embody some values. His presence must offer some meaning to their being there together, or else the client is left alone to find meaning for his existence in the presence of another who is denying his own moral concerns and struggle to find purpose in life. From this context I said to Rev. Miller: "No, I don't believe what you have done is enough!"

Speaking from a deep conviction in what I regard as the bedrock of moral wisdom in the writings of the social philosopher Martin Buber, I suggested that Rev. Miller by his own continued suffering was indicating that it wasn't punishment but something else that he needed to attend but had not yet done.

Buber's (1953) writings reveal an important distinction between Jewish and Christian notions of sin and redemption. Christian theology emphasizes redemption of wrongdoing by confession to God. Judaism focuses instead on acting in ways to correct the wrong. The distinction, I believe, stems from the fact that Christian theology holds that a person can have direct contact with God and on this basis personally reestablish a proper moral relationship with Him. Judaism, in contrast, maintains that human beings cannot know God directly; therefore, they must show their godliness through their proper conduct with other people. Accordingly, from this perspective, preoccupation with one's wrongful behavior leads to a shameful avoidance of others. In this regard, Buber stresses that the violation of a moral law is a lesser sin than the more serious one of recognizing that one has done wrong and yet not tried to do anything to correct that wrong with the people harmed by one's behavior.

Following upon Buber's ideas, the German American psychoanalyst Erich Fromm (1964) suggests that real sin is to act as a partial person and not take into consideration one's entire existential and spiritual needs, that is to say, to separate one's self into observed and observing parts. The observed self is labeled the sinner and is split off from the responsible/ emotive, observing self. In contrast, a morally healthy person recognizes that his sin represents the error of not responding fully and constructively to a moral dilemma, and as such, his suffering is intended not as punishment, but as *signal anxiety* to alert himself that he needs to constructively and responsibly undo (or lessen) the harm caused by his improper behavior. In other words, it is true that there were psychological issues that Rev.

Miller eventually needed to deal with—such as his sense of narcissistic entitlement because of the deprivations he suffered as a child and his sense of alienation from other people who lacked his level of intellect. Nevertheless, a recognition and an understanding of his psychological issues would not alleviate his suffering unless he took resolute and responsible *action* to constructively address the suffering he had caused himself and others.

With these thoughts in mind, I indicated to Rev. Miller that I believed that his continuing to suffer wasn't the way to properly address his moral dilemma. "After all," I indicated, "in what way do you believe that your suffering and guilt will help the woman and her son in their plight?" Consequently, I told him that I believed that he had a moral responsibility to undo or at least in some way lessen the suffering he has caused by direct active conduct toward those he has affected.

"How should I do that?"

I discussed with him commonsense empathy—that is to say, what he might want if he were in the shoes of the other, in this instance, the woman and her son.

He claimed that he simply couldn't do that. He regarded them as weak, inferior people. How could he with his superior intellect and blameless life—except for his single moral failing—identify with simple-minded people like them?

Rev. Miller's response struck me as so utterly naive and unfeeling that I was for a long moment stunned, unsure how I should respond and convey to this overly defended man that he was actually like all of the rest us—much of the time vulnerable, weak, fearful, unsure, and hungering for genuine concern from others.

It then occurred to me that as a rather intellectualized man, he might be more open to the wisdom of one of the great literary psychologists than to my psychological probing. I asked him whether he was familiar with the writings of Leo Tolstoy, the brilliant Russian novelist and essayist whose work is pervaded by the question of how best to live the virtuous life. All of Tolstoy's writings reflect the moral imperatives that he struggled with in his own life. He was an anti-romantic, staunch realist, who liberated the presentation of the personality and the behavior of the individual from the ideal artistic model of previous generations of writers by describing the events in his stories in their concrete, perceptible reality. In this regard, Tolstoy was less concerned with the story plot than with character description that he believed accurately mirrored the multifold nature of real life in its complexity. As a writer who regarded himself as more of a social philosopher than an artist, the psychological problem for Tolstoy was that in his depiction of character he tried to give comparable attention both to the strict demands of the conditionality of individual personality and to the liberation of free will implicit in individual responsibility.

"Yes, of course I am intimately familiar with Tolstoy. I have read all that he has written from my college days to the present and have found much wisdom in his struggle to find a path to the good life."

"Then you must have read his remarkable short story *Father Sergius*?"

"Of course!"

Literary commentators, I reminded Rev. Miller, have generally described the story of *Father Sergius* as Tolstoy's psychological inquiry as to whether the conditionality of our personality is a more powerful author of our life script than that of our willful intentions. And, despite the actual ending of the story in which Tolstoy tells us that Father Sergius succeeds in helping people so that "little by little God began to reveal Himself in him" (1967, p. 545), the literary critics claim that Father Sergius was a prisoner of his own pride of superiority in regard to other people, and as a result his life was a failure.

"Do you disagree?" Rev. Miller asked.

"Yes, I view the story differently. I regard it as Tolstoy's inquiry into whether he who seeks to live the virtuous life does best to channel his efforts to the welfare of other people or to perfect his own selfhood by his devotion to God, and, in so doing, remain aloof from other people in the belief, shared by many saints, that he who seeks to be aligned with God must be lonely and alone.[1] That also seems to be your *fixed idea*—that is to say, your unique perception that there is only one way of living that is morally acceptable: a life egocentrically devoted to perfection—that must be lived in isolated ascetic melancholy—in order to resist learning anything from anyone except those imports that are congruent with what you regard as the voice of God."

"What is wrong with that?"

"Let's take the case of Father Sergius, and then see whether it also applies to you. Because he lacked curiosity about himself and his place in the world of other people, Father Sergius slights, perhaps even ignores, the evidence that could validly confirm or disconfirm the appropriateness of his belief. Father Sergius' shame-prone personality is crucial to an understanding of his lack of curiosity. So, for example, only insofar as he was unreflective about his emotional reactions to the stressful and shameful events in his life—dedicating all of his energy instead to spiritual accomplishments—could Father Sergius's extreme reactions to his disillusionment with significant people in his life seem to him to be a natural and inevitable course of events."

"But just what am I missing by not being curious about myself in the way you seem to suggest?"

"Each of us has a dark side: the hurts, angers, and vulnerabilities that result from our experiences with shame, humiliation, and the reactive feelings of self-contempt. What differentiates Father Sergius from people who seem to find meaning in their lives is his unwillingness to be curious about his dark side. Unawareness of his own motives may shield him from a probing and disturbing confrontation with his own limitations, and perhaps, even his fear of his own finitude, but, on the other hand, it also renders him a victim of his untoward instinctual urges—such as his rage and his need to be first and foremost in all that he does. In short, it is his unwillingness to introspect his narcissistic wounds that keeps Father Sergius a prisoner of his own toxic self-contempt. And I believe that there is nothing in the world as painful and unendurable as severe self-contempt. Nor is there anything as conducive to finding life meaningless than the despair of self-contempt."

"I cannot really disagree with you about self-contempt, but nevertheless, what does all of this have to do with my moral dilemma with that woman?"

I asked him what he knew of the woman's background, her upbringing, her life up until the time he started the affair with her. He told of a life of neglect, an abusive father, a well-meaning but weak and ineffectual mother, and a fervent wish for warmth and companionship with another loving person.

"Who besides her does that description fit to a 'T'?"

"I don't know!" he snorted.

"You don't know. How honest and self-observant are you being now if you claim that you really don't know?"

He seemed to be taken aback for the first time by what I regarded as his dishonesty. He reflected on my question to him, but this time his answer wasn't swift and perfunctory. "I'm ashamed," he replied, "at what you are saying to me. I am beginning to see that it might be my feelings of shame that I have been trying to disguise and hide from myself that has been the source of my moral dilemma. What I mean to say is that I have not allowed myself the recognition that I am morally weak, prone to common human failings. The real reason I guess that I haven't been able to reach my parishioners in any meaningful way is because I didn't want to stir up my early deprivations as a child or the loneliness and aloneness I experienced as an adult. I imagine that I'm more comfortable with feeling guilty—with guilt feeling at least there are clear-cut rules for how to morally respond:

admit my guilt, ask for forgiveness, accept punishment, and hope for redemption from God."

"But, of course, all the guilt stuff doesn't do much for the victims of your wrongdoings, especially if it is God—not the afflicted—from whom you are asking forgiveness."

"You may be right. My religious teachings strongly suggest that if moral responsibility has any valid meaning it is in the sense that each of us is responsible for one another. The answer to your question, I guess, is the person who is like my description of that woman is *me.*"

"So you aren't so different from other people; apparently you co-occupy a common humanity and shared fate with the rest of humanity. If so, the answer to what you would want if you were in the place of the woman and her son shouldn't be so difficult to answer."

Over the next few sessions Rev. Miller decided that the question of whether he was or was not the actual father of the young man wasn't the paramount issue. His life, he was now willing to admit, had been aimless and unfitting his religious mission. He made a decision about how to handle his situation in California based on what I regard as a *functional* choice. This is to say, his decision was not only morally rectifiable, but also the fulfillment of his humanity. By accepting the young man as his own son and demonstrating personal concern and responsibility for him, he hoped to be able to give his life a sense of purpose and fulfillment that it heretofore lacked. Accordingly, he returned to California and took responsibility for helping the young man as a real father would—letting the chips (in regard to his ministerial reputation) fall as they would. In California he prevailed upon the authorities to provide counseling for the young man and made a home for the young man in which he took up parental responsibilities. In a letter to me, Rev. Miller indicated to me that the position he took was in keeping with what he regarded as the existential wisdom of the philosopher Friedrich Nietzsche, the son of a Protestant minister, who had been in his writings a stern critic of Christianity. Nevertheless, Nietzsche's ideas appealed to him because of Nietzsche's ardent struggle to find an authentic way of living. "Nietzsche," he told me, "was supposed to have said, 'Every truth must be confronted with the question: Can it be lived?' " His decision to accept the young man as his son was something he could accept because it would render his life a sense of purpose that had until now eluded him.

CONCLUSION

This clinical case offers us several important considerations. I focus on two here. Living with a *fixed idea* about the need for superiority and perfection seems to be our desperate defense against our own feared future; it is tantamount to living with unquestioned certainty, despite the unreasonableness of our beliefs. Phenomenologically, we experience no need to critically examine our ideas and to match their appropriateness with the world of others. Only the imperative of curiosity demands self-examination and dialogue with others about their own experiences—so that we can match theirs with our own. In other words, our capacity for choice is predicated on our awareness of possibilities. It is our curiosity about our inner life and that of others that portends possibility. And it is this same curiosity that serves to remove the fictional notion of the inevitability of our behavior.

Secondly, this case study seems to show that our prevailing notions of guilt are faulty and are at the heart of our moral failings as a society. As California-based writer Peter Marin (1981) indicates, "We seem as a society to have few useful ways to approach moral pain . . . it remains for us a form of neurosis or a pathological symptom, something to escape rather than something to learn from. . . ."

Feeling guilty and expecting punishment and redemption from either God and/or society is a rather selfish and, for the most part, useless process. It is in no way helpful to the victim(s) of one's wrongful acts. Nor does it instruct the perpetrator about proper and constructive social behavior necessary to become a morally responsible person. Moral responsibility involves a curious and courageous reflection about oneself and others. It requires us to know our limitations, to accept ourselves as less than perfect, to live to the best of our abilities, and to come caringly together with others to heal the wounds of loneliness, shame, and self-hatred. In this way, a person assumes *personal agency*. A moral agent is a person who takes responsibility for his actions and inactions. So when he finds himself in adverse situations, he investigates the factors within himself that might have caused the untoward occurrence. This is quite different from seeking blame and accepting guilt. By using his self-inquiry as a guide, he attempts to redress and correct those attitudes on his part that are incongruous with what he regards as his intended behavior.

BOOK CONCLUSION

I have shown in this book that there are built-in barriers that psychotherapeutic theory and practice have imposed upon themselves that currently stand in the way of enlightened clinical practice. In other words, a number of serious dilemmas in how practitioners view human existence cast an oscillating shadow on the significance of psychotherapy's impact on contemporary society. I am referring to the host of important metapsy-chological and philosophical issues that I have explored in this book that psychology and psychotherapy have not dealt with successfully. It is pre-cisely a deficiency of knowledge in regard to these issues that lies at the heart of the limitations of current psychotherapeutic practice. For exam-ple, psychotherapy has not yet formulated a model of behavior that emphasizes the values of sharing and cooperating rather than highlighting the obstacles of fear and resistance to psychotherapeutic work. A related problem is the glaring omission of social, moral, and community respon-sibilities of the client in psychotherapy's concept of constructive mental health. From the beginning of their craft psychotherapists have focused on what was done to the client while largely ignoring the client's respon-sibilities to others. This misconceived theoretical perspective is often reinforced by a serious deficiency in the training of psychotherapists: They are oriented to look for and to accept as the most credible that which is wrong with their clients. In other words, most training programs focus far too exclusively on what is hidden, denied, or pathological in the client's life. As a result, the client's strengths and virtues are regarded as masking serious psychological conflict rather than something of which to be proud and to be used responsibly.

I also have shown that having available the language of health is crucial to clinical work. This is because a client's overriding need in struggling with shame (central to all serious psychological afflictions) is to find pos-itive qualities about himself, and his situation, so that he can establish his personal identity in a self-enhanced way. My own clinical experience has revealed that the most difficult task, and when achieved the turning point in healing, is enabling a client to believe in and trust his own goodness. The absence of a sense of personal goodness is the major cause of depres-sion and despair. If clients cannot secure the recognition of their own worth from interactions with their therapists, then from whence will it come initially?

No less important to psychology's place as a significant social agent, as its clinical services, is the relevance of the subject matter of its scientific investigations. Too few studies in contemporary psychology have intellec-tual value or social significance. If the aim of psychology is to understand important human issues, psychologists must turn away from contrived experimental situations now common to psychological studies and pursue instead relevant investigations of the actual world in which we live. An investigation of how to best live the compassionate life is one of the most pressing issues of our world.

In this regard, I have shown here that traveling by the standard psychotherapy carriage of the past more than a century—knowledge by self-examination insulated from one's social and moral responsibility—cannot traverse the road to the life lived fully and well. Only a life borne of compassion and concern for other people, concretely *enacted* in such ways that one has a constructive impact on others' existence, leads to a meaningful and satisfying life.

NOTE

1. This issue has been a perennial controversy in moral philosophy. One of the basic premises of ethical theory, at least since the Jewish Bible, is that virtue is primarily a commitment to improving the well-being of other people. But an even more ancient concept of morality, found in the ideas of the ancient Greek philosophers, is that the highest form of moral perfection is found in a frank and concentrated concern about the conditions of one's own personality, because self-development, it is claimed, is the best means for a person to promote the commonweal. "The most famous example of this classic conception is Socrates' parting plea to his Athenian jurors [at his trial for corrupting the youth of Athens] to recognize that *psuches epimeleia* (care of one's soul) is the highest moral obligation" (Louden, 1988).

REFERENCES

Acocella, J. (1998, 6 April). The politics of hysteria. *New Yorker, 64–79.*

Ainsworth, M.D. (1962). Patterns of attachment behavior shown by the infant in interaction with the mother. *Merrill-Palmer Quarterly, 10,* 51–58.

Allport, G. (1950). *The nature of personality.* Cambridge, MA: Addison-Wesley.

Arendt, H. (1963). *Eichmann in Jerusalem.* New York: Viking.

Aronoff, J. (1962). Freud's conception of the origin of curiosity. *Journal of Psychology, 54,* 39–45.

Bakan, D. (1968). *Disease, pain, and sacrifice.* Boston: Beacon Press.

Baker, R.A. (1992). *Hidden memories.* Buffalo, NY: Prometheus.

Baumeister, R. (1991). *Meanings of life.* New York: Guilford.

Beck, S., Beck, A., Levitt, E., & Molish, H. (1961). *Rorschach's Test: I. Basic processes.* New York: Grune & Stratton.

Becker, E. (1973). *The denial of death.* New York: Free Press.

Benoit, H. (1955). *The supreme doctrine.* New York: Viking.

Bigelow, R. (1992). *Unusual personal experiences.* Las Vegas, NV: Bigelow Holding Company.

Bion, W.R. (1962). *Learning from experience.* London: Heinemann.

Bion, W.R. (1967). Notes on memory and desire. *Psychoanalytic Forum, 2,* 271–280.

Bloecher, T., Clammar, A., & Hopkins, A. (1985). *Summary report on the psychological testing of nine individuals reporting UFO experiences.* Mt. Rainer, MD: Fund for UFO Research.

Blythe, R. (1981). Introduction. *The Death of Ivan Illyich.* New York: Bantam.

Bowlby, J. (1953). Some pathological processes set in train by early mother-child separation. *Journal of Medical Science, 99,* 265–272.

Brofsky, G.L., & Brand, D.J. (1980). Personality and psychological functioning of the Nuremberg war criminals: The Rorschach data. In J.E. Dimsdale (Ed.), *Survivors, victims, and perpetrators: Essays on the Nazi Holocaust* (pp. 359–403). Washington, DC: Hemisphere.

Brown, G.S. (1972). *Laws of form.* New York: Julian Press.

Bruner, J. (1986). *Actual minds, possible worlds.* Cambridge, MA: Harvard University Press.

Brunswick, R.M. (1940). The preoedipal phase of the libido development. *Psychoanalytic Quarterly, 9,* 307–308.

Bryan, J.H. (1972). Why children help: A review. *Journal of Social Issues, 28,* 87–104.

Bryan, J.H., & Walbek, H. (1970). The impact of words and deeds concerning altruism upon children. *Child Development, 41,* 747–757.

Buber, M. (1953). *Good and evil.* New York: Scribner & Sons.

Buber, M. (1965). *Between man and man.* New York: Macmillan.

Buber, M. (1970). *I and thou.* New York: Scribner.

Buber, M. (1999). *Martin Buber on psychology and psychotherapy.* Syracuse, NY: Syracuse University Press.

Cantril, H. (1941). *The psychology of social movements.* New York: Wiley.

Clarke, B. (1980). Beyond "The Banality of Evil." *British Journal of Political Science, 10,* 417–439.

Clary, E.G., & Miller, J. (1986). Socialization and situational influences on sustained altruism. *Child Development, 57,* 1358–1369.

Clines, D.J. (1993). Job, the book of. In B.M. Metzer & M.D. Coogan (Eds.), *The Oxford companion to the Bible* (pp. 297–335). New York: Oxford University Press.

Cohen, J. (1962). *Humanistic psychology.* New York: Collier.

Coles, R. (1981). Psychoanalysis and moral development. *American Journal of Psychoanalysis, 41,* 101–113.

Dewey, J. (1980). *The theory of the moral life.* New York: Irvington Press.

Dhorme, E.A. (1984). *Commentary on the book of Job.* Nashville: Thomas Nelson.

Eakin, P.J. (1999). *How our lives become stories: Making selves.* Ithaca, NY: Cornell University Press.

Edwards, A.L. (1944). The signs of incipient fascism. *Journal of Abnormal & Social Psychology, 39,* 301–316.

Eigen, M. (1993). *The electrified tightrope.* Northvale, NJ: Jason Aronson.

Erikson, E. (1950). *Childhood and society.* New York: Norton.

Feinstein, D., & Krippner, S. (1988). *Personal mythology: The psychology of your evolving self.* Los Angeles: Jeremy Tarcher.

Fenichel, O. (1945). *The psychoanalytic theory of neurosis.* New York: Norton.

Fogelman, E. (1994). *Conscience and courage.* New York: Doubleday.

Freud, S. (1905). Three essays on sexuality. In J. Strachey (Ed.), *Standard edition of the complete works of Sigmund Freud, Vol. 23* (pp. 135–244). New York: Norton.

Freud, S. (1908). Creative writers and day-dreamers. In J. Strachey (Ed.), *Standard edition of the complete works of Sigmund Freud, Vol. 9* (pp. 142–156). New York: Norton.

Freud, S. (1909). Analysis of a phobia in a five-year-old boy. In J. Strachey (Ed.), *Standard edition of the complete works of Sigmund Freud, Vol. 10* (pp. 3–141). New York: Norton.

Freud, S. (1915). Our attitude toward death. In J. Strachey (Ed.), *Standard edition of the complete works of Sigmund Freud, Vol. 14* (pp. 289–300). New York: Norton.

Freud, S. (1923). The ego and the id. In J. Strachey (Ed.), *Standard edition of the complete works of Sigmund Freud, Vol. 19* (pp. 3–42). New York: Norton.

Freud, S. (1930). *Civilization and its discontents.* New York: Norton.

Freud, S. (1937). Analysis terminable and interminable. In J. Strachey (Ed.), *Standard edition of the complete works of Sigmund Freud, Vol. 7* (pp. 231–243). New York: Norton.

Freud, S. (1965). *The interpretation of dreams.* New York: Avon Books [1900].

Fromm, E. (1963). *Escape from freedom.* New York: Holt, Rinehart & Winston.

Fromm, E. (1964). *The heart of man.* New York: Harper & Row.

Fromm-Reichman, F. (1959). Loneliness. *Psychiatry, 22,* 1–15.

Fuller, J. G. (1966). *The interrupted journey.* New York: Dial.

Furer, M. (1967). Some developmental aspects of the superego. *International Journal of Psycho-Analysis, 48,* 277–280.

Gardner, R. (1971). *Therapeutic communication with children: The mutual story telling technique.* New York: Science House.

Gilman, N. (1990). *Sacred fragments.* Philadelphia: Jewish Publication Society.

Ginzsburg, L. (1991). *On psychological prose.* Princeton, NJ: Princeton University Press.

Goldberg, C. (1991). *Understanding shame.* Northvale, NJ: Jason Aronson.

Goldberg, C. (1992). *The seasoned psychotherapist.* New York: Norton.

Greenacre, P. (1954). The role of transference. *Journal of the American Psychoanalytic Association, 2,* 671–684.

Greenson, R. (1953). On boredom. *Journal of the American Psychoanalytic Association, 1,* 7–21.

Greenson, R. R. (1971). The "real" relationship between the patient and the psychoanalyst. In M. Kanzer (Ed.), *The unconscious today* (pp. 213–232). New York: International Universities Press.

Grinker, R. R. (1957). On identification. *International Journal of Psycho-Analysis, 38,* 379–390.

Grinker, R. R. (1964). Relations between behavioral and cognitive dimensions of conscience in middle childhood. *Child Development, 35,* 881–891.

Grinspan, L., & Persky, A.D. (1972). Psychiatry and UFO reports. In C. Sagan & T. Page (Eds.), *UFOs: A scientific debate* (pp. 233–246). Ithaca, NY: Cornell University Press.

Gruber, H.E. (1985). Giftedness and moral responsibility: Creative thinking and human survival. In F.D. Horowitz & M.O. O'Brien (Eds.), *The gifted and talented: Developmental perspectives* (pp. 301–330). Washington, DC: American Psychological Association Press.

Harris, M.B. (1972). The effects of performing one altruistic act on the likelihood of performing another. *Journal of Social Psychology, 88*, 65–73.

Harrower, M. (1976). Rorschach records of the Nazi war criminals: An experimental study after thirty years. *Journal of Personality Assessment, 40*, 341–351.

Hartocollis, P. (1983). *Time and timelessness.* Madison, CT: International Universities Press.

Hegel, D. (1892). *The logic of Hegel.* Translated from the *Encyclopedia of philosophical science,* Oxford, England: William Wallace.

Heidegger, M. (1972). *Time and being.* New York: Harper.

Hibbert, C. (1963). *The roots of evil.* Boston: Little, Brown.

Hillman, J., & Ventura, M. (1993). *We've had a hundred years of psychotherapy and the world's getting worse.* San Francisco: HarperCollins.

Hoffman, M.L. (1963). Parent discipline and the child's consideration for others. *Child Development, 34*, 573–588.

Hoffman, M.L. (1975). Altruistic behavior and the parent-child relationship. *Journal of Personality and Social Psychology, 31*, 937–943.

Hopkins, B. (1981). *Missing time.* New York: Marek.

Hufford, D. (1982). *The terror that comes in the night.* Philadelphia: University of Pennsylvania Press.

Hynek, J.A. (1972). *The UFO experience: A scientific inquiry.* Chicago: Henry Regnery.

Inner-Smith, J. (1987). Pre-oedipal identification and the cathexis of autistic objects in the aetiology of adult psychopathology. *International Journal of Psychoanalysis, 68*, 405–413.

Jacobs, D. (1992). *The secret life.* New York: Simon & Schuster.

Jaspers, K. (1957). *Socrates, Buddha, Confucius, Jesus.* New York: Harcourt, Brace, & World.

Jimack, P.D. (2000). Introduction. In J-J. Rousseau, *Emile* (pp. 3–10). North Claredon, VT: Everyman [1762].

Jung, C.G. (1956). *Symbols of transformation.* New York: Pantheon Press.

Jung, C.G. (1971). Answer to Job. In J. Campbell (Ed.), *The portable Jung* (pp. 519–650). New York: Penguin.

Jung, C.G. (1976). *The portable Jung.* New York: Penguin.

Kant, I. (1956). *Critique of pure reason.* New York: Liberal Arts Press [1781].

Kierkegaard, S. (1974). *Fear and trembling and sickness unto death.* Princeton, NJ: Princeton University Press.

Kierkegaard, S. (1999). *The living thoughts of Kierkegaard.* New York: New York Review of Books.

King, C.W. (1956). *Social movements in the United States.* New York: Random House.

Kohut, H. (1977). *The restoration of the self.* New York: International Universities Press.

Krishnamurti, J. (1972). *You are the world.* New York: Harper & Row.

Kristof, N.D. (1999, 6 July). Alien-abductions? Science calls it Sleep Paralysis. *The New York Times,* Section F, 1–2.

Krutch, J.W. (1926). *Edgar Allan Poe: A study in genius.* New York: Russell & Russell.

La Barre, W. (1980). *Culture in context.* Durham, NC: Duke University Press.

Laing, R.D. (1967). *The politics of experience.* New York: Ballantine.

Levinson, D.J., Darrow, C.N., Kleen, E.B., Levenson, H.H., & McKee, B. (1978). *The seasons of a man's life.* New York: Ballintine.

Levy, D.M. (1946). The German Anti-Nazi: A case study. *American Journal of Orthopsychiatry, 16,* 507–515.

Levy, D.M. (1948). Anti-Nazis: Criteria of differentiation. *Psychiatry, 11,* 125–167.

Lewis, H.B. (1987). The role of shame in depression over the life span. In H.B. Lewis (Ed.), *The role of shame in symptom formation* (pp. 29–50). New York: Lawrence Erlbaum.

Lifton, R.J. (1963). *Thought reform and the psychology of totalism.* New York: Norton.

Lifton, R.J. (1993). *The protean self.* New York: Basic Books.

Loevinger, J. (1976). *Ego development.* San Francisco: Jossey-Bass.

Lottman, H. (1980). *Albert Camus: A biography.* New York: Braziller.

Louden, R.B. (1988). Can we be too moral? *Ethics, 98,* 361–378.

Lynd, H. (1958). *On shame and the search for identity.* New York: Harcourt, Brace.

Macalpine, I. (1950). The development of the transference. *Psychoanalytic Quarterly, 19,* 501–539.

Mack, J. (1994). *Abductions.* New York: Scribner.

Macmurray, J. (1957). *The self as agent.* London: Faber.

Maier, N.R. (1942). The role of frustration in social movements. *Psychoanalytic Review, 42,* 586–599.

Manwell, R., & Fraenkel, H. (1965). *Heinrich Himmler.* Paris: Stock.

Marin, P. (1981, November). Living in moral pain. *Psychology Today,* 68–80.

Maslow, A.H. (1963). The need to know and the fear of knowing. *Journal of General Psychology, 68* (111–115).

May, R. (1978). *The courage to create.* New York: Bantam.

May, R., Angel, E., & Ellenberger, H.F. (Eds.). (1959). *Existence.* New York: Basic Books.

McAdam, D.P. (1993). *Stories we live by: Personal myths and the making of the self.* New York: William Morrow.

McDevitt, J.B. (1979). The role of internalization in the development of object relations during separation-individualization phase. *Journal of the American Psychoanalytic Association, 27,* 327–344.

McGill, A. (1982). Human suffering and the passion of Christ. In F. Doughert (Ed.), *The meaning of human suffering* (pp. 159–193). New York: Human Sciences Press.

Meerloo, J.A. (1968). The flying saucer syndrome and the need for miracles. *Journal of the American Medical Association, 170,* 501–540.

Mendelson, M.D. (1990). Reflections on loneliness. *Contemporary Psychoanalysis, 26,* 330–353.

Menninger, K. (1968). *The crime of punishment.* New York: Viking.

Midlarsky, E., & Byran, J. (1967). Training charity in children. *Journal of Personality and Social Psychology, 5,* 408–415.

Monroe, K.R., Barton, M.C., & Klingemann, U. (1990). Altruism and the theory of rational action: Rescuers of Jews in Nazi Europe. *Ethics, 101,* 103–122.

Morin, A., & Evertt, J. (1991). Self-awareness and "introspective" private speech in six-year-old children. *Psychological Reports, 68,* 1299–1306.

Natanson, M. (1981). An editorial fragment. *Journal of Medical Philosophy. 6,* 3.

Nersessian, E. (1995). Some reflections on curiosity and psychoanalytic technique. *Psychoanalytic Quarterly, 54,* 113–135.

Parnell, J. (1988). Measured personality characteristics of persons who claim UFO experiences. *Psychotherapy in Private Practice, 6,* 159–165.

Polonoff, D. (1987). Self-deception. *Social Research, 54,* 45–53.

Randi. J. (1982). *Flim-flam.* Buffalo, NY: Prometheus.

Randle, J. (1994). *Strange & unexplained mysteries of the 20th century.* New York: Sterling.

Ring, K. (1992). *The omega project.* New York: William Morrow.

Ritzler, B.A. (1978). The Nuremberg mind revisited: A quantitative approach to Nazi Rorschachs. *Journal of Personality Assessment, 42,* 344–353.

Rogers, C. (1961). *On becoming a person.* Boston: Houghton-Mifflin.

Rokeach, M. (1960). *The open and closed mind.* New York: Basic Books.

Rosenhan, D.L., Salovey, P., & Hargis, K. (1981). The joys of helping: Focus of attention mediates the impact of positive affect on altruism. *Journal of Personality and Social Psychology, 40,* 899–905.

Rosenhan, D.L., Underwood, B., & Moore, B. (1974). Affect moderates self-gratification and altruism. *Journal of Personality and Social Psychology, 30,* 546–552.

Rousseau, J-J. (1954). *The social contract.* Chicago: Henry Regnery.

Rousseau, J-J. (2000). *Emile*. Translated: Foxley, B. Introduction: Jimack, P. A. North Clarendon, VT: Everyman [1762].

Rushton, J.P. (1976). Socialization and the altruistic behavior of children. *Psychology Bulletin, 83,* 899–913.

Sagan, E. (1988). *Freud, women, and morality.* Englewood, NJ: Fish Drum Press.

Sagi, A., & Hoffman, M.L. (1976). Empathic distress in newborns. *Developmental Psychology, 12,* 175–176.

Sartre, J.P. (1966). *Being and nothingness.* New York: Washington Square Press [1943].

Schafer, R. (1960). The loving and beloved superego in Freud's structural theory. *Psychoanalytic Study of the Child, 15,* 163–188.

Schank, R.C. (1990). *Tell me a story.* New York: Charles Schribner.

Schneider, C. (1977). *Shame, exposure, and privacy.* Boston: Beacon Press.

Schneider, P. (2000, 13 Feb.). Saving Konrad Latte. *The New York Times Magazine,* 14–20.

Schulweis, H.M. (1990). The fear and suspicion of goodness. *Dimensions, 5,* 22–25.

Searles, H. (1961). Schizophrenia and the inevitability of death. *Psychiatric Quarterly, 35,* 631–665.

Searles, H. (1975). The patient as therapist to his analyst. In P. Giovacchi (Ed.), *Tactics and techniques in psychoanalytic thought, Vol. II* (pp. 95–151). New York: Jason Aronson.

Shane, M., & Shane, E. (1989). Child analysis and adult analysis. In A. Goldberg (Ed.), *Dimensions of self-experience, Vol. 5* (pp. 59–73). Hillsdale, NJ: Analytic Books.

Sheaffer, R. (1986). *The UFO verdict: Examining the evidence.* Buffalo, NY: Prometheus.

Silberman, C. (1978). *Criminal violence/criminal justice.* New York: Random House.

Simner, M.L. (1971). Newborn's responses to the cry of another infant. *Developmental Psychology, 5,* 136–150.

Singer, J.A., & Salovey, P. (1993). *The remembered self: Emotion and memory in personality.* New York: The Free Press.

Smith, A. (1973). The psychological text of three tales by Poe. *American Studies, 7,* 279–289.

Spanos, N., Cross, P.A., Dickerson, K., & DuBreuil, S.C. (1993). Close encounters: An examination. *Journal of Abnormal Psychology, 102,* 624–632.

Spinoza, B. (1949). *The ethics.* New York: Hafner Press [1677].

Spitz, R.A. (1958). On the genesis of superego components. *Psychoanalytic Study of the Child, 13,* 375–414.

Sprinkle, R.L. (1976). Hypnotic and psychotic implications in the investigation of UFO reports. In C. Lorenzen & J. Lorenzen (Eds.), *Encounters with UFO occupants* (pp. 256–329). New York: Berkeley.

Stern, D. (1985). *The interpersonal world of the infant.* New York: Basic Books.

Straus, E. W. (1966). Shame as a historeological problem. In E. W. Straus (Ed.), *Phenomenological psychology: Selected papers* (pp. 217–223). New York: Basic Books.

Strean, H. S. (1988). The patient as a consultant: The boy who prescribed his own treatment. In H. S. Strean, *Behind the couch: Revelations of a psychoanalyst* (pp. 95–106). New York: Wiley.

Sullivan, H. S. (1953). *The interpersonal theory of personality.* New York: Norton.

Target, M., & Fonagy, P. (1996). Play with reality. II The development of psychic reality from a theoretical perspective. *International Journal of Psychoanalysis, 77,* 459–479.

Tec, N. (1986). The rescuer-rescued relationship: How did it begin? *Dimensions, 1,* 4–7.

Thompson, W. C., Cowan, C. L., & Rosenhan, D. L. (1980). Focus of attention mediates the impact of negative affect on altruism. *Journal of Personality and Social Psychology, 38,* 291–300.

Tillich, P. (1952). *The courage to be.* New Haven, CT: Yale University Press.

Tolstoy, L. (1987). *The death of Ivan Illyich.* New York: Bantam [1886].

Tolstoy, L. Father Sergius. In L. Tolstoy, *Great works of Leo Tolstoy* (pp. 523–567). New York: Harper & Row.

Vallee, J. (1991). *Revelations: Alien contact and human deception.* New York: Ballantine.

Walsh, J. (1968). *Poe, the detective and the mysterious circumstances behind the mystery of Marie Roget.* New Brunswick, NJ: Rutgers University.

Warren, D. I. (1970). Status inconsistency theory and flying saucer sightings. *Science, 153,* 269–277.

Watts, A. (1961). *Psychotherapy: East and West.* New York: Ballantine.

Werman, D. S. (1983). Suppression as a defense. *Journal of the American Psychoanalytic Association, 31,* 405–415.

Wheelis, A. (1960). *The seeker.* New York: New American Library.

White, R. W. (1963). Sense of incompetence. In R. W. White, *The Study of Lives* (pp. 73–93). New York: Prentice Hall.

Winnicott, D. W. (1958). *Collected papers.* New York: Basic Books.

Wright, B. (1942). Altruism in children and perceived conduct of others. *Journal of Abnormal and Social Psychology, 37,* 218–233.

Yarrow, M. R., Scott, P. M., & Waxler, C. Z. (1973). Learning concern for others. *Developmental Psychology, 8,* 240–260.

Yochelson, Samuel, & Samenow, Stanton. (1993). *The criminal personality.* Northvale, NJ: Jason Arenson.

Zahn-Waxler, C., Radke-Yarrow, M., & King, R. C. (1979). Child rearing and children's presocial initiations toward victims of distress. *Child Development, 50,* 319–330.

INDEX

ABOUT THE SERIES EDITOR
AND ADVISORS

J. HAROLD ELLENS is a Research Scholar at the University of Michigan, Department of Near Eastern Studies. He is a retired Presbyterian theologian and ordained minister, a retired U.S. Army Colonel, and a retired Professor of Philosophy, Theology, and Psychology. He has authored, coauthored, and/or edited 72 books and 148 professional journal articles. He served 15 years as Executive Director of the Christian Association for Psychological Studies, and as Founding Editor and Editor-in-Chief of the *Journal of Psychology and Christianity*. He holds a Ph.D. from Wayne State University in the Psychology of Human Communication, a Ph.D. from the University of Michigan in Biblical and Near Eastern Studies, and master's degrees from Calvin Theological Seminary, Princeton Theological Seminary, and the University of Michigan. He was born in Michigan, grew up in a Dutch-German immigrant community, and determined at age seven to enter the Christian Ministry as a means to help his people with the great amount of suffering he perceived all around him. His life's work has focused on the interface of psychology and religion.

ARCHBISHOP DESMOND TUTU is best known for his contribution to the cause of racial justice in South Africa, a contribution for which he was recognized with the Nobel Peace Prize in 1984. Archbishop Tutu has been an ordained priest since 1960. Among his many accomplishments are being named the first black General Secretary of the South African Council of Churches and serving as Archbishop of Cape Town. Once a high school teacher in South Africa, he has also taught theology in college and holds honorary degrees from universities including Harvard, Oxford, Columbia, and Kent State. He has been awarded the Order for Meritorious Service presented by President Nelson Mandela, the Archbishop of Canterbury's Award for outstanding service to the Anglican community, the Family of Man Gold Medal Award, and the Martin King Jr. Non-Violent Peace Award. The publications Archbishop Tutu has authored, co-authored, or made contributions to include *No Future Without Forgiveness* (2000), *Crying in the Wilderness: The Struggle for Justice in South Africa* (1982), and *The Rainbow People of God: The Making of a Peaceful Revolution* (1994).

LEROY H. ADEN is Professor Emeritus of Pastoral Theology at the Lutheran Theological Seminary in Philadelphia, Pennsylvania. He taught full-time at the seminary from 1967 to 1994 and part-time from 1994 to 2001. He served as Visiting Lecturer at Princeton Theological Seminary, Princeton, New Jersey on a regular basis. In 2002, he co-authored *Preaching God's Compassion: Comforting Those Who Suffer* with Robert G. Hughes. Previously, he edited four books in a Psychology and Christianity series with J. Harold Ellens and David G. Benner. He served on the Board of Directors of the Christian Association for Psychological Studies for six years.

DONALD CAPPS, Psychologist of Religion, is William Hart Felmeth Professor of Pastoral Theology at Princeton Theological Seminary. In 1989, he was awarded an honorary doctorate from the University of Uppsala, Sweden, in recognition of the importance of his publications. He served as president of the Society for the Scientific Study of Religion from 1990 to 1992. Among his many significant books are *Men, Religion and Melancholia: James, Otto, Jung and Erikson;* also *Freud and Freudians on Religion: A Reader;* also *Social Phobia: Alleviating Anxiety in an Age of Self-Promotion;* and *Jesus: A Psychological Biography.* He also authored *The Child's Song: The Religious Abuse of Children.*

ZENON LOTUFO JR. is a Presbyterian minister (Independent Presbyterian Church of Brazil), a philosopher, and a psychotherapist, specialized in Transactional Analysis. He has lectured both to undergraduate and graduate courses in universities in São Paulo, Brazil. He coordinates the course of specialization in Pastoral Psychology of the Christian Psychologists and Psychiatrists Association. He is the author of the books, *Relações Humanas* [Human Relations], *Disfunções no Comportamento Organizacional* [Dysfunctions in Organizational Behavior], and co-author of *O Potencial Humano* [Human Potential]. He has also authored numerous journal articles.

DIRK ODENDAAL is South African; he was born in what is now called the Province of the Eastern Cape. He spent much of his youth in the Transkei in the town of Umtata, where his parents were teachers at a seminary. He trained as a minister at the Stellenbosch Seminary for the Dutch Reformed Church and was ordained in 1983 in the Dutch Reformed Church in Southern Africa. He transferred to East London in 1988 to minister to members of the Uniting Reformed Church in Southern Africa in one of the huge suburbs for Xhosa-speaking people. He received his doctorate (D.Litt.) in 1992 at the University of Port Elizabeth in Semitic Languages. At present, he is enrolled in a Masters course in Counselling Psychology at Rhodes University.

WAYNE G. ROLLINS is Professor Emeritus of Biblical Studies at Assumption College, Worcester, Massachusetts, and Adjunct Professor of Scripture at Hartford Seminary, Hartford, Connecticut. His writings include *The Gospels: Portraits of Christ* (1964), *Jung and the Bible* (1983), and *Soul and Psyche, The Bible in Psychological Perspective* (1999). He received his Ph.D. in New Testament Studies from Yale University and is the founder and chairman (1990–2000) of the Society of Biblical Literature Section on Psychology and Biblical Studies

About the Authors

CARL GOLDBERG was a clinical psychologist and psychoanalyst for 35 years. He has authored 12 books, as well as more than 170 journal articles. He was Editor-for-the-Americas of the *International Journal of Psychotherapy*. His book, *Speaking with the Devil: Exploring Senseless Acts of Evil* earned the H.M. Moss Achievement Award in 1997.

VIRGINIA CRESPO is a medical and psychiatric social worker who has treated chronically ill and terminal patients at Columbia-Presbyterian Medical Center, New York University Hospital, St. Luke's-Roosevelt Hospital, and New York State Psychiatric Institute. She has been a field instructor at Columiba-Presbyterian and Roosevelt hospitals, and an Adjunct Faculty Member for Columbia University School of Social Work. She is a member of the Editorial Board for the *International Journal of Psychotherapy*. She has conducted numerous workshops with Carl Goldberg on interpersonal relations.